A-Z SOUTHA...

C000201983

CONTENT...

Key to Map Pages   2-3

Large Scale Pages   4-5

Map P...

Index to Streets   56-80

REFERENCE

Motorway	**M27**
A Road	A335
B Road	B3038
Dual Carriageway	
One-way Street Traffic flow on A Roads is indicated by a heavy line on the driver's left.	→
Large Scale Pages Only	⇒
Restricted Access	
Pedestrianized Road	
Track	
Footpath	
Residential Walkway	
Railway	Level Crossing Station Tunnel
Built-up Area	CENTRAL RD.
Local Authority Boundary	—·—·—
National Park Boundary	
Postcode Boundary	— — —

Map Continuation	16 Large Scale City Centre 4
Car Park Selected	ℙ
Church or Chapel	†
Cycle Route Selected	⊶
Dock Gate Number	⑨
Fire Station	■
Hospital	⊞
House Numbers A & B Roads only	83 96
Information Centre	🛈
National Grid Reference	4 45
Berth Number	101
Police Station	▲
Post Office	★
Toilet With facilities for the Disabled	▽ ♿
Educational Establishment	◪
Hospital or Hospice	◪
Industrial Building	◪
Leisure or Recreational Facility	◪
Place of Interest	◪
Public Building	◪
Shopping Centre or Market	◪
Other Selected Buildings	◪

SCALE

Map Pages 6-55
1:15,840   4 inches to 1 mile

0	¼	½ Mile
0 250 500 750 Metres		

6.31 cm to 1 km   10.16 cm to 1 mile

Map Pages 4-5
1:7,920   8 inches to 1 mile

0	⅛	¼ Mile
0 100 200 300 Metres		

12.63 cm to 1 km   20.32 cm to 1 mile

Copyright of Geographers' A-Z Map Company Ltd.

Head Office :
Fairfield Road, Borough Green, Sevenoaks, Kent TN15 8PP
Tel: 01732 781000 (Enquiries & Trade Sales)
Tel: 01732 783422 (Retail Sales)

www.a-zmaps.co.uk

Copyright © Geographers' A-Z Map Co. Ltd.

Ordnance Survey® This product includes mapping data licensed from Ordnance Survey® with the permission of the Controller of Her Majesty's Stationery Office.

© Crown Copyright 2001. All rights reserved. Licence number 100017302

EDITION 5 2001   EDITION 5A* 2004 (Part revision)

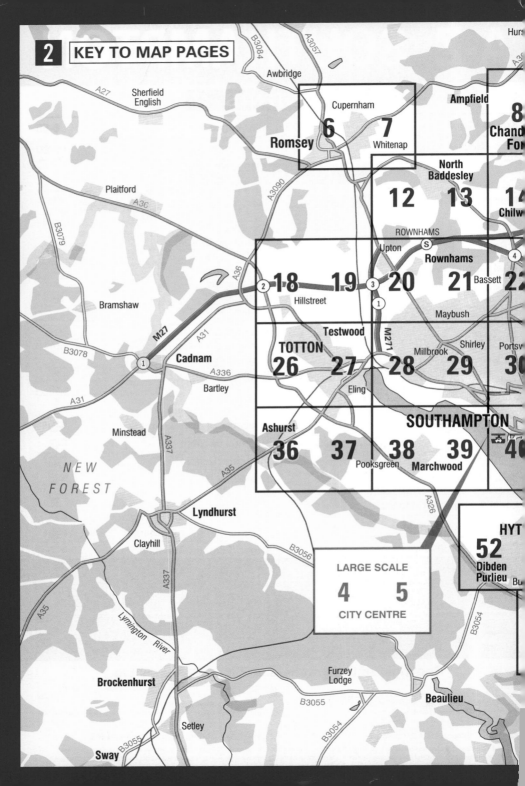

2 **KEY TO MAP PAGES**

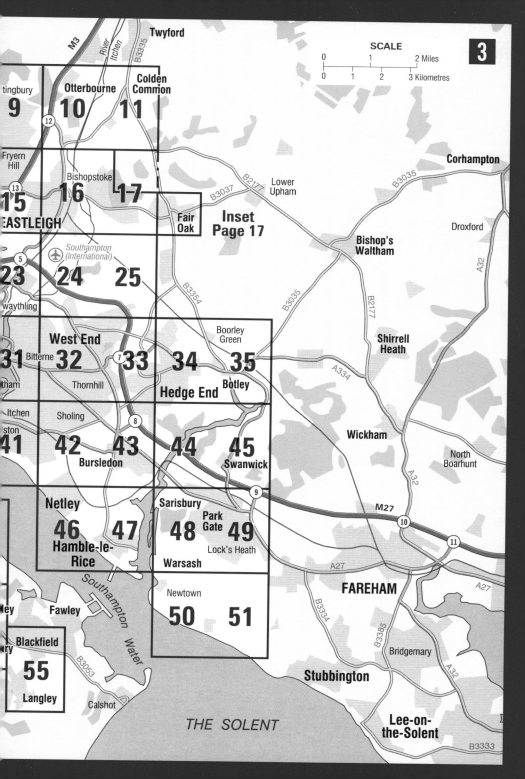

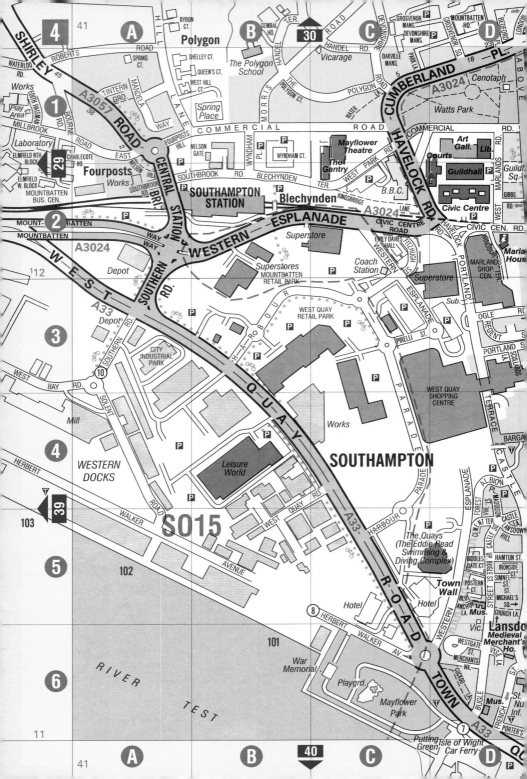

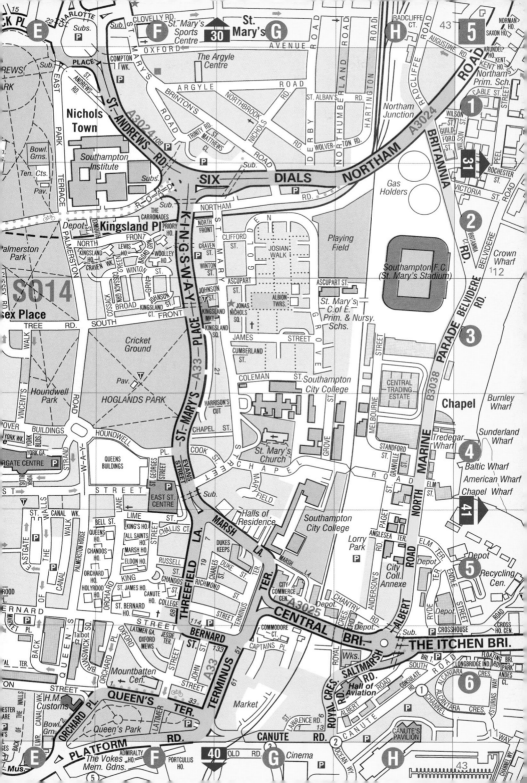

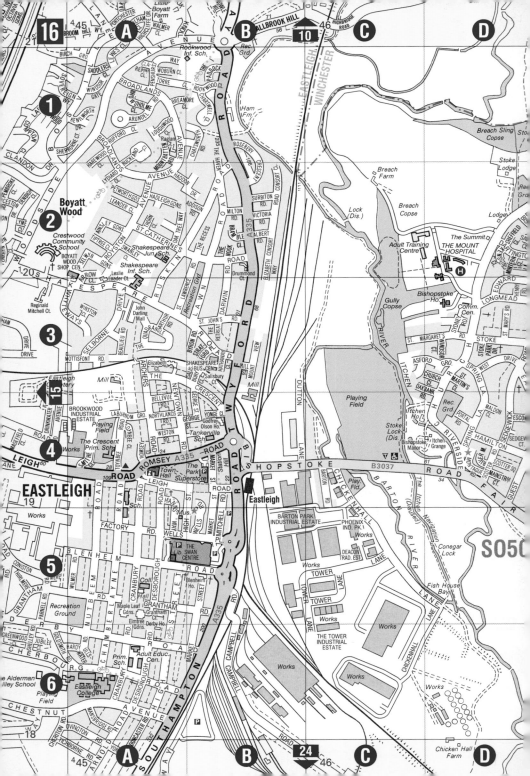

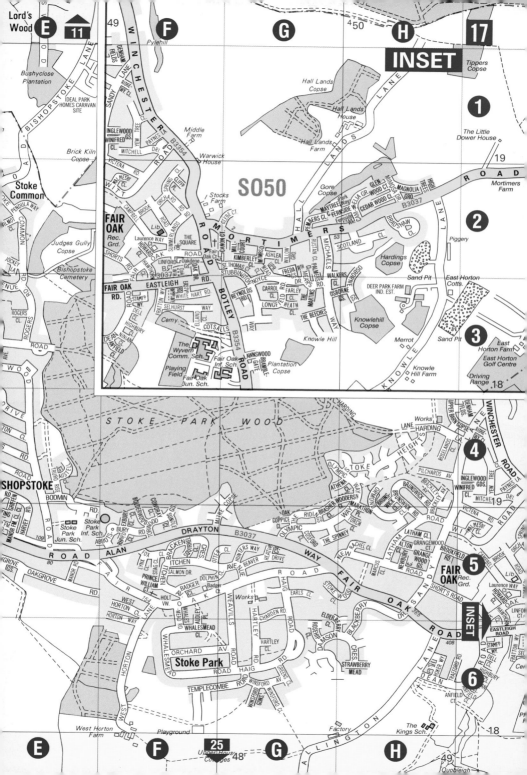

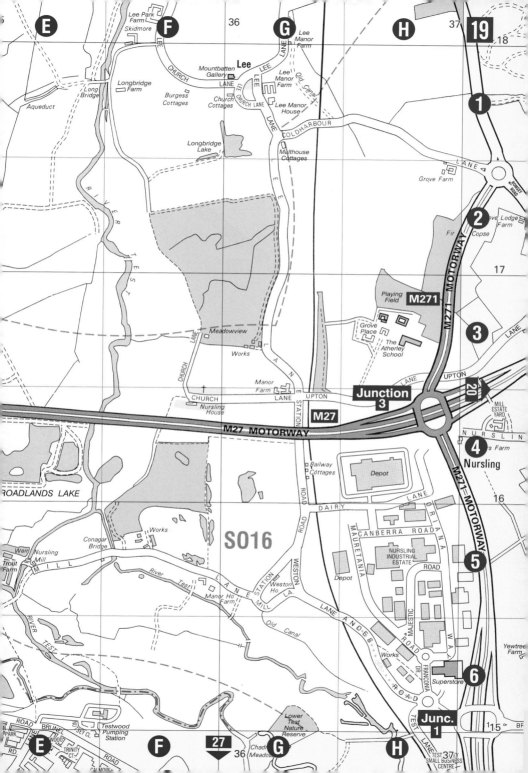

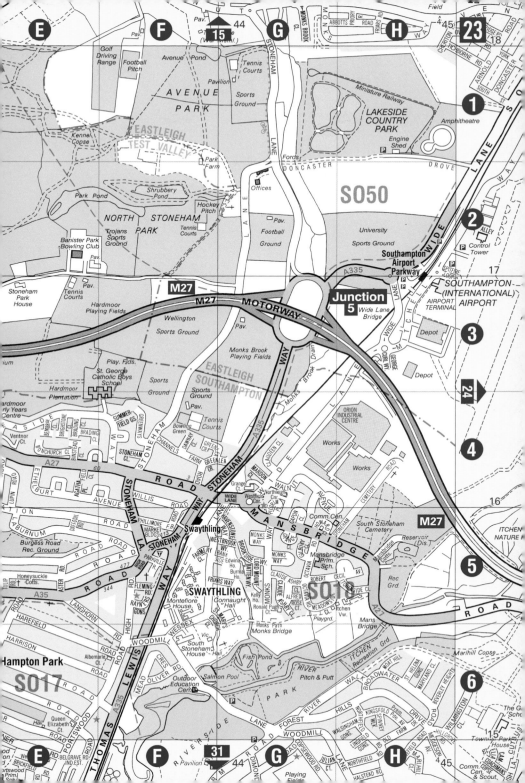

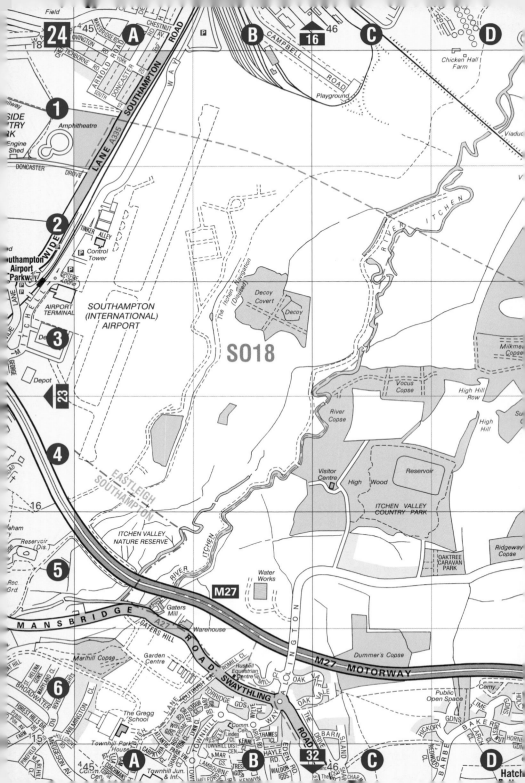

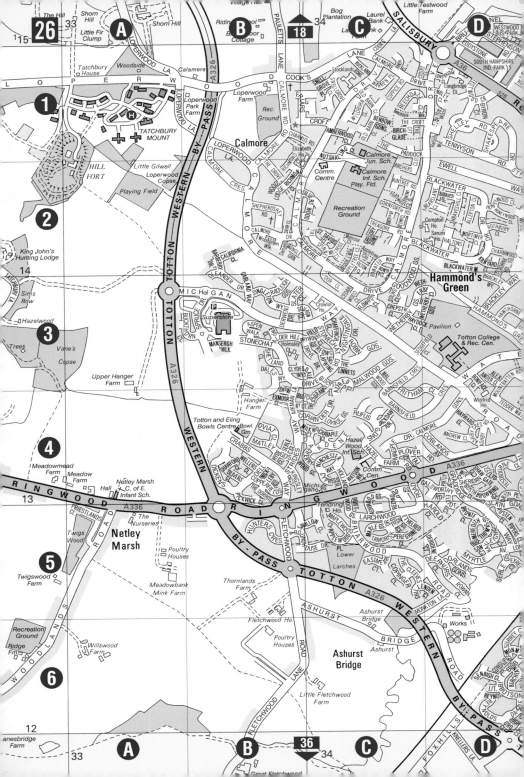

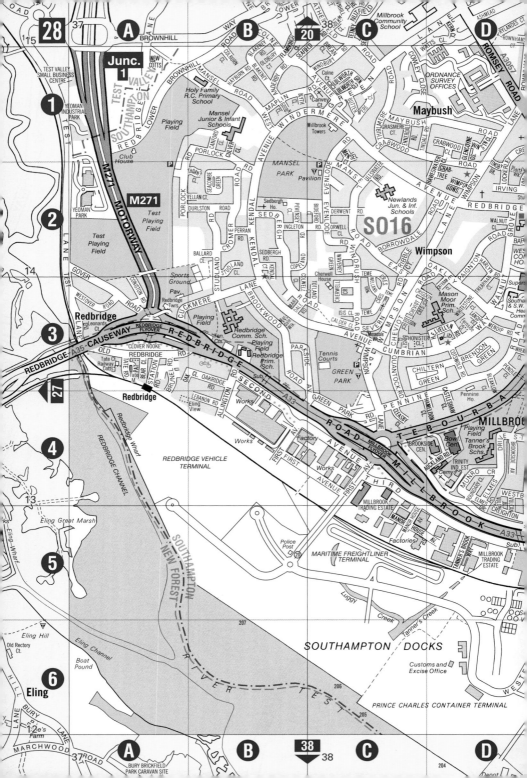

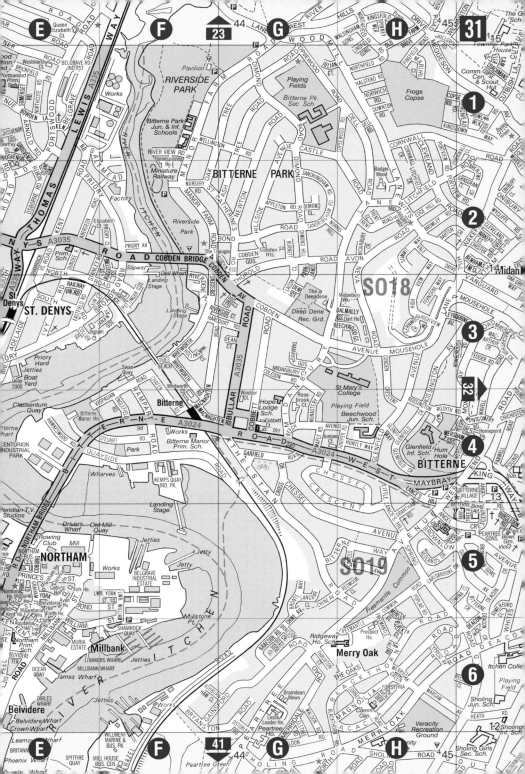

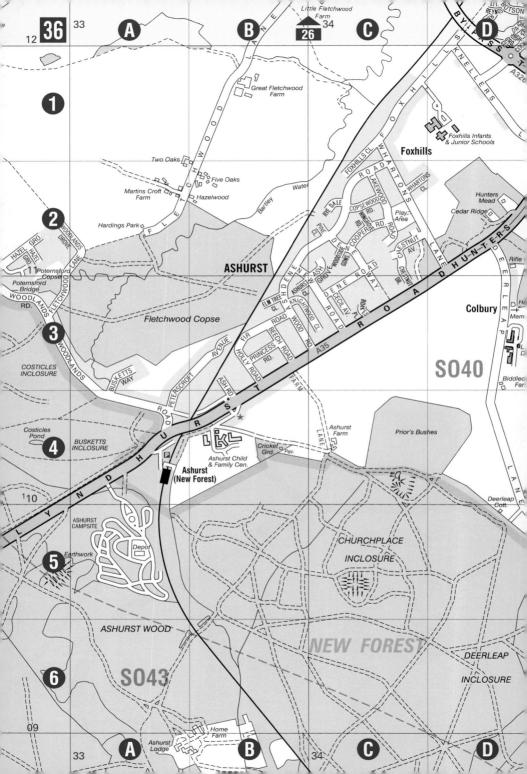

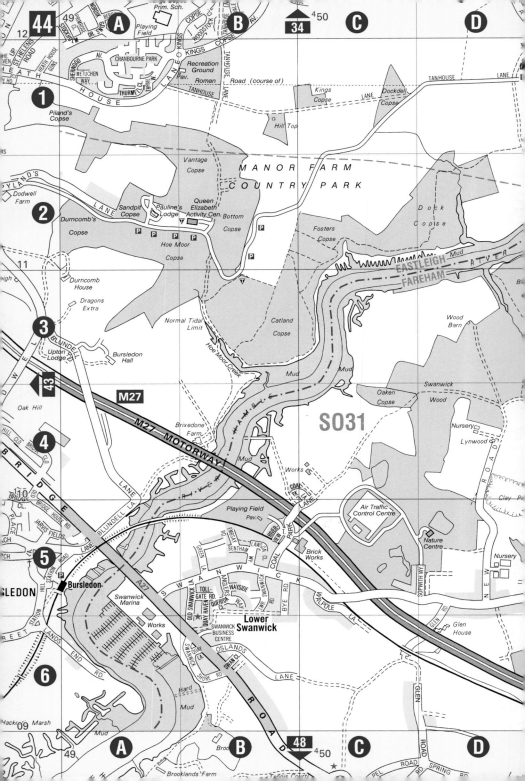

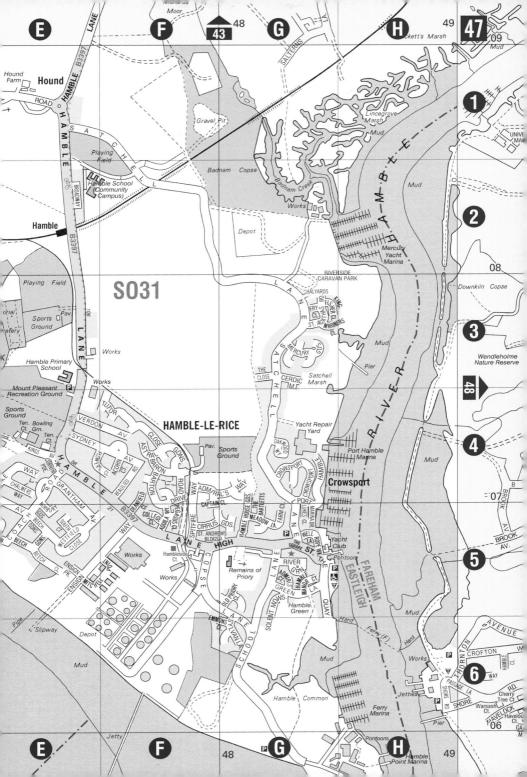

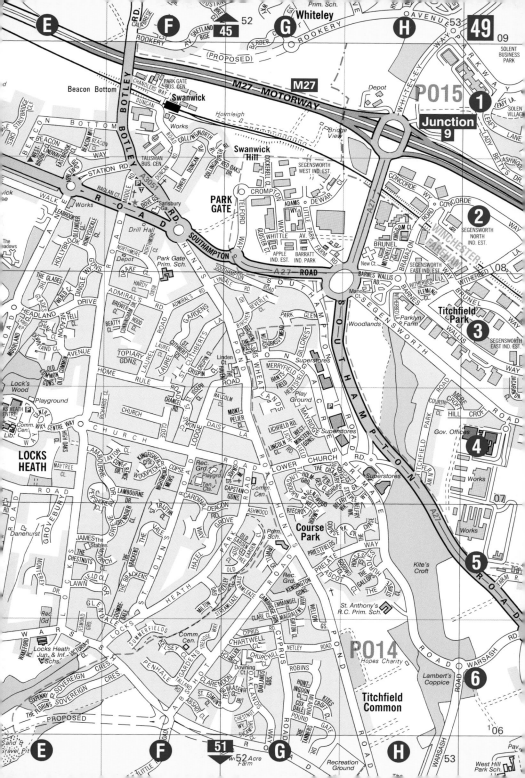

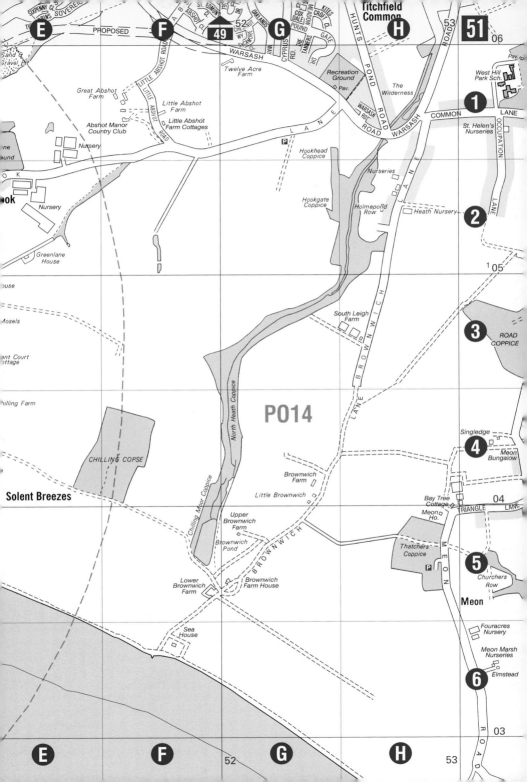

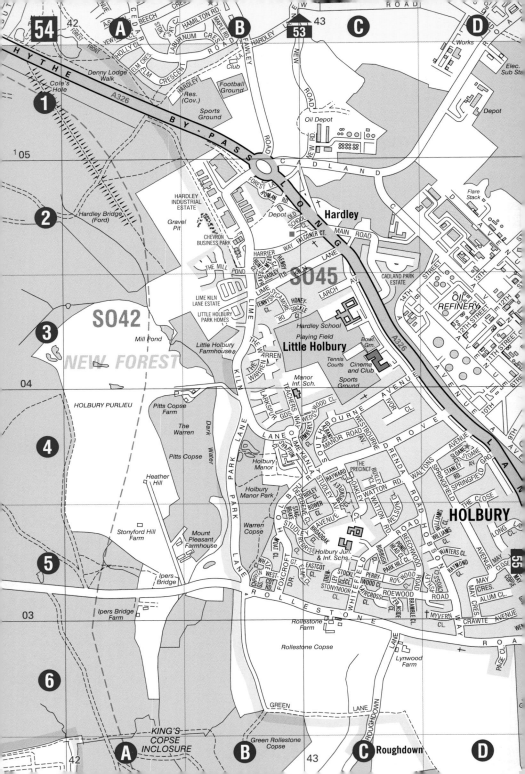

INDEX

Including Streets, Industrial Estates and
Selected Flats & Walkways

HOW TO USE THIS INDEX

1. Each street name is followed by its Posttown or Postal Locality and then by its map reference; e.g. Abbey Fields Clo. *Net A* . . . .1D **46** is in the Netley Abbey Postal Locality and is to be found in square 1D on page **46**. The page number being shown in bold type. A strict alphabetical order is followed in which Av., Rd., St., etc. (though abbreviated) are read in full and as part of the street name; e.g. Abbotswood Clo. appears after Abbots Way but before Abbotts Rd.

2. Streets and a selection of Subsidiary names not shown on the Maps, appear in the index in *Italics* with the thoroughfare to which it is connected shown in brackets; e.g. *Abbey Wlk. Roms . . . .5B* **6** *(off Church St.)*

3. Map references shown in brackets; e.g. Above Bar St. *Sotn* . . . .6B **30** (1D **4**) refer to entries that also appear on the large scale pages 4 & 5.

GENERAL ABBREVIATIONS

All : Alley
App : Approach
Arc : Arcade
Av : Avenue
Bk : Back
Boulevd : Boulevard
Bri : Bridge
B'way : Broadway
Bldgs : Buildings
Bus : Business
Cvn : Caravan
Cen : Centre
Chu : Church
Chyd : Churchyard
Circ : Circle
Cir : Circus
Clo : Close
Comn : Common
Cotts : Cottages

Ct : Court
Cres : Crescent
Cft : Croft
Dri : Drive
E : East
Embkmt : Embankment
Est : Estate
Fld : Field
Gdns : Gardens
Gth : Garth
Ga : Gate
Gt : Great
Grn : Green
Gro : Grove
Ho : House
Ind : Industrial
Info : Information
Junct : Junction
La : Lane

Lit : Little
Lwr : Lower
Mc : Mac
Mnr : Manor
Mans : Mansions
Mkt : Market
Mdw : Meadow
M : Mews
Mt : Mount
Mus : Museum
N : North
Pal : Palace
Pde : Parade
Pk : Park
Pas : Passage
Pl : Place
Quad : Quadrant
Res : Residential
Ri : Rise

Rd : Road
Shop : Shopping
S : South
Sq : Square
Sta : Station
St : Street
Ter : Terrace
Trad : Trading
Up : Upper
Va : Vale
Vw : View
Vs : Villas
Vis : Visitors
Wlk : Walk
W : West
Yd : Yard

POSTTOWN AND POSTAL LOCALITY ABBREVIATIONS

Amp : Ampfield
Asht : Ashurst
Bish W : Bishops Waltham
Black : Blackfield
Bot : Botley
Bourn : Bournemouth
Bram : Brambridge
Bur : Burridge
Burs : Bursledon
Cal : Calmore
Chan F : Chandler's Ford
Chilw : Chilworth
Col C : Colden Common
Comp : Compton
Cram : Crammpmoor
Curd : Curdridge
Dib : Dibden

Dib P : Dibden Purlieu
E Dock : Eastern Docks
Eastl : Eastleigh
E Wel : East Wellow
F Oak : Fair Oak
Fare : Fareham
Fawl : Fawley
Fern : Ferndown
Fish P : Fishers Pond
Gos : Gosport
Hamb : Hamble
H End : Hedge End
Highb : Highbridge
Highc : Highcliffe
Holb : Holbury
H Hth : Horton Heath
Hurs : Hursley

Hythe : Hythe
Lee : Lee
L Hth : Locks Heath
Lwr S : Lower Swanwick
March : Marchwood
Net A : Netley Abbey
N Bad : North Baddesley
Nurs : Nursling
Ocn V : Ocean Village
Ott : Otterbourne
Ower : Ower
Park G : Park Gate
Ports : Portsmouth
Roms : Romsey
Rown : Rownhams
Sar G : Sarisbury Green
Seg W : Segensworth West

Shaw : Shawford
Sotn : Southampton
Sotn I : Southampton
International Airport
S'sea : Southsea
Swanw : Swanwick
Titch : Titchfield
Tot : Totton
Twy : Twyford
Wal C : Waltham Chase
Wars : Warsash
W End : West End
W Dock : Western Docks
White : Whiteley
Win : Winchester
W'lnds : Woodlands

1st Street. *Hythe* 2G **55**
2nd Street. *Hythe* 2F **55**
3rd Street. *Hythe* 2F **55**
4th Street. *Hythe* 2F **55**
(in two parts)
5th Street. *Hythe* 2E **55**
6th Street. *Hythe* 1E **55**
7th Street. *Hythe* 2E **55**
(in three parts)
8th Street. *Hythe* 1E **55**
9th Street. *Hythe* 4D **54**
10th Street. *Hythe* 4D **54**
11th Street.
Hythe 3D **54**

12th Street. *Hythe* 3D **54**
(in two parts)
13th Street. *Hythe* 3D **54**
14th Street. *Hythe* 3C **54**

A

Aaron Ct. *March* 3D **38**
A Avenue. *Hythe* 3C **54**
(in two parts)
Abbey Clo. *Hythe* 3E **53**
Abbey Ct. *Sotn* 4B **30**
Abbey Enterprise Cen.
Roms 2B **12**
Abbey Fields Clo. *Net A* . .1D **46**
Abbey Hill. *Net A* 6H **41**

Abbey Pk. Ind. Est. *Roms* . .6G **7**
Abbey, The. *Roms* 5B **6**
Abbey Wlk. Roms *5B* **6**
(off Church St.)
Abbey Water. *Roms* 5B **6**
Abbotsbury Rd. *Eastl* 5F **17**
Abbotsfield. *Tot* 4E **27**
Abbotsfield Clo. *Sotn* 4G **21**
Abbots Way. *Net A* 1D **46**
Abbotswood Clo. *Roms* 3F **7**
Abbotts Rd. *Eastl* 6G **15**
Abbotts Way. *Sotn* 2D **30**
Abercrombie Gdns. *Sotn* . .5E **21**
Aberdeen Rd. *Sotn* 2E **31**
Aberdour Clo. *Sotn* 3B **32**
Abingdon Gdns. *Sotn* . . .6A **22**

Above Bar St.
Sotn 6B **30** (1D **4**)
Abraham Clo. *Bot* 6C **34**
Abshot Clo. *Fare* 6F **49**
Abshot Rd. *Fare* 6F **49**
Acacia Rd. *Sotn* 6H **31**
Acorn Clo. *March* 4E **39**
Acorn Ct. *Hamb* 4F **47**
Acorn Dri. *Rown* 2C **20**
Acorn Gro. *Chan F* 3B **14**
Acorns, The. *Burs* 5F **43**
Acorn Workshops.
Sotn 4D **30**
Adams Clo. *H End* 6H **25**
Adamson Clo. *Chan F* 5F **9**
Adams Rd. *Hythe* 4E **53**

Adams Way. *Fare* 2G **49**
Adams Wood Dri.
  March 4D **38**
Adcock Ct. *Sotn* 2C **20**
Addison Clo. *Roms* 3E **7**
Addison Rd. *Eastl* 2B **16**
Addison Rd. *Sar G* 1D **48**
Addis Sq. *Sotn* 2D **30**
  (in two parts)
Adelaide Rd. *Sotn* 3E **31**
Adela Verne Clo. *Sotn* .2E **43**
Adey Clo. *Sotn* 3B **42**
Admirals Clo. *Fawl* 2H **55**
Admirals Ct. *Hamb* 5G **47**
Admiral's Rd. *L Hth* . . .3F **49**
Admiral's Way. *Hamb* . .4F **47**
Admirals Way. *Hythe* 1E **53**
Admiralty Ho. *Sotn* 3C **40**
Admiralty Way. *March* .2D **38**
Adur Clo. *W End* 2B **32**
Africa Dri. *March* 4D **38**
Agitator Rd. *Hythe* 1H **55**
Agwi Rd. *Hythe* 1H **55**
Aikman La. *Tot* 4B **26**
Ailsa La. *Sotn* 1F **41**
Ainsley Gdns. *Eastl* 2A **16**
Aintree Ct. *White* 5F **45**
Aintree Rd. *Cal* 2C **26**
Alandale Rd. *Sotn* 1D **42**
Alan Drayton Way.
  Eastl 5F **17**
Albacore Av. *Wars* 6C **48**
Albany Pk. Ct. *Sotn* . . .3B **30**
Albany Rd. *Holb* 4C **54**
Albany Rd. *Roms* 5C **6**
Albany Rd. *Sotn* 5G **29**
Albemarle Ct. *Sotn* 6E **23**
Albert Clo. *Net A* 2C **46**
  (in two parts)
Albert Rd. *Eastl* 2B **16**
Albert Rd. *H End* 6H **33**
Albert Rd. N.
  Sotn 2D **40** (5H **5**)
Albert Rd. S.
  Sotn 2D **40** (6H **5**)
Albion Pl. *Sotn* 1B **40** (4D **4**)
  (in two parts)
Albion Towers.
  Sotn 1D **40** (3G **5**)
Albury Pl. *Chan F* 4D **8**
Alcantara Cres.
  Sotn 2E **41** (6H **5**)
Alder Clo. *Col C* 5G **11**
Alder Clo. *Dib P* 3A **52**
Alder Clo. *March* 3D **38**
Alder Clo. *Roms* 6G **7**
Alder Hill Dri. *Tot* 3B **26**
Aldermoor Av. *Sotn* . . .5E **21**
Aldermoor Clo. *Sotn* . .5G **21**
Aldermoor Rd. *Sotn* . . .5E **21**
Alderney Clo. *Sotn* 5C **20**
Alder Rd. *Sotn* 5D **20**
Alderwood Av. *Chan F* .1C **14**
Alexander Clo. *Tot* 3D **26**
Alexander Ct. *Sotn* 5H **29**
Alexandra Clo. *Hythe* .2E **53**
Alexandra Rd. *Chan F* .5G **9**
Alexandra Rd. *H End* . .6H **33**
Alexandra Rd. *Hythe* . .2E **53**
Alexandra Rd. *Sotn* . . .5H **29**
Alexandra Way. *Bot* . . .4E **35**
Alfred Clo. *Tot* 3C **26**
Alfred Rose Ct. *Sotn* . .5G **23**
Alfred St. *Sotn* 5D **30**
Alfriston Gdns. *Sotn* . .1B **42**
Allan Gro. *Roms* 5E **7**
Allbrook Hill. *Eastl* . . .6B **10**
Allbrook Knoll. *Eastl* . .6A **10**

Allbrook Way. *Eastl* 5A **10**
Allen Rd. *H End* 4A **34**
Allerton Clo. *Tot* 2D **26**
Allington La.
  W End & F Oak 6B **24**
Allington Mnr. Farm Bus. Cen.
  F Oak 2E **25**
Allington Rd. *Sotn* 4B **28**
Allison Ho. *H End* 3A **34**
Allotment Rd. *H End* . .5H **33**
Allotment Rd. *Sar G* . .2C **48**
All Saints Ho. *Sotn* . . .5F **5**
Alma Rd. *Roms* 5C **6**
Alma Rd. *Sotn* 3C **30**
Almatade Rd. *Sotn* 4A **32**
Almond Ct. *Sotn* 5G **29**
Almond Rd. *Sotn* 5G **29**
Alpha Ho. *Sotn* 6G **13**
Alpine Clo. *Sotn* 3B **32**
Alton Clo. *F Oak* 5H **17**
Alum Clo. *Holb* 5D **54**
Alum Way. *Sotn* 4B **32**
Alyne Ho. *Sotn* 3B **30**
Amberley Clo. *Bot* 4E **35**
Amberley Clo. *N Bad* . .2C **12**
Amberley Ct. *Tot* 6E **27**
Amberslade Wlk. *Dib P* .5D **52**
Amberwood Clo. *Cal* . . .1C **26**
Ambledale. *Sar G* 3C **48**
Ambleside. *Bot* 6B **34**
Ambleside Gdns. *Sotn* .2A **42**
Amoy St. *Sotn* 5B **30**
Ampthill Rd. *Sotn* 4F **29**
Ancasta Rd. *Sotn* 4D **30**
Anchor Bus. Cen.
  Chan F 2D **14**
Andalusian Gdns.
  White 5F **45**
Anderby Rd. *Sotn* 1B **28**
Andersen Clo. *White* . .5G **45**
Anderson Clo. *Roms* . . .2F **7**
Anderson's Rd.
  Sotn 2D **40** (5H **5**)
Andes Clo. *Sotn* 2E **41**
Andes Rd. *Nurs* 6H **19**
Andover Rd. *Sotn* 5H **29**
Andrew Clo. *Dib P* 5E **53**
Andrew Clo. *Tot* 4D **26**
Andromeda Rd. *Sotn* . .5C **20**
Anfield Clo. *F Oak* 3F **17**
Anfield Ct. *F Oak* 6H **17**
Angel Cres. *Sotn* 5H **31**
Angelica Way. *White* . .5H **45**
Anglers Way. *Lwr S* . . .5B **44**
Anglesea Ct. *Sotn* 2F **29**
Anglesea Rd. *Sotn* 2F **29**
Anglesea Ter.
  Sotn 2D **40** (5H **5**)
Anson Dri. *Sotn* 1C **42**
Anstey Rd. *Roms* 3E **7**
Anton Clo. *Roms* 5F **7**
Anvil Clo. *W End* 1C **32**
Apollo Pl. *Sotn* 3A **32**
Apollo Rd. *Chan F* 6H **9**
Apple Ind. Est. *Fare* . .2G **49**
Appleton Rd. *Sotn* 2G **31**
Appletree Clo. *Cal* 2C **26**
  (in two parts)
Appletree Ct. *Bot* 4E **35**
Applewood. *Park G* 2E **49**
Applewood Gdns.
  Sotn 2A **42**
Applewood Pl. *Tot* 5C **26**
April Clo. *Sotn* 4B **32**
April Gro. *Sar G* 4C **48**
Apsley Pl. *Chan F* 4D **8**
Aquila Way. *Hamb* 5F **47**
Aquitania Ho. *Sotn* 6E **31**

Arabian Gdns. *White* . .6G **45**
Arcadia Clo. *Sotn* 6G **21**
Archers. *Sotn* 5A **30**
Archers Clo. *Cal* 2C **26**
Archers Rd. *Eastl* 3A **16**
Archers Rd. *Sotn* 4A **30**
Archery Gdns. *Sotn* . . .3H **41**
Archery Gro. *Sotn* 3G **41**
Archery Rd. *Sotn* 4G **41**
Arden Clo. *Sotn* 2B **32**
Ardingly Cres. *H End* .1B **34**
Ardnave Cres. *Sotn* . . .4B **22**
Argosy Clo. *Wars* 6D **48**
Argyle Rd. *Sotn* . .6C **30** (1F **5**)
Arliss Rd. *Sotn* 2E **29**
Arlott Ct. *Sotn* 3A **30**
Armada Clo. *Rown* 2C **20**
Armada Dri. *Hythe* 4D **52**
Armadale Ho. *Sotn* 5E **31**
  (off Princes Ct.)
Armitage Av. *Dib P* . . .5D **52**
Armstrong Ct. *Sotn* . . .4D **20**
Arnheim Clo. *Sotn* 5G **21**
Arnheim Rd. *Sotn* 5H **21**
Arnold Rd. *Eastl* 1A **24**
Arnold Rd. *Sotn* 1E **31**
Arnwood Av. *Dib P* 6D **52**
Arreton. *Net A* 6C **42**
Arrow Clo. *Eastl* 2A **16**
Arrow Clo. *Sotn* 4F **41**
Arters Lawn. *March* . . .6G **37**
Arthur Rd. *Eastl* 3A **16**
Arthur Rd. *Sotn* 4H **29**
Arthurs Gdns. *H End* . .6H **25**
Arundel Ho. *Sotn* 5E **31**
  (SO14)
Arundel Ho. *Sotn* 3B **30**
  (SO15)
Arundel Rd. *Eastl* 1A **16**
Arundel Rd. *Tot* 3G **27**
Arun Rd. *W End* 6B **24**
Ascot Clo. *Fare* 5G **49**
Ascupart St.
  Sotn 1D **40** (3G **5**)
  (in two parts)
Asford Gro. *Eastl* 3C **16**
Ashbridge Ri. *Chan F* . .4C **8**
Ashburnham Clo. *Sotn* .6F **31**
Ashburton Clo. *Dib* . . .3B **52**
Ashby Cres. *Tot* 4D **26**
Ashby Rd. *Sotn* 2B **42**
Ashby Rd. *Tot* 4D **26**
Ash Clo. *Burs* 5F **43**
Ash Clo. *Col C* 4F **11**
Ash Clo. *Hythe* 6E **53**
Ash Clo. *N Bad* 2D **12**
Ash Clo. *Roms* 6F **7**
Ash Clo. *Sotn* 5C **32**
Ash Ct. *Sotn* 2H **41**
Ashdene. *Sotn* 3F **29**
Ashdene Rd. *Asht* 3B **36**
Ashdown. *Fawl* 2F **55**
Ashdown Clo. *Chan F* . .3E **9**
Ashdown Dri. *Chan F* . .3E **9**
Ashdown Rd. *Chan F* . .3E **9**
Ashdown Rd. *Fawl* 3F **55**
Ashdown Way. *Roms* . .5E **7**
Ashen Clo. *Chan F* 5E **9**
Ashford Cres. *Hythe* . .3F **53**
Ash Gro. *Asht* 2C **36**
Ashlea Clo. *F Oak* 2G **17**
Ashleigh Clo. *Hythe* . .6E **53**
Ashlett Clo. *Fawl* 2H **55**
Ashlett M. *Fawl* 2H **55**
Ashlett Rd. *Fawl* 2H **55**
Ashley Clo. *Swanw* 6F **45**
Ashley Ct. *Burs* 3G **43**
Ashley Cres. *Sotn* 3C **42**

Ashley Cross Clo.
  Holb 5D **54**
Ashley Gdns. *Chan F* . .2G **15**
Ashley Ho. *Roms* 6B **6**
Ashley Meadows.
  Roms 4D **6**
Ashmead Rd. *Sotn* 6D **20**
Ashridge Clo. *Sotn* 3B **30**
Ash Rd. *Asht* 3B **36**
Ashton Ho. *Sotn* 4H **41**
Ashton Pl. *Chan F* 4D **8**
Ashtree Ct. *Chan F* 4E **15**
Ash Tree Rd. *Sotn* 2G **31**
Ashurst Bri. Rd. *Tot* . . .5C **26**
Ashurst Campsite.
  Asht 5A **36**
Ashurst Clo. *Asht* 3B **36**
Ashurst Clo. *Sotn* 4A **42**
Ashwood. *L Hth* 5G **49**
Ashwood. *White* 2H **49**
Ashwood Gdns. *Sotn* . .6A **22**
Ashwood Gdns. *Tot* . . .5C **26**
Aspen Av. *Wars* 1B **50**
Aspen Clo. *Col C* 5G **11**
Aspen Clo. *H End* 4B **34**
Aspen Holt. *Sotn* 4C **22**
Aspen Wlk. *Tot* 3B **26**
Aster Rd. *Sotn* 5E **23**
Astra Ct. *Hythe* 1E **53**
Astral Gdns. *Hamb* 4F **47**
Asturias Way. *Sotn* . . .2E **41**
Asylum Rd. *Sotn* 5C **30**
Atheling Rd. *Hythe* . . .2E **53**
Athelstan Rd. *Sotn* 4G **31**
Athena Clo. *F Oak* 4G **17**
Atherfield Rd. *Sotn* . . .6C **20**
Atherley Ct. *Sotn* 3A **30**
Atherley Rd. *Sotn* 5H **29**
Atlantic Clo. *Sotn* 3D **40**
Atlantic Pk. Vw.
  W End 6A **24**
Auckland Rd. *Sotn* 4D **28**
Audley Pl. *Eastl* 5F **17**
Augustine Rd. *Sotn* . . .5D **30**
Augustus Clo. *Chan F* .6G **9**
Augustus Way.
  Chan F 6G **9**
Austen Clo. *Tot* 5D **26**
Austen Gdns. *White* . . .5G **45**
Autumn Pl. *Sotn* 2C **30**
Autumn Rd. *March* 4E **39**
Avebury Gdns. *Chan F* .4C **8**
Avenger Clo. *Chan F* . .2D **14**
Avenue C. *Hythe* 6H **53**
Avenue D. *Hythe* 6H **53**
Avenue E. *Hythe* 6H **53**
Avenue Rd. *Sotn* 3C **30**
Avenue, The. *Sotn* 6B **22**
Avington Clo. *Eastl* . . .2D **16**
Avington Ct. *Sotn* 5B **22**
Avonborne Way.
  Chan F 5D **8**
Avon Ct. *Net A* 2B **46**
Avon Cres. *Roms* 5F **7**
Avon Grn. *Chan F* 2F **15**
Avon Ho. *Sotn* 5E **31**
Avon Rd. *Sotn* 2H **31**
Avon Way. *W End* 1E **33**
Avondale Mobile Home Pk.
  Col C 4G **11**
Aynsley Ct. *Sotn* 4H **29**

B

Bk. of the Walls.
  Sotn 3C **40** (6E **5**)
  (in two parts)

Bacon Clo. *Sotn* 4H **41**
Baddesley Clo. *N Bad* 2D **12**
Baddesley Pk. Ind. Est.
   N Bad 3F **13**
Baddesley Rd. *N Bad* 5C **8**
Baden Powell Ho.
   Roms 5C **6**
   (off Winchester Rd.)
Baden Powell Way.
   Roms 5C **6**
Bader Clo. *H End* 3A **34**
Badger Clo. *Eastl* 5F **17**
Badger Ct. *Eastl* 5F **17**
Badgers, The. *Net A* 1C **46**
Badgers Wlk. *Dib P* 4D **52**
Badger Wood Pl. *Sotn* . . .2H **31**
Badminton La. *Fawl* 4H **55**
Bagber Rd. *Tot* 4F **27**
Bagshot M. *Sotn* 2H **41**
Bailey Clo. *Bot* 5E **35**
Bailey Grn. *Sotn* 1A **32**
Bakers Drove. *Rown* 4C **20**
Bakers Wharf. *Sotn* 6E **31**
Balaclava Rd. *Sotn* 4A **32**
Balfour Rd. *Sotn* 6C **32**
Ballard Clo. *Sotn* 2B **28**
Balliol Clo. *Fare* 6G **49**
Balmoral Clo. *Chan F* 5D **8**
Balmoral Clo. *Sotn* 4G **21**
Balmoral Ct. *Sotn* 5E **29**
Balmoral Way. *Rown* 3B **20**
Baltic Rd. *W End* 1E **33**
Banbury Av. *Sotn* 1C **42**
Bangor Rd. *Sotn* 5F **29**
Banister Gdns. *Sotn* 4B **30**
Banister Grange. *Sotn* 4B **30**
Banister M. *Sotn* 4B **30**
Banister Rd. *Sotn* 4B **30**
Bank Side. *Sotn* 5G **23**
Banning St. *Roms* 6B **6**
Bannister Ct. *Tot* 4G **27**
Barbe Baker Av.
   W End 1C **32**
Barberry Dri. *Tot* 2B **26**
Barclay M. *Hythe* 6E **53**
Barford Clo. *Chan F* 5D **8**
Bargate Shop. Cen.
   Sotn 1C **40** (4E **5**)
Bargate St.
   Sotn 1B **40** (4D **4**)
Barker Mill Clo. *Rown* 3C **20**
Bark Mill M. *Roms* 6B **6**
Barle Clo. *W End* 1B **32**
Barnbrook Rd. *Sar G* 3C **48**
Barnes Clo. *Sar G* 3B **48**
Barnes Clo. *Sotn* 5C **32**
Barnes La. *Sar G* 4B **48**
Barnes Rd. *Sotn* 5C **32**
Barnes Wallis Rd. *Fare* . . .3H **49**
Barnfield Clo. *Sotn* 4G **41**
Barnfield Ct. *Sotn* 4H **41**
Barnfield Flats. *Sotn* 4H **41**
Barnfield Rd. *Sotn* 4H **41**
Barnfield Way. *Sotn* 4H **41**
Barn Piece. *Chan F* 1B **14**
Barnsfield Cres. *Tot* 4C **26**
Barnsland. *W End* 6C **24**
Baron Rd. *Hamb* 4F **47**
Barons Mead. *Sotn* 6C **20**
Barratt Ind. Pk. *White* 2G **49**
Barrie Clo. *White* 5G **45**
Barrington Clo. *Eastl* 2H **15**
Barrow Down Gdns.
   Sotn 2E **43**
Barry Rd. *Sotn* 5B **32**
Barters Clo. *Sotn* 2D **28**
Bartletts, The. *Hamb* 5G **47**
Bartley Av. *Tot* 5E **27**

Barton Clo. *Roms* 4E **7**
Barton Cres. *Sotn* 2H **31**
Barton Dri. *Hamb* 4F **47**
Barton Dri. *H End* 4B **34**
Barton Pk. Ind. Est.
   Eastl 5B **16**
Barton Rd. *Eastl* 4C **16**
Bartons, The. *H End* 5G **33**
Bartram Rd. *Tot* 5G **27**
   (in two parts)
Barwell Ter. *H End* 5B **34**
Basing Way. *Chan F* 3C **14**
Bassett Av. *Sotn* 6B **22**
Bassett Clo. *Sotn* 5B **22**
Bassett Ct. *Sotn* 5B **22**
Bassett Cres. E. *Sotn* 5B **22**
Bassett Cres. W. *Sotn* 6B **22**
Bassett Dale. *Sotn* 3B **22**
Bassett Gdns. *Sotn* 5B **22**
Bassett Grn. *Sotn* 4D **22**
Bassett Grn. Clo. *Sotn* . . .4C **22**
Bassett Grn. Ct. *Sotn* 4D **22**
Bassett Grn. Dri. *Sotn* 3C **22**
Bassett Grn. Rd. *Sotn* 2C **22**
Bassett Heath Av. *Sotn* . . .2B **22**
Bassett Lodge. *Sotn* 5B **22**
Bassett Mdw. *Sotn* 5B **22**
Bassett M. *Sotn* 4B **22**
Bassett Row. *Sotn* 3B **22**
Bassett Wood Dri.
   Sotn 3B **22**
Bassett Wood M. *Sotn* 5B **22**
Bassett Wood Rd.
   Sotn 3B **22**
Batchelor Grn. *Burs* 5G **43**
Bath Clo. *Sotn* 5B **32**
Bath Rd. *Sotn* 5B **32**
Bath St. *Sotn* 4C **30**
Batten Way. *Sotn* 5G **23**
Battle Clo. *Sar G* 3D **48**
B Avenue. *Hythe* 3C **54**
   (in three parts)
Baxter Rd. *Sotn* 6E **33**
Bay Clo. *Sotn* 2A **42**
Bay Rd. *Sotn* 2A **42**
Bay Tree Gdns. *March* 4D **38**
Bay Trees. *Sotn* 5E **33**
Beach La. *Net A* 1A **46**
Beacon Bottom.
   Park G 1E **49**
Beacon Clo. *Park G* 1E **49**
Beacon Clo. *Rown* 3B **20**
Beacon M. *W End* 3D **32**
Beacon Mt. *Park G* 1E **49**
Beacon Rd. *W End* 2D **32**
Beacon Way. *Park G* 1E **49**
Bealing Clo. *Sotn* 5D **22**
Bearslane Clo. *Tot* 2D **26**
Beatrice Rd. *Sotn* 4G **29**
Beattie Ri. *H End* 1A **34**
Beatty Clo. *L Hth* 3F **49**
Beatty Ct. *Sotn* 6C **32**
Beaulieu Clo. *Sotn* 4F **21**
Beaulieu Ct. *Sotn* 2C **30**
Beaulieu Rd.
   Dib P & Hythe 6C **52**
Beaulieu Rd. *Eastl* 3A **16**
Beaulieu Rd. *Hamb* 4F **47**
Beaumaris Clo. *Chan F* . . .3C **14**
Beaumaris Gdns.
   Hythe 1D **52**
Beaumont Clo. *Sotn* 6A **22**
Beaumont Rd. *Tot* 4G **27**
Beauworth Av. *Sotn* 3C **32**
Beaver Dri. *Eastl* 5G **17**
Beck Clo. *Sar G* 4C **48**
Bedford Av. *Sotn* 3G **41**
Bedford Clo. *H End* 5B **34**

Bedford Pl. *Sotn* 5B **30**
Bedwell Clo. *Rown* 3D **20**
Beech Av. *Sotn* 4G **31**
Beech Clo. *Chan F* 4F **9**
Beech Clo. *Hamb* 5E **47**
Beech Clo. *Roms* 6F **7**
Beech Ct. *Sotn* 2H **41**
Beech Cres. *Hythe* 6E **53**
Beechcroft Clo. *Chan F* . . .2F **15**
Beechcroft Way.
   Chan F 1F **15**
Beechdale Clo. *Cal* 1C **26**
Beechdale Wlk. *Cal* 1C **26**
Beeches, The. *F Oak* 3G **17**
Beechfield Ct. *Sotn* 3F **29**
Beech Gdns. *Hamb* 5E **47**
Beechmount Rd. *Sotn* 4B **22**
Beech Rd. *Asht* 3B **36**
Beech Rd. *Chan F* 5F **9**
Beech Rd. *H End* 4B **34**
Beech Rd. *Sotn* 5F **29**
Beechwood Clo. *Chan F* . . .4C **8**
Beechwood Clo. *Wars* 1B **50**
Beechwood Cres.
   Chan F 4C **8**
Beechwood Gdns.
   Sotn 3H **31**
Beechwood Ri. *W End* 2C **32**
Beechwood Rd. *Holb* 5C **54**
Beechwood Way.
   Dib P 4A **52**
Begonia Rd. *Sotn* 5D **22**
Belbins Bus. Pk. *Roms* 1D **6**
Belfry Wlk. *Fare* 5G **49**
   (in two parts)
Belgrave Ind. Est. *Sotn* . . .5F **31**
Belgrave Rd. *Sotn* 1E **31**
Belgrave Rd. Ind. Est.
   Sotn 1E **31**
Bellamy Ct. *Sotn* 3F **31**
Bell Clo. *Fawl* 3F **55**
Bellemoor Rd. *Sotn* 2G **29**
Bellevue Rd. *Eastl* 4A **16**
Bellevue Rd. *Sotn* 5C **30**
Bellevue Ter. *Sotn* 5C **30**
Bellflower Way. *Chan F* 6B **8**
Bell St. *Roms* 5B **6**
Bell St. *Sotn* 2C **40** (5F **5**)
Belmont Clo. *Dib P* 4E **53**
Belmont Rd. *Chan F* 4E **15**
Belmont Rd. *Sotn* 3D **30**
Belstone Rd. *Tot* 4E **27**
Belton Rd. *Sotn* 2B **42**
Belvedere Rd. *Dib P* 4E **53**
Belvidere Ho. *Sotn* 5E **31**
Belvidere Rd. *Sotn* 1E **41**
Belvidere Ter. *Sotn* 6E **31**
   (in two parts)
Bembridge. *Net A* 1C **46**
Bembridge Clo. *Sotn* 4E **23**
Benbow Gdns. *Cal* 1C **26**
Bencroft Ct. *Sotn* 4D **22**
Benedict Clo. *Roms* 5F **7**
Benhams Farm Clo.
   Sotn 2A **32**
Benhams Rd. *Sotn* 1A **32**
Ben More Gdns. *Chan F* . . .5D **8**
Bennett Wlk. *Black* 3F **55**
Benson Rd. *Sotn* 3F **29**
Bentham Ct. *Sotn* 5C **22**
Bentham Way. *Swanw* 5B **44**
Bentley Ct. *Sotn* 2C **30**
Bentley Grn. *Sotn* 3C **32**
Berber Clo. *White* 1G **49**
Bere Clo. *Chan F* 5C **8**
Beresford Clo. *Chan F* 2G **15**
Beresford Gdns.
   Chan F 2G **15**

Beresford Rd. *Chan F* 2G **15**
Bergen Cres. *H End* 6A **34**
Berkeley Clo. *Sotn* 4A **30**
Berkeley Gdns. *H End* 6A **34**
Berkeley Rd. *Sotn* 5B **30**
Bernard St. *Sotn* . . .2C **40** (5E **5**)
Bernwood Gro. *Black* 6E **55**
Berry Clo. *H End* 5B **34**
Berrywood Gdns.
   H End 4H **33**
Berthon Ho. *Roms* 6B **6**
Beta Ho. *Sotn* 6G **13**
Betteridge Dri. *Rown* 3B **20**
Beulah Rd. *Sotn* 2E **29**
Bevan Clo. *Sotn* 4G **41**
Beverley Clo. *Park G* 3G **49**
Beverley Gdns. *Burs* 4E **43**
Beverley Gdns. *Roms* 3F **7**
Beverley Heights.
   Sotn 6H **23**
Beverley Rd. *Dib P* 6D **53**
Bevis Clo. *Fawl* 3F **55**
Bevis Clo. *Wars* 1B **50**
Bevois Gdns. *Sotn* 4C **30**
Bevois Hill. *Sotn* 3D **30**
Bevois M. *Sotn* 4C **30**
Bevois Valley Rd.
   Sotn 4D **30**
Biddlesgate Ct.
   Sotn 2B **40** (5D **4**)
Bideford Clo. *Sotn* 2C **28**
Bilberry Clo. *L Hth* 5D **49**
Bilberry Dri. *March* 3C **38**
Billington Gdns.
   H End 1B **34**
Bindon Clo. *Sotn* 1E **29**
Bindon Rd. *Sotn* 1E **29**
Binsey Clo. *Sotn* 3C **28**
Binstead Clo. *Sotn* 4E **23**
Birch Clo. *Col C* 5F **11**
Birch Clo. *Roms* 6G **7**
Birch Dale. *Hythe* 4F **53**
Birchdale Clo. *Wars* 1B **50**
Birchen Clo. *Park G* 3G **49**
Birchen Rd. *Park G* 3G **49**
Birches Clo., The.
   N Bad 2D **12**
Birches, The. *Sotn* 3B **32**
Birchglade. *Cal* 1C **26**
Birch Gro. *Eastl* 1A **16**
Birchlands. *Tot* 6D **26**
Birch Rd. *Chilw* 1B **22**
Birch Rd. *H End* 4B **34**
Birch Rd. *Sotn* 6E **21**
Birch Wood. *Sotn* 6E **33**
Birchwood Gdns.
   H End 3A **34**
Birdfield. *Chan F* 6A **8**
Bishops Clo. *Tot* 3E **27**
Bishops Ct. *Eastl* 2D **16**
Bishops Cres. *Sotn* 1H **41**
Bishops Ga. *Fare* 4G **49**
Bishops Rd. *Sotn* 2G **41**
Bishopstoke La. *Bram* 1E **17**
Bishopstoke Mnr.
   Eastl 4C **16**
Bishopstoke Rd. *Eastl* 4B **16**
Bisley Ct. *Sotn* 2B **42**
Bitterne Cres. *Sotn* 5A **32**
Bitterne Mnr. Ho.
   Sotn 4E **31**
Bitterne Rd. *Sotn* 5H **31**
   (in three parts)
Bitterne Rd. E. *Sotn* 4A **32**
Bitterne Rd. W. *Sotn* 4E **31**
Bitterne Village. *Sotn* 4A **32**
Bitterne Way. *Sotn* 5G **31**

Blackberry Dri. *F Oak* 6H **17**
Blackberry Ter. *Sotn* 4D **30**
Blackbird Rd. *Eastl* 6F **15**
Blackbushe Clo. *Sotn* 4D **20**
Blackdown Clo. *Dib P* 4B **52**
Blackfield Rd.
   Black & Fawl 4E **55**
Blackthorn Clo. *Sotn* 6H **31**
Blackthorn Grn. *Col C* 5G **11**
Blackthorn Rd. *Sotn* 6H **31**
Blackwater Dri. *Tot* 2D **26**
Blackwater M. *Tot* 2D **26**
Bladon Rd. *Sotn* 1G **29**
Blake Clo. *Nurs* 4B **20**
Blakeney Rd. *Sotn* 1B **28**
Blann Clo. *Nurs* 4A **20**
Bleaklow Clo. *Sotn* 3D **28**
Blechynden Ter.
   Sotn 6A **30** (2B **4**)
Blencowe Dri. *Chan F* 2A **14**
Blendworth La. *Sotn* 4C **32**
Blenheim Av. *Sotn* 2C **30**
Blenheim Clo. *Chan F* 3B **14**
Blenheim Clo. *Tot* 5D **26**
Blenheim Ct. *Sotn* 2C **30**
Blenheim Gdns. *Dib P* 4B **52**
Blenheim Gdns. *Sotn* 1D **30**
Blenheim Ho. *Eastl* 5B **16**
Blenheim Ho. Roms 5E **7**
   (off Chambers Av.)
Blenheim Rd. *Eastl* 5A **16**
Blighmont Av. *Sotn* 5F **29**
Blighmont Cres. *Sotn* 5F **29**
Blind La. *Curd* 1H **35**
Blind La. *W End* 4H **25**
Bloomsbury Wlk.
   Sotn 3G **41**
Blossom Clo. *Bot* 5C **34**
Blue Anchor La.
   Sotn 2B **40** (5D **4**)
Bluebell Copse. *L Hth* ...5D **48**
Bluebell Rd. *Sotn* 5D **22**
Bluestar Gdns. *H End* ...1A **34**
Blundell La. *Burs* 3H **43**
Blyth Clo. *Sotn* 1B **28**
Boakes Pl. *Asht* 3C **36**
Bodmin Rd. *Eastl* 4E **17**
Bodycoats Rd. *Chan F* 1F **15**
Bolderwood Clo. *Eastl* 5F **17**
Boldrewood Rd. *Sotn* 5A **22**
Bolhinton Av. *March* 4B **38**
Bonchurch Clo. *Sotn* 4E **23**
Bond Rd. *Sotn* 2G **31**
Bond St. *Sotn* 5E **31**
Boniface Clo. *Tot* 3D **26**
Boniface Cres. *Sotn* 6B **20**
Boothby Clo. *Tot* 5G **27**
Borrowdale Rd. *Sotn* 2C **28**
Bossington Clo. *Rown* 4C **20**
Boston Ct. *Chan F* 6F **9**
Bosville. *Eastl* 1H **15**
Boswell Clo. *Bot* 4E **35**
Boswell Clo. *Sotn* 5C **32**
Botany Bay Rd. *Sotn* 2B **42**
Botley Gdns. *Sotn* 2E **43**
Botley Hill. *Bot* 5F **35**
Botley Ind. Est. *Bot* 4F **35**
Botley Mills Craft And Bus. Cen.
   Bot 4E **35**
Botley Rd.
   Curd & Bish W 4G **35**
Botley Rd.
   F Oak & H Hth,Durl ..3G **17**
Botley Rd.
   N Bad & Chilw 2E **13**
Botley Rd. *Roms* 5D **6**
Botley Rd.
   Roms & N Bad 6G **7**

Botley Rd. *Sotn* 3C **42**
   (in two parts)
Botley Rd.
   Swanw & Park G 5E **45**
Botley Rd.
   W End & H End 2E **33**
Bottings Ind. Est.
   Curd 4G **35**
Boundary Clo. *Sotn* 4D **28**
Boundary Rd. *Burs* 5F **43**
Boundstone. *Hythe* 3D **52**
Bourne Av. *Sotn* 2G **29**
Bourne Clo. *Ott* 1C **10**
Bournemouth Rd.
   Chan F 5D **14**
Bourne Rd.
   Sotn 6H **29** (1A **4**)
Bowater Clo. *Cal* 2C **26**
Bowater Way. *Cal* 2C **26**
Bowcombe. *Net A* 6C **42**
Bowden La. *Sotn* 1E **31**
Bower Clo. *Holb* 5C **54**
Bower Clo. *Sotn* 4H **41**
Bowland Ri. *Chan F* 6C **8**
Bowland Way. *Black* 6E **55**
Bowman Ct. *Sotn* 2B **42**
   (Butts Rd.)
Bowman Ct. *Sotn* 2F **41**
   (Florence Rd.)
Boyatt Cres. *Eastl* 5A **10**
Boyatt La. *Ott & Eastl* ...4A **10**
   (in three parts)
Boyatt Shop. Cen.
   Eastl 2H **15**
Boyes La. *Col C* 4G **11**
Boynton Clo. *Chan F* 5D **8**
Brabant Clo. *White* 6F **45**
Brabazon Rd. *Fare* 2H **49**
Bracken Clo. *N Bad* 4E **13**
Bracken Cres. *Eastl* 5F **17**
Bracken La. *Sotn* 2E **29**
Bracken Pl. *Chilw* 2C **22**
Bracken Rd. *N Bad* 4E **13**
Brackens, The. *Dib P* 3B **52**
Brackens, The. *L Hth* 5F **49**
Brackenway Rd. *Chan F* ...5E **9**
Bracklesham Clo.
   Sotn 2H **41**
Brackley Av. *F Oak* 4H **17**
Brackley Way. *Tot* 3D **26**
Brading Clo. *Sotn* 4E **23**
Bradley Grn. *Sotn* 5F **21**
Bradshaw Clo. *F Oak* 2H **17**
Braehead. *Hythe* 4D **52**
Braeside Clo. *Sotn* 6G **31**
Braeside Cres. *Sotn* 6G **31**
Braeside Rd. *Sotn* 6G **31**
Braishfield Clo. *Sotn* 2D **28**
Bramble Clo. *Eastl* 2B **16**
Bramble Clo. *Holb* 5C **54**
Bramble Dri. *Roms* 3F **7**
Bramblegate. *F Oak* 3G **17**
Bramble Hill. *Chan F* 1D **14**
Bramble La. *Sar G* 2C **48**
Bramble M. *Sotn* 3A **32**
Brambles Clo. *Col C* 5G **11**
Brambling Clo. *Sotn* 3F **21**
Bramblings, The. *Tot* 4C **26**
Brambridge. *Col C* 5E **11**
Bramdean M. *Sotn* 6G **31**
Bramdean Rd. *Sotn* 3D **32**
Bramley Cres. *Sotn* 3B **42**
Bramley Gdns. *H Hth* 3H **25**
Bramley Ho. *H End* 5H **33**
Brampton Ct. *Chan F* 1E **15**
Brampton Mnr. *Sotn* 4B **22**
Brampton Tower. *Sotn* ...4B **22**
Bramshott Hill. *Dib* 1A **52**

Bramshott Rd. *Sotn* 5H **41**
Bramston Rd. *Sotn* 3G **29**
Branksome Av. *Sotn* 2G **29**
Bransbury Clo. *Sotn* 5G **21**
Bransley Clo. *Roms* 3E **7**
Brasenose Clo. *Fare* 6G **49**
Brasher Clo. *Eastl* 5G **17**
Breamore Clo. *Eastl* 1A **16**
Breamore Rd. *Sotn* 4D **32**
Brean Clo. *Sotn* 1C **28**
Brecon Clo. *Chan F* 4D **14**
Brecon Clo. *Dib P* 3C **52**
Brecon Clo. Roms 4E **7**
   (off Viney Av.)
Brecon Rd. *Sotn* 6C **32**
Brendon Clo. *Dib P* 4B **52**
Brendon Grn. *Sotn* 3D **28**
Brentwood Cres. *Sotn* ...2A **32**
Breton Clo. *White* 6F **45**
Brewer Clo. *L Hth* 3F **49**
Briardene Ct. *Tot* 4E **27**
Briarswood. *Sotn* 2F **29**
Briarswood Ri. *Dib P* 4B **52**
Briar Way. *Roms* 3F **7**
Briarwood Rd. *Tot* 5C **26**
Brickfield La. *Chan F* 2D **14**
Brickfield Rd. *Sotn* 1E **31**
Brickfield Trad. Est.
   Chan F 2E **15**
Brickwoods Clo. *Roms* ...4E **7**
Bridge Clo. *Burs* 4H **43**
Bridge Ct. *Roms* 6B **6**
Bridge Rd.
   Burs & Swanw 4H **43**
Bridge Rd. *Roms* 5D **6**
Bridge Rd.
   Sar G & Park G 1C **48**
Bridge Rd. *Sotn* 2F **41**
Bridgers Clo. *Rown* 4C **20**
Bridges Clo. *Eastl* 4H **15**
Bridge Ter.
   Sotn 2D **40** (6H **5**)
Bridgwater Ct. *Sotn* 5G **29**
Bridlington Av. *Sotn* 3H **29**
Bridport Ct. *Sotn* 6G **29**
Brigantine Rd. *Wars* 6C **48**
Brighstone Clo. *Sotn* 4E **23**
Brighton Rd. *Sotn* 4B **30**
Brightside Rd. *Sotn* 1D **28**
Brindle Clo. *Sotn* 4C **22**
Brinton La. *Hythe* 1E **53**
Brinton's Rd.
   Sotn 6C **30** (1F **5**)
Brinton's Ter. *Sotn* 5C **30**
Britannia Ct. *Sotn* 6E **31**
Britannia Gdns. *H End* ...6H **25**
Britannia Rd.
   Sotn 6D **30** (1H **5**)
Britannia Wharf. *Sotn* ...1E **41**
Britannic Ho. Sotn 6E **31**
   (off Kent St.)
Briton St. *Sotn* 2C **40** (6E **5**)
Broadbent Clo. *Sotn* 3B **20**
Broad Grn.
   Sotn 1C **40** (3F **5**)
Broadlands Av. *Eastl* 1A **16**
Broadlands Rd. *Sotn* 5D **22**
Broad La. *N Bad* 2C **12**
Broadley Clo. *Holb* 4C **54**
Broadmeadow Clo. *Tot* ...4E **27**
Broadmead Rd. *Nurs* 3B **20**
Broad Oak. *Bot* 4C **34**
Broadoak Clo. *Holb* 5C **54**
Broadwater Rd. *Roms* ...6B **6**
Broadwater Rd. *Sotn* 6H **23**
Broadway. *Hamb* 2E **47**
Broadway, The. *Sotn* 2D **30**
   (SO17)

Broadway, The. *Sotn* 4D **32**
   (SO18)
Brocks Clo. *Dib P* 4B **52**
Brokenford Av. *Tot* 4G **27**
Brokenford Bus. Cen.
   Tot 4F **27**
Brokenford La. *Tot* 4F **27**
Bromley Rd. *Sotn* 2H **31**
Bronte Clo. *Tot* 5D **26**
Bronte Gdns. *White* 5G **45**
Bronte Way. *Sotn* 5G **31**
Brook Av. *Wars* 4A **48**
Brook Clo. *N Bad* 4E **13**
Brook Clo. *Sar G* 4B **48**
Brook Ct. *Sotn* 6H **29**
Brookes Hill Ind. Est.
   Cal 5B **18**
Brookfield Gdns.
   Sar G 3D **48**
Brookfield Pl. *Sotn* 1D **30**
Brookfield Rd. *F Oak* 5H **17**
Brook Ho. *Sotn* 2A **42**
Brook La. *Bot* 4D **34**
Brook La. *Wars* 6A **48**
Brooklyn Clo. *Ott* 2C **10**
Brook Rd. *F Oak* 2F **17**
Brook Rd. *Sotn* 4A **32**
Brookside. *Tot* 6F **27**
Brookside Av. *Sotn* 4D **28**
Brookside Cen. *Sotn* 4C **28**
Brookside Dri. *Sar G* 4B **48**
Brookside Way. *Sotn* 5G **23**
Brookside Way. *W End* ..1E **33**
Brooks Way. *Win* 1D **8**
Brookvale Ct. *Sotn* 2C **30**
Brookvale Rd. *Sotn* 2C **30**
Brook Valley. *Sotn* 1E **29**
Brook Wlk. *Cal* 2C **26**
Brook Way. *Roms* 3D **6**
Brookwood Av. *Eastl* 4H **15**
Brookwood Ind. Est.
   Eastl 4A **16**
Brookwood Rd. *Sotn* 3B **28**
Broom Hill Way. *Eastl* ...6A **10**
Brooms Gro. *Sotn* 2D **42**
Broomy Clo. *Dib* 2A **52**
Broughton Clo. *Sotn* 2E **29**
Brownhill Clo. *Chan F* ...6E **9**
Brownhill Ct. *Sotn* 6C **20**
Brownhill Gdns. *Chan F* ..6E **9**
Brownhill Ho. *Sotn* 6C **20**
Brownhill Rd. *Chan F* 6E **9**
Brownhill Rd. *N Bad* 3E **13**
   (in two parts)
Brownhill Way. *Sotn* 6A **20**
Browning Av. *Sotn* 5D **32**
Browning Clo. *Eastl* 4H **15**
Browning Clo. *Tot* 4D **26**
Browning Clo. *White* 4G **45**
Brownlow Av. *Sotn* 5H **31**
Brownlow Gdns. *Sotn* ...5A **32**
Brownwich La. *Fare* 5G **51**
Browsholme Clo. *Eastl* ...1A **16**
Broxburn Clo. *Chan F* ...4G **9**
Brue Clo. *Chan F* 6D **8**
Brunei Ho. *Sotn* 4C **22**
Brunel Clo. *H End* 2B **34**
Brunel Rd. *Sotn* 3A **28**
Brunel Rd. *Tot* 6D **18**
Brunel Way. *Fare* 2H **49**
Brunswick Clo. *F Oak* ...4H **17**
Brunswick Pl. *Sotn* 5B **30**
Brunswick Rd. *F Oak* 4H **17**
Brunswick Sq.
   Sotn 2C **40** (6E **5**)
Bryanston Rd. *Sotn* 6F **31**
Bryony Clo. *L Hth* 5D **48**
Bubb La. *W End* 6G **25**

Buchanan Rd. *Sotn* 4D **20**
Buchan Av. *White* 5G **45**
Buchan Ct. *Dib P* 4A **52**
Buckland Clo. *Eastl* 1A **16**
Buckland Gdns. *Cal* 1C **26**
Buckley Ct. *Sotn* 2F **29**
Buckthorn Clo. *Tot* 3B **26**
Budds La. *Roms* 3B **6**
Budds La. Ind. Est.
  Roms 3B **6**
Bugle St. *Sotn* . . .2B **40** (6D **4**)
Bullar Rd. *Sotn* 4G **31**
Bullar St. *Sotn* 5D **30**
Bullfinch Clo. *Tot* 4C **26**
Bullrush Clo. *Dib P* 5D **52**
Burbush Clo. *Holb* 5C **54**
Burgess Ct. *Sotn* 5D **22**
Burgess Gdns. *Sotn* 6A **22**
Burgess Rd. *Sotn* 6H **21**
  (in two parts)
Burghclere Rd. *Sotn* 5H **41**
Burgoyne Rd. *Sotn* 1E **43**
Burgundy Clo. *L Hth* 5D **48**
Burke Dri. *Sotn* 5C **32**
Burley Clo. *Chan F* 3D **14**
Burley Down. *Chan F* 3D **14**
Burlington Ct. *Sotn* 6B **32**
Burlington Mans. *Sotn* . . .4G **29**
Burlington Rd. *Sotn* 5A **30**
Burma Ho. *Sotn* 5G **23**
Burma Rd. *Roms* 6C **6**
Burma Way. *March* 4D **38**
Burmese Clo. *White* 6F **45**
Burnbank Gdns. *Tot* 4E **27**
Burnett Clo. *Hythe* 4F **53**
Burnett Clo. *Sotn* 2G **31**
Burnetts La.
  W End & H Hth 6G **25**
Burnham Beeches.
  Chan F 1D **14**
Burnham Chase. *Sotn* 4B **32**
Burns Clo. *Eastl* 6G **15**
Burns Pl. *Sotn* 1E **29**
Burns Rd. *Eastl* 6H **15**
Burns Rd. *Sotn* 5D **32**
Burr Clo. *Col C* 5F **11**
Burridge Rd. *Bot* 5G **35**
Burridge Rd. *Bur* 3E **45**
Bursledon Heights.
  Burs 4H **43**
Bursledon Rd. *H End* 1H **43**
Bursledon Rd.
  Sotn & Burs 5A **32**
Burton Rd. *Sotn* 5A **30**
Bury Brickfield Pk. Cvn. Site.
  Tot 1A **38**
Bury La. *Tot* 6H **27**
Bury Rd. *March* 2B **38**
Busketts Way. *Asht* 3A **36**
Buttercup Clo. *H End* 5G **33**
Buttercup Clo. *Hythe* 5E **53**
Buttercup Wlk. *Tot* 6D **26**
Buttercup Way. *L Hth* 4C **48**
Butterfield Rd. *Sotn* 6A **22**
Buttermere Clo. *Sotn* 1C **28**
Butts Ash Av. *Hythe* 6E **53**
Butts Ash Gdns. *Hythe* . . .5E **53**
Butts Ash La. *Hythe* 6D **52**
Butts Bri. Hill. *Hythe* 4E **53**
Buttsbridge Rd. *Hythe* 5E **53**
Butt's Clo. *Sotn* 1D **42**
Butt's Cres. *Sotn* 1C **42**
Butt's Rd. *Sotn* 3B **42**
Butt's Sq. *Sotn* 1C **42**
Byam's La. *March* 3E **39**
Bye Rd. *Swanw* 5B **44**
Byeways. *Hythe* 4D **52**
Byron Rd. *Sotn* 5A **30**

Byron Rd. *Eastl* 3B **16**
Byron Rd. *Sotn* 5C **32**
By-the-Wood. *Cal* 1D **26**

C

Cable St. *Sotn* 6E **31**
Cabot Dri. *Dib* 3A **52**
Cadland Ct. *Ocn V* 2E **41**
Cadland Pk. Est. *Hythe* . .3C **54**
Cadland Rd. *Hythe* 2B **54**
Caerleon Av. *Sotn* 5C **32**
Caerleon Dri. *Sotn* 5B **32**
Caernarvon Gdns.
  Chan F 3C **14**
Caistor Clo. *Sotn* 5E **21**
Calabrese. *Swanw* 6F **45**
Calbourne. *Net A* 6C **42**
Calder Clo. *Sotn* 3C **28**
Calderwood Dri. *Sotn* 1A **42**
Caledonia Dri. *Dib* 3B **52**
California Clo. *Tot* 2B **26**
Calmore Cres. *Cal* 1B **26**
Calmore Dri. *Cal* 1C **26**
Calmore Gdns. *Tot* 4C **26**
Calmore Ind. Est. *Tot* 1E **27**
  (in two parts)
Calmore Rd. *Cal & Tot* . . .1B **26**
Calshot Ct. *Ocn V* 3E **41**
Calshot Dri. *Chan F* 4C **14**
Calshot Rd. *Fawl* 2H **55**
Camargue Clo. *White* 5F **45**
Cambria Dri. *Dib* 3B **52**
Cambrian Clo. *Burs* 3G **43**
Cambridge Dri. *Chan F* . .4E **15**
  (in two parts)
Cambridge Grn.
  Chan F 4E **15**
Cambridge Grn. *Fare* 5G **49**
Cambridge Rd. *Sotn* 3C **30**
Camelia Gdns. *Sotn* 1A **32**
Camelia Gro. *F Oak* 2H **17**
Camellia Clo. *N Bad* 2E **13**
Cameron Ct. *Sotn* 4D **20**
Camley Clo. *Sotn* 4G **41**
Campbell Rd. *Eastl* 6B **16**
Campbell St. *Sotn* 5E **31**
Campbell Way. *F Oak* 2F **17**
Campion Clo. *Wars* 6C **48**
Campion Dri. *Roms* 3F **7**
Campion Rd. *Sotn* 6D **32**
Canada Pl. *Sotn* 5A **22**
Canada Rd. *Sotn* 3G **41**
Canal Clo. *Roms* 3D **6**
Canal Wlk.
  Sotn 2C **40** (5E **5**)
Canberra Rd. *Nurs* 5H **19**
Canberra Towers.
  Sotn 5H **41**
Candlemas Pl. *Sotn* 5D **30**
Candover Ct. *Sotn* 5A **42**
Candy La. *Sotn* 4E **33**
Canford Clo. *Sotn* 1B **28**
Cannon St. *Sotn* 3G **29**
Canoe Clo. *Wars* 6D **48**
Canon Ct. *Eastl* 2F **17**
Canterbury Av. *Sotn* 2C **42**
Canterbury Dri. *Dib* 3A **52**
Canton St. *Sotn* 5B **30**
Canute Ho. *Sotn* 5F **5**
Canute Rd.
  Sotn 2D **40** (6G **5**)
Canutes Pavilion.
  Ocn V 3D **40**
Canvey Ct. *Sotn* 1C **28**
Capella Gdns. *Dib* 3B **52**
Capon Clo. *Sotn* 5G **23**
Capstan Gdns. *L Hth* 4G **49**

Captain's Pl.
  Sotn 2D **40** (6G **5**)
Caraway. *White* 6H **45**
Cardinal Way. *L Hth* 4F **49**
Cardington Ct. *Sotn* 5D **20**
Carey Rd. *Sotn* 6C **32**
Carisbrooke. *Net A* 6C **42**
Carisbrooke Ct. *Roms* 3D **6**
Carisbrooke Cres.
  Chan F 2G **15**
Carisbrooke Dri. *Sotn* 5H **31**
Carlisle Rd. *Sotn* 3F **29**
Carlton Commerce Cen., The.
  Sotn 4D **30**
Carlton Ct. *Sotn* 3B **30**
Carlton Cres. *Sotn* 5B **30**
Carlton Pl. *Sotn* 5B **30**
Carlton Rd. *Sotn* 4B **30**
Carlyn Dri. *Chan F* 6C **9**
Carnation Rd. *Sotn* 4E **23**
Carne Clo. *Chan F* 5E **9**
Caroline Ct. *Sotn* 3F **29**
Carolyn Clo. *Sotn* 3G **41**
Carpathia Clo. *W End* 1A **32**
Carpenter Clo. *Hythe* 2E **53**
Carpenter Wlk. *Black* 3F **55**
Carrington Ho. *Sotn* 2C **30**
Carrol Clo. *F Oak* 3G **17**
Carronades, The.
  Sotn 6C **30** (2F **5**)
Carthage Clo. *Chan F* 6H **9**
Caspian Clo. *White* 6F **45**
Castle Ct. *Sotn* 5E **29**
Castle La. *Chan F* 3C **14**
Castle La. *N Bad* 3F **13**
Castle La. *Sotn* . . .2B **40** (5D **4**)
  (in two parts)
Castle Rd. *Net A* 1B **46**
Castle Sq. *Sotn* . . .2B **40** (5D **4**)
Castleshaw Clo. *Sotn* 4D **28**
Castle St. *Sotn* 4C **30**
Castle Way.
  Sotn 1B **40** (4D **4**)
Castlewood La.
  Chan F 3D **14**
Catamaran Clo. *Wars* 6D **48**
Cateran Clo. *Sotn* 3D **28**
Cathay Gdns. *Dib* 3A **52**
Catherine Clo. *W End* 1E **33**
Catherine Gdns.
  W End 1E **33**
Catmint Clo. *Chan F* 6B **8**
Causeway. *Roms* 6A **6**
Causeway Cres. *Tot* 3G **27**
Cavalier Clo. *Dib* 3B **52**
Cavendish Clo. *Roms* 2E **7**
Cavendish Gro. *Sotn* 3B **30**
Cavendish M. *Sotn* 3B **30**
C Avenue. *Hythe* 2C **54**
Caversham Clo. *Sotn* 1A **42**
Caversham Clo.
  W End 3D **32**
Cawte Rd. *Sotn* 5G **29**
Caxton Av. *Sotn* 5B **32**
Cecil Av. *Asht* 3C **36**
Cecil Av. *Sotn* 2F **29**
Cecil Rd. *Sotn* 2H **41**
Cedar Av. *Sotn* 3G **29**
Cedar Clo. *Burs* 5F **43**
Cedar Clo. *H End* 4A **34**
Cedar Cres. *N Bad* 2D **12**
Cedar Gdns. *Sotn* 3C **30**
Cedar Lawn. *Roms* 3F **7**
Cedar Rd. *Eastl* 6G **15**
Cedar Rd. *Hythe* 6E **53**
Cedar Rd. *Sotn* 3C **30**
Cedarwood Clo. *Cal* 3C **26**

Cedarwood Clo. *F Oak* 2H **17**
Cedric Clo. *Black* 5F **55**
Celandine Av. *L Hth* 5D **48**
Celandine Clo. *Chan F* . . .2B **14**
Cement Ter.
  Sotn 2B **40** (5D **4**)
Cemetery Rd. *Sotn* 3A **30**
Central Bri.
  Sotn 2D **40** (5G **5**)
Central Precinct, The.
  Chan F 1F **15**
Central Rd. *Sotn* 3C **40**
Central Sta. Bri.
  Sotn 6A **30** (2A **4**)
Central Trad. Est.
  Sotn 1D **40** (3H **5**)
Centre Ct. *Sotn* 3F **29**
Centre 27 Retail Pk.
  H End 2G **33**
Centre Way. *L Hth* 4D **48**
Centurion Ind. Pk.
  Sotn 4E **31**
Cerdic M. *Hamb* 3G **47**
Cerne Clo. *N Bad* 3D **12**
Cerne Clo. *W End* 2B **32**
Chadwell Av. *Sotn* 1B **42**
Chadwick Rd. *Eastl* 5H **15**
Chafen Rd. *Sotn* 3F **31**
Chaffinch Clo. *Tot* 3C **26**
Chalcroft Distribution Cen.
  W End 4H **35**
Chalewood Rd. *Black* 6E **55**
Chalfont Ct. *Sotn* 2E **29**
Chalice Ct. *H End* 5G **33**
Chalk Hill. *W End* 3C **32**
Challenger Way. *Dib* 3B **52**
Challenger Way. *Hythe* . . .2B **52**
Challis Ct. *Sotn* 2C **40** (5F **5**)
Chalmers Way. *Hamb* 4E **47**
Chaloner Cres. *Dib P* 5E **53**
Chalvington Rd.
  Chan F 2E **15**
Chalybeate Clo. *Sotn* 1F **29**
Chamberlain Rd. *Sotn* 6C **22**
Chamberlayne Ct.
  N Bad 2F **13**
Chamberlayne Rd.
  Burs 5F **43**
Chamberlayne Rd.
  Eastl 6A **16**
Chamberlayne Rd.
  Net A 1B **46**
Chambers Av. *Roms* 5E **7**
Chambers Clo. *Nurs* 4A **20**
Chancel Rd. *L Hth* 4F **49**
Chandlers Ford Ind. Est.
  Chan F 2D **15**
Chandlers Way. *Park G* . . .1F **49**
Chandos Ho.
  Sotn 2C **40** (5E **5**)
Chandos St.
  Sotn 2C **40** (5F **5**)
Channels Farm Rd.
  Sotn 4F **23**
Channel Way.
  Ocn V 2D **40** (6H **5**)
Chantry Rd.
  Sotn 2D **40** (5H **5**)
Chantry, The. *Fare* 4G **49**
Chapel Clo. *W End* 1D **32**
Chapel Cres. *Sotn* 1A **42**
Chapel Drove. *H End* 5H **33**
  (in two parts)
Chapel La. *Black* 5E **55**
Chapel La. *Curd* 2H **35**
Chapel La. *Fawl* 2G **55**
Chapel La. *Ott* 4B **10**
Chapel La. *Tot* 6E **27**

Chapel Rd. Sar G 1C 48
Chapel Rd.
  Sotn 1D 40 (4G 5)
Chapel Rd. W End 1D 32
Chapel St. Sotn ...1C 40 (4F 5)
Charden Ct. Sotn 4B 32
Charden Rd. Eastl 5G 17
Charlecote Dri. Chan F 5C 8
Charlecote Ho. Sotn 1A 4
Charles Knott Gdns.
  Sotn 4B 30
Charles Ley Ct. Fawl 2H 55
Charles St.
  Sotn 2C 40 (5F 5)
Charleston Rd. Hythe ...6H 53
Charles Watts Way.
  H End 4E 33
Charles Wyatt Ho.
  Sotn 4C 30
Charliejoy Gdns. Sotn ...5D 30
Charlotte Ct. Chan F 6G 9
Charlotte Ct. Sotn 3H 41
Charlotte Pl.
  Sotn 5C 30 (1E 5)
Charlton Rd. Sotn 3H 29
Charmus Rd. Cal 1B 26
Charmwen Cres.
  W End 1C 32
Charnwood Clo. Chan F 3E 9
Charnwood Clo. Tot 2D 26
Charnwood Cres.
  Chan F 3E 9
Charnwood Gdns.
  Chan F 3E 9
Charnwood Way. Black ..6E 55
Charterhouse Way.
  H End 2A 34
Chartwell Clo. Eastl 1B 16
Chartwell Clo. Fare 6G 49
Chase, The. Fare 5H 49
Chatsworth Rd. Eastl 1B 16
Chatsworth Rd. Sotn 5A 32
Chaucer Rd. Sotn 5D 32
Chaveney Clo. Dib P 5D 52
Chawton Clo. Sotn 3D 32
Cheam Way. Tot 2D 26
Cheddar Clo. Sotn 2G 41
Cheltenham Gdns.
  H End 1A 34
Chelveston Cres. Sotn ...5E 21
Chelwood Ga. Sotn 4B 22
Cheping Gdns. Bot 5E 35
Chepstow Clo. Chan F ...1D 14
Chepstow Clo. Tot 3C 26
Cherbourg Rd. Eastl 6H 15
Cheriton Av. Sotn 4C 32
Cheriton Rd. Eastl 6H 15
Cherryton Gdns. Holb ...5B 54
Cherry Tree Ct. Wars ...6A 48
Cherry Wlk. Sotn 3G 29
Cherry Wlk. Wars 1A 50
Cherrywood. H End 5H 33
Cherrywood Gdns. Tot ...4C 26
Cherville Ct. Roms 5B 6
Cherville St. Roms 5B 6
Cherwell Cres. Sotn 3C 28
Cherwell Gdns. Chan F ..2F 15
Cherwell Ho. Sotn 2C 28
Chessel Av. Sotn 4G 31
Chessel Cres. Sotn 4G 31
Chester Rd. Sotn 2A 32
Chesterton Pl. White 5G 45
Chestnut Av.
  Chan F & Eastl 4E 15
Chestnut Av. Col C 4F 11
Chestnut Clo. Chan F 4E 15
Chestnut Clo. Roms 6G 7

Chestnut Clo. W End 6D 24
Chestnut Dri. Asht 2C 36
Chestnut Lodge. Sotn ...6A 22
Chestnut Ri. Eastl 6F 15
Chestnut Rd. Sotn 1E 29
Chestnuts, The. L Hth ...5E 49
Chestnut Wlk. Bot 4D 34
Chestnut Way. Fare 6G 49
Chettle Rd. Sotn 6E 33
Chetwynd Dri. Sotn 5B 22
Chetwynd Rd. Sotn 5B 22
Cheviot Cres. Sotn 3C 28
Cheviot Dri. Dib 3B 52
Cheviot Grn. Wars 1B 50
Cheviot Rd. Sotn 3C 28
Chevron Bus. Pk. Holb ..2B 54
Chichester Clo. H End ...2A 34
Chichester Clo. Sar G ..4C 48
Chichester Rd. Sotn 4A 32
Chickenhall La. Eastl 4C 16
Chidden Holt. Chan F 2C 14
Chilcomb Rd. Sotn 3C 32
Chilham Clo. Eastl 6A 10
Chillenden Ct. Tot 5C 26
Chillerton. Net A 6C 42
Chilling La. Wars 4C 50
Chillington Gdns.
  Chan F 4D 8
Chiltern Clo. Tot 6D 26
Chiltern Grn. Sotn 3C 28
Chilworth Clo. Chilw ...6H 13
Chilworth Drove. Chilw ..4F 21
Chilworth Rd. Chilw 6A 14
Chine Av. Sotn 6G 31
  (in two parts)
Chine Clo. L Hth 3E 49
Chisholm Clo. Sotn 4D 20
Christie Av. White 5G 45
Church Clo. Eastl 3D 16
Church Clo. L Hth 4F 49
Church Clo. N Bad 3E 13
Church Clo. Sotn 3G 29
Chu. Farm Cvn. Site.
  Dib 6F 39
Chu. Farm Clo. Dib 6F 39
Churchfields. Fawl 2H 55
Church Hill. W End 1C 32
Churchill Clo. Fare 6G 49
Churchill Ho. Sotn 3C 32
Church La. Bot 6E 35
Church La. Burs 5H 43
Church La. Col C 5F 11
Church La. Curd 3H 35
Church La. Fawl 2G 55
Church La. H End 6H 33
Church La. Nurs 3F 19
Church End. Sotn 3G 29
Church La. Roms 5B 6
Church La.
  Sotn 2B 40 (5D 4)
  (SO14)
Church La. Sotn 1D 30
  (SO17)
Church Path. Sotn 1D 30
  (SO17)
Church Path. Sotn 2A 42
  (SO19)
Church Pl. Roms 5B 6
Church Rd. Eastl 4D 16
Church Rd. L Hth 4F 49
Church Rd. Roms 5B 6
Church Rd. Sotn 4F 41
Church Rd. Wars 6B 48
Church St. Roms 5B 6
Church Vw. Sotn 3F 29
Churchview. Sotn 2A 42
Church Vw. Clo. Sotn ...2A 42
Churchward Gdns.
  H End 1A 34

Cinnamon Ct. Sotn 5A 30
Circle, The. S'sea 4F 5
Cirrus Gdns. Hamb 5F 47
City Commerce Cen.
  Sotn 2D 40 (5G 5)
City Ind. Pk.
  Sotn 1A 40 (3A 4)
Civic Cen. Rd.
  Sotn 6B 30 (2C 4)
Clamp Grn. Col C 5F 11
Clandon Dri. Eastl 1H 15
Clanfield Clo. Chan F 1F 15
Clanfield Dri. Chan F 1F 15
Clanfield Rd. Sotn 4C 32
Clanfield Way. Chan F ...1F 15
Clare Clo. Fare 5G 49
Clare Gdns. Black 6F 55
Claremont Clo. Eastl 1A 16
Claremont Cres. Sotn ...4E 29
Claremont Rd. Sotn 4E 29
Clarence Ho. Sotn 5E 31
Clarendon Clo. Roms 3E 7
Clarendon Cres. Fare ...6F 49
Clarendon Rd. Sotn 3E 29
Claude Ashby Clo.
  Sotn 5G 23
Claudeen Clo. Sotn 4G 23
Claudius Clo. Chan F 6H 9
Claudius Gdns. Chan F ..6H 9
Clausentum Clo.
  Chan F 6G 9
Clausentum Rd. Sotn ...4C 30
Claypits La. Dib 3A 52
Cleasby Clo. Sotn 4C 28
Cleethorpes Rd. Sotn ...1B 42
Cleeves, The. Tot 5C 26
Cleric Ct. Fare 4H 49
Cleveland Ct. Sotn 2A 32
Cleveland Dri. Dib P 4B 52
Cleveland Rd. Sotn 1H 31
Clevelands Clo. Chan F ..4D 8
Cliffe Av. Hamb 4E 47
Clifford Dibben M.
  Sotn 3C 30
Clifford Pl. F Oak 2F 17
Clifford St.
  Sotn 6D 30 (2G 5)
Cliff Rd. Sotn 6H 29
Cliff, The. Sotn 2F 41
  (off Jackman's Clo.)
Clifton Gdns. Sotn 3E 29
Clifton Gdns. W End 2C 32
Clifton Rd. Sotn 3E 29
Clipper Clo. Wars 6C 48
Cloisters, The. Roms 3B 6
Cloisters, The. Sotn 6C 22
Close, The. Bram 4D 10
Close, The. Hamb 3G 47
Close, The. H End 5H 33
Close, The. Holb 5D 54
Close, The. Sotn 4D 32
Clovelly Rd. Sotn 5C 30
Clover Clo. L Hth 5C 48
Clover Nooke. Sotn 3A 28
Clover Way. H End 5G 33
Clover Way. Roms 4F 7
Clyde Ho. Sotn 6E 31
Clydesdale Rd. White ...6F 45
Clydesdale Way. Tot 3B 26
Coach Hill Clo. Chan F ...6D 8
Coachmans Copse.
  Sotn 1A 32
Coach Rd. Hamb 5E 47
Coal Pk. La. Swanw 4B 44
Coalville Rd. Sotn 1B 42
Coates Rd. Sotn 1D 42
Coat Gdns. Hythe 3E 53
Cobbett Ct. Sotn 4G 31

Cobbett Rd. Sotn 4G 31
Cobbett Way. Bot 4D 34
Cobden Av. Sotn 2F 31
Cobden Bri. Sotn 2F 31
Cobden Ct. Sotn 3G 31
Cobden Cres. Sotn 3H 31
Cobden Gdns. Sotn 2G 31
Cobden Heights. Sotn ...2G 31
Cobden Ri. Sotn 2G 31
Coblands Av. Tot 4D 26
Coburg Ho. Sotn 5E 31
Coburg St. Sotn 5E 31
Cockerell Clo. Fare 2G 49
Cockleshell Clo. Wars ...6C 48
Cocklydown La. Tot 1D 36
Colburn Clo. Sotn 1B 28
Colchester Av. Eastl 3E 17
Coldeast Clo. Sar G 2C 48
Coldeast Way. Sar G 2D 48
Coldharbour La. Nurs ...1G 19
Colebrook Av. Sotn 2G 29
Coleman St.
  Sotn 1D 40 (3G 5)
Coleridge Clo. Wars 6B 48
Coleridge Ct. Sotn 6D 32
Coles Mede. Ott 2B 10
  (in two parts)
Coleson Rd. Sotn 3G 31
Coleville Av. Fawl 2H 55
College Clo. Hamb 5F 47
College Pl. Sotn 5C 30
College Rd. Sotn 3F 41
College St.
  Sotn 2C 40 (5F 5)
Collett Clo. H End 1H 33
Collier Clo. Sotn 3E 31
Collingbourne Dri.
  Chan F 1C 14
Collingworth Ri.
  Park G 1F 49
Collins Clo. Chan F 1B 14
Collins Ho. Chan F 1F 15
Colne Av. Sotn 6B 20
Colne Ct. Sotn 1C 28
Colonnade, The. Sotn ...2F 41
Colt Clo. Rown 4D 20
Colton Copse. Chan F ...1B 14
Coltsfoot Clo. H End 4H 33
Coltsfoot Dri. L Hth 5C 48
Coltsfoot Wlk. Roms 3F 7
Colts Rd. Rown 2C 20
Columbine Wlk. Tot 6D 26
Colvedene Clo. Col C 4F 11
Colwell Clo. Sotn 3B 28
Comfrey Clo. Roms 3F 7
Comines Way. H End 5E 33
Commercial Rd.
  Sotn 6A 30 (1B 4)
Commercial Rd. Tot 4G 27
Commercial St. Sotn 4A 32
Commodore Ct.
  Sotn 2D 40 (6G 5)
Common Clo. Chan F 5E 9
Common Fields. H End ...5F 33
Common Gdns. Chan F ...5E 9
Common La. Titch 1H 51
Common Rd. Chan F 5D 8
Common, The. Sotn 2A 30
Compass Clo. Sotn 1A 42
Compton Clo. Eastl 1H 15
Compton Ho. Sotn 3F 29
Compton Ho. Tot 2D 26
Compton Rd. Tot 3G 27
Compton Wlk.
  Sotn 6C 30 (1F 5)
Concorde Way. Fare 2H 49
Condor Clo. Sotn 2F 41
Conference Dri. L Hth ...4F 49

Conifer Clo. *Hythe* 3C **52**
Conifer Rd. *Sotn* 5E **21**
Coniston Gdns. *H End* 6H **33**
Coniston Rd. *Eastl* 5H **15**
Coniston Rd. *Sotn* 3A **28**
Connemara Cres.
   White 6F **45**
Conrad Gdns. *White* 5G **45**
Consort Clo. *Eastl* 2B **16**
Consort Rd. *Eastl* 2B **16**
Constable Clo. *Sotn* 3C **42**
Constantine Av.
   Chan F 1G **15**
Constantine Clo.
   Chan F 1H **15**
Consulate Ho.
   Sotn 2D **40** (6H **5**)
Conway Clo. *Chan F* 4D **14**
Cook's La. *Cal* 1B **26**
Cook St. *Sotn* 1C **40** (4F **5**)
Coombedale. *L Hth* 5F **49**
Cooper Rd. *Asht* 2C **36**
Cooper's Clo. *W End* 2C **32**
Cooper's La. *Sotn* 2F **41**
Copeland Rd. *Sotn* 2B **28**
Copenhagen Towers.
   Sotn 5G **41**
Copinger Clo. *Tot* 5C **26**
Copperfield Rd. *Sotn* 4C **22**
Copperfields. *Tot* 4B **26**
Coppice Rd. *Cal* 1C **26**
Copse Clo. *N Bad* 3D **12**
Copse Clo. *Ott* 1C **10**
Copse Clo. *Tot* 5F **27**
Copse La. *Chilw* 6B **14**
Copse La. *Hamb* 5F **47**
Copse Rd. *Sotn* 1H **31**
Copse, The. *Chan F* 2G **15**
Copse, The. *Roms* 3F **7**
Copse Vw. *Sotn* 6E **33**
Copsewood Rd. *Asht* 2C **36**
Copsewood Rd. *Hythe* 3D **52**
Copsewood Rd. *Sotn* 1G **31**
Copthorne La. *Fawl* 2H **55**
Coracle Clo. *Wars* 6D **48**
Corbiere Clo. *Sotn* 6C **20**
Corbould Rd. *Dib P* 5D **52**
Cordelia Clo. *Dib* 3B **52**
Coriander Dri. *Tot* 4C **26**
Coriander Way. *White* 5H **45**
Corinna Gdns. *Dib* 3B **52**
Corinthian Rd. *Chan F* 6G **9**
Cork La. *March* 3D **38**
Cormorant Dri. *Hythe* 4G **53**
Cornel Rd. *Sotn* 6H **31**
Cornfield Clo. *Chan F* 1B **14**
Cornflower Clo. *L Hth* 4C **48**
Cornforth Rd. *Cal* 2C **26**
Corn Mkt. *Roms* 5B **6**
Cornwall Clo. *Sotn* 1A **32**
Cornwall Cres. *Sotn* 1H **31**
Cornwall Rd. *Chan F* 4E **15**
Cornwall Rd. *Sotn* 1H **31**
Coronation Av. *Sotn* 6A **22**
Coronation Homes.
   Sotn 3D **32**
Coronation Pde. *Hamb* . . .4E **47**
Corsair Dri. *Dib* 3B **52**
Cortina Way. *H End* 6B **34**
Corvette Av. *Wars* 6D **48**
Cosford Clo. *Eastl* 5G **17**
Cossack Grn.
   Sotn 1C **40** (3F **5**)
Cosworth Dri. *Dib* 3B **52**
Cotsalls. *F Oak* 3F **17**
Cotswold Clo. *Dib P* 3B **52**
Cotswold Rd. *Sotn* 3D **28**
Cotton Clo. *Eastl* 4E **17**

Coulsdon Rd. *H End* 5A **34**
Coultas Rd. *Chan F* 3G **9**
Course Pk. Cres. *Fare* 5G **49**
Court Clo. *Cal* 1D **26**
Court Clo. *Sotn* 5A **32**
Courtenay Clo. *Fare* 4H **49**
Court Ho. Clo. *Hythe* 2E **53**
Courtier Clo. *Dib* 3A **52**
Courtland Gdns. *Sotn* 4D **22**
Court Rd. *Sotn* 4B **30**
Court Royal M. *Sotn* 3B **30**
Coventry Rd. *Sotn* 5B **30**
Covert, The. *Roms* 6E **7**
Cowdray Clo. *Eastl* 5F **17**
Cowdray Clo. *Sotn* 5F **21**
Cowes La. *Wars* 4B **50**
Cowley Clo. *Sotn* 1C **28**
Cowper Rd. *Sotn* 5D **32**
Cowslip Clo. *L Hth* 5C **48**
Cowslip Wlk. *Tot* 6D **26**
   (in two parts)
Cowslip Way. *Roms* 3F **7**
Coxdale. *Fare* 6G **49**
Coxford Clo. *Sotn* 1E **29**
Coxford Drove. *Sotn* 6E **21**
Coxford Rd. *Sotn* 1D **28**
Cox Row. *Chan F* 4E **15**
Cox's Dri. *Sotn* 3B **42**
Cox's La. *Sotn* 3F **41**
Cozens Clo. *Sotn* 4G **41**
Crabapple Clo. *Tot* 4C **26**
Crabbe La. *Sotn* 4C **22**
   (in two parts)
Crabbs Way. *Tot* 4B **26**
Crableck La. *Sar G* 2A **48**
Crabtree. *Sotn* 2D **28**
Crabwood Clo. *Sotn* 1D **28**
Crabwood Dri. *W End* 2E **33**
Crabwood Rd. *Sotn* 1C **28**
Cracknorehard La.
   March 3E **39**
Cracknore Rd. *Sotn* 6H **29**
Crampmoor La. *Cram* 3G **7**
Cranberry Clo. *March* 4D **38**
Cranborne Gdns. *Chan F* . . .4D **8**
Cranbourne Clo. *Sotn* 2H **29**
Cranbourne Dri. *Ott* 2B **10**
Cranbourne Pk. *H End* 1A **44**
Cranbury Av. *Sotn* 5C **30**
Cranbury Clo. *Ott* 2B **10**
Cranbury Ct. *Sotn* 2H **41**
Cranbury Gdns. *Burs* 4F **43**
Cranbury Pl. *Sotn* 5C **30**
Cranbury Rd. *Eastl* 6A **16**
   (in two parts)
Cranbury Rd. *Sotn* 2H **41**
Cranbury Ter. *Sotn* 5C **30**
*Cranbury, The. Sotn 5C **30***
   (off Cranbury Ter.)
Cranbury Towers.
   Sotn 5C **30**
   (off Cranbury Pl.)
Cranford Gdns. *Chan F* 5D **8**
Cranford Ho. *Sotn* 1C **30**
Cranford Way. *Sotn* 1C **30**
Cranleigh Ct. *Sotn* 3C **30**
Cranleigh Rd. *H End* 5A **34**
Cranmer Dri. *Nurs* 4A **20**
Cranmore. *Net A* 6C **42**
Cranwell Ct. *Sotn* 4D **20**
Cranwell Cres. *Sotn* 4E **21**
Craven Rd. *Chan F* 1F **15**
Craven St. *Sotn* 6C **30** (2F **5**)
Craven Wlk.
   Sotn 6C **30** (2E **5**)
Crawford Clo. *Nurs* 4B **20**
Crawte Av. *Holb* 6D **54**
Creedy Gdns. *W End* 6A **24**

Creighton Rd. *Sotn* 5D **28**
Crescent Rd. *L Hth* 4D **48**
Crescent Rd. *N Bad* 2D **12**
Crescent, The. *Eastl* 3A **16**
Crescent, The. *March* 4C **38**
Crescent, The. *Net A* 1C **46**
Crescent, The. *Roms* 4E **7**
Crescent, The. *Sotn* 3A **42**
Cressey Rd. *Roms* 5C **6**
Crest Way. *Sotn* 1C **42**
Crete Cotts. *Dib P* 6C **52**
Crete La. *Dib P* 5D **52**
Crete Rd. *Dib P* 6D **52**
Crigdon Clo. *Sotn* 3C **28**
Crispin Clo. *H Hth* 3H **25**
Crispin Clo. *L Hth* 3F **49**
Crofton Clo. *Sotn* 2C **30**
Crofton Way. *Wars* 6A **48**
Croft, The. *Cal* 1C **26**
Croft, The. *Chan F* 4E **15**
Cromalt Clo. *Dib P* 4B **52**
Cromarty Rd. *Sotn* 4C **20**
Cromer Rd. *Sotn* 2B **28**
Crompton Way. *Fare* 2G **49**
Cromwell Rd. *Sotn* 4B **30**
Crooked Hays Clo.
   March 4D **38**
Crookham Rd. *Sotn* 5H **41**
Cross Ho. Cen. *Sotn* 2E **41**
Crosshouse Rd.
   Sotn 2E **41** (6H **5**)
Crossley Ct. *Sotn* 5G **29**
Cross Rd. *Sotn* 4G **31**
Crosstrees. *Sar G* 1D **48**
Crosswell Clo. *Sotn* 6C **32**
Crowders Grn. *Col C* 5F **11**
Crown St. *Sotn* 3F **29**
Crowsnest La. *Bot* 2D **34**
Crowsport. *Hamb* 4G **47**
Crowther Clo. *Sotn* 1C **42**
Croydon Clo. *Sotn* 5E **21**
Crummock Rd. *Chan F* 5C **8**
Crusader Rd. *H End* 6B **34**
Crusaders Way.
   Chan F 1B **14**
Cuckmere La. *Sotn* 3A **28**
Cuckoo Bushes La.
   Chan F 5D **8**
Cuckoo La.
   Sotn 2B **40** (6D **4**)
Cudworth Mead.
   H End 2B **34**
Culford Av. *Tot* 5F **27**
Culford Way. *Tot* 5F **27**
Culver. *Net A* 6C **42**
Culver Clo. *Sotn* 1B **28**
Culvery Gdns. *W End* 2A **32**
Cumberland Av.
   Chan F 1G **15**
Cumberland Clo.
   Chan F 1G **15**
Cumberland Pl.
   Sotn 6B **30** (1C **4**)
Cumberland St.
   Sotn 1D **40** (3G **5**)
Cumberland Way. *Dib* 3A **52**
Cumber Rd. *L Hth* 4C **48**
Cumbrian Way. *Sotn* 3C **28**
Cummins Grn. *Burs* 4G **43**
Cunard Av. *Sotn* 3G **29**
Cunard Rd. *Sotn* 3C **40**
Cunningham Cres.
   Sotn 1A **42**
Cunningham Dri.
   L Hth 3F **49**
Cunningham Gdns.
   Burs 5F **43**
Cupernham Clo. *Roms* 3D **6**

Cupernham La. *Roms* 1D **6**
Curlew Clo. *Hythe* 4F **53**
Curlew Clo. *Sotn* 4F **21**
Curlew Dri. *Hythe* 4F **53**
Curlew Sq. *Eastl* 5G **15**
Curlew Wlk. *Hythe* 4F **53**
Curzon Ct. *Sotn* 5H **21**
Cutbush La.
   Sotn & W End 1A **32**
   (in two parts)
Cutter Av. *Wars* 6C **48**
Cygnus Gdns. *Dib* 3A **52**
Cypress Av. *Sotn* 6H **31**
Cypress Gdns. *Bot* 4E **35**
Cypress Gdns. *Tot* 4C **26**
Cyprus Rd. *Fare* 6G **49**

D

Daffodil Rd. *Sotn* 5E **23**
Dahlia Rd. *Sotn* 5C **22**
Daintree Clo. *Sotn* 2D **42**
Dairy La. *Sotn* 5G **19**
Daisy La. *L Hth* 4F **49**
Daisy Rd. *Sotn* 5D **22**
Dale Grn. *Chan F* 4D **8**
Dale Rd. *Hythe* 3D **52**
Dale Rd. *Sotn* 1G **29**
Dales Way. *Tot* 3B **26**
Dale Valley Clo. *Sotn* 1G **29**
Dale Valley Gdns.
   Sotn 1G **29**
Dalmally Gdns. *Sotn* 3H **31**
Damen Clo. *H End* 6H **33**
Damson Cres. *F Oak* 6G **17**
Danebury Gdns.
   Chan F 3C **14**
Danebury Way. *Nurs* 6B **20**
Dane Clo. *Black* 4F **55**
Daniels Wlk. *Cal* 2B **26**
Dapple Pl. *March* 4E **39**
Dark La. *Black* 4E **55**
   (in two parts)
Darlington Gdns. *Sotn* 2H **29**
Dart Ho. *Sotn* 3H **31**
Dartington Rd. *Eastl* 2D **16**
Dart Rd. *W End* 6B **24**
Darwin Rd. *Eastl* 3B **16**
Darwin Rd. *Sotn* 4H **29**
D Avenue. *Hythe* 2D **54**
David Ct. *Roms* 6D **6**
Dawlish Av. *Sotn* 3H **29**
Dawnay Clo. *Sotn* 4F **23**
Dawson Lodge.
   W End 2F **33**
Dawson Rd. *Sotn* 3C **42**
Dawtrey Ct. *Sotn* 1E **31**
Dayrell Clo. *Cal* 2B **26**
Deacon Clo. *Sotn* 6A **32**
Deacon Cres. *Sotn* 6A **32**
Deacon Rd. *L Hth* 5F **49**
Deacon Rd. *Sotn* 6A **32**
Deacon Trad. Est.
   Eastl 5C **16**
Dean Ct. *H End* 4H **33**
Dean Ct. *Sotn* 3G **31**
Deanery, The. *Chan F* 4D **8**
Deanfield Clo. *Hamb* 5F **47**
Dean Rd. *F Oak* 6H **17**
Dean Rd. *Sotn* 3A **32**
Deansfield Clo. *Roms* 4E **7**
Dee Clo. *Chan F* 2D **14**
Deepdene, The. *Sotn* 3G **31**
Deeping Clo. *Sotn* 4H **41**
Deerhurst Clo. *Tot* 5D **26**
Deerleap Clo. *Hythe* 3E **53**
Deerleap La. *Tot* 2D **36**
Deerleap Way. *Hythe* 3E **53**

Deer Pk. Farm Ind. Est.
  F Oak 3H 17
Defender Rd. Sotn 2F 41
Defender Wlk. Sotn 2F 41
Defoe Clo. White 5G 45
De Grouchy La. Sotn 2C 30
Delft Clo. L Hth 4D 48
Delius Av. Sotn 2D 42
Dell Clo. F Oak 3F 17
Dell Rd. Sotn 1H 31
Delta Ho. Sotn 6G 13
Dempsey Clo. Sotn 1B 42
Denbigh Clo. Eastl 2H 15
Denbigh Clo. Tot 6D 26
Denbigh Gdns. Sotn 5B 22
Dene Clo. Chilw 2B 22
Dene Clo. Sar G 3C 48
Dene Rd. Asht 3C 36
Dene Way. Asht 2C 36
Denham Fields. Eastl 1F 17
Denham Gdns. Net A 2B 46
Denmead Rd. Sotn 3C 32
Dennison Ct. Sotn 3F 29
Denny Clo. Fawl 2H 55
Denzil Av. Net A 1C 46
Denzil Av. Sotn 5C 30
Depedene Clo. Holb 4B 54
Derby Ho. Eastl 6A 16
Derby Rd. Eastl 5G 15
Derby Rd. Sotn 6D 30 (1G 5)
Deridene Ct. Tot 5D 26
Derwent Clo. W End 2B 32
Derwent Dri. Tot 3B 26
Derwent Rd. Sotn 2C 28
Desborough Rd. Eastl 6A 16
Devine Gdns. Eastl 5D 16
Devon Clo. Chan F 4E 15
Devon Dri. Chan F 4E 15
Devonshire Gdns.
  Burs 3G 43
Devonshire Gdns.
  Hythe 6E 53
Devonshire Mans.
  Sotn 5B 30
    (off Devonshire Rd.)
Devonshire Rd.
  Sotn 5B 30 (1C 4)
Dewar Clo. Fare 2G 49
Dew La. Eastl 4H 15
Dewsbury Ct. Sotn 1A 32
Dibben Wlk. Roms 3F 7
Dibble Dri. N Bad 4D 12
Dibden Lodge Clo.
  Hythe 1D 52
Dibles Pk. Cvn. Site.
  Wars 6C 48
Dibles Rd. Wars 6B 48
Dibles Wharf. Sotn 6E 31
Dickens Dell. Tot 4B 26
Dickens Dri. White 4G 45
Didcot Rd. Sotn 2G 29
Diligence Clo. Burs 4G 43
Dimond Clo. Sotn 2G 31
Dimond Hill. Sotn 2G 31
Dimond Rd. Sotn 1G 31
Dingle Way. L Hth 3E 49
Dirty Dri. N Bad 2H 13
Disa Ho. Sotn 5A 30
    (off Handell Ter.)
Dodwell La. Burs 4H 43
Dodwell Ter. Burs 4H 43
Dolphin Clo. Eastl 5F 17
Dolton Rd. Sotn 6D 20
Dominy Clo. Hythe 2F 53
Doncaster Drove.
  Eastl 2G 23
Doncaster Rd. Eastl 1A 24
Donkey La. Bot 4E 35

Donnington Dri.
  Chan F 4C 14
Donnington Gro. Sotn 1D 30
Dorchester Ct. Sotn 3B 30
Doric Clo. Chan F 6H 9
Dorland Gdns. Tot 5D 26
Dormy Clo. Sar G 4B 48
Dornan Ho. Sotn 4C 30
Dorrick Ct. Sotn 4B 30
Dorrits, The. Tot 4B 26
Dorset Rd. Chan F 4E 15
Dorset St. Sotn 5C 30
Dorval Ho. Sotn 4A 30
Dorval Mnr. Sotn 4A 30
Douglas Cres. Sotn 5C 32
Douglas Way. Hythe 2D 52
Dove Dale. Eastl 5F 15
Dove Gdns. Park G 2F 49
Dover St. Sotn 4C 30
Dowds Clo. H End 3H 33
Downing Ct. Titch 6G 49
Downland Clo. Bot 4D 34
Downland Clo. L Hth 3E 49
Downland Pl. H End 6H 33
Down La. Roms 4E 7
Downscroft Gdns.
  H End 4H 33
Downside Av. Sotn 5A 32
Downs Pk. Av. Tot 5G 27
Downs Pk. Cres. Tot 5G 27
Downs Pk. Rd. Tot 5G 27
Downton Rd. Sotn 1H 31
Downwood Clo. Dib P 4A 52
Doyle Ct. Sotn 4H 41
Dragoon Clo. Sotn 1C 42
Drake Clo. L Hth 2F 49
Drake Clo. March 3E 39
Drake Rd. Eastl 3E 17
Drakes Clo. Hythe 4D 52
Drakes Ct. March 2D 38
Drapers Copse Mobile Home Pk.
  Dib 2B 52
Drayton Clo. Sotn 5H 41
Drayton Pl. Tot 4D 26
Driftwood Gdns. Tot 5C 26
Drinkwater Clo. Eastl 4H 15
Drive, The. Dib 3B 52
Drive, The. Tot 6F 27
Drive, The. W End 6B 24
Drove Rd. Sotn 6B 32
Drove, The. Black 4E 55
Drove, The. Cal 2B 26
Drove, The. Sotn 4A 32
Drove, The. W End 6F 25
Drummond Ct. Eastl 2B 16
Drummond Ct. Sotn 2G 41
Drummond Dri. Sotn 3E 31
Drummond Rd. H End 2A 34
Drummond Rd. Hythe 2E 53
Drummond Way.
  Chan F 5D 8
Dryden Rd. Sotn 6E 33
Duddon Clo. W End 2B 32
Duke Rd. H End 6B 34
Dukes Keeps. Sotn 5G 5
Dukes Mill Cen. Roms 5B 6
Dukes Rd. Sotn 3D 30
Duke St. Sotn 2D 40 (5G 5)
Dukeswood Dri. Dib P 5D 52
Dumbleton Clo. Sotn 6F 33
Dumbleton's Towers.
  Sotn 1E 43
Dunbar Clo. Sotn 4D 20
Duncan Clo. Sotn 4G 41
Duncan Ct. Sotn 6C 32
Duncan Rd. Park G 1F 49
Dundee Rd. Sotn 2E 31

Dundonald Clo. Sotn 4F 41
Dundry Way. H End 4A 34
Dunkirk Clo. Sotn 5H 21
Dunkirk Rd. Sotn 5G 21
Dunnings La. N Bad 2C 12
Dunster Clo. Sotn 4G 21
Dunvegan Dri. Sotn 4G 21
Durban Clo. Roms 3D 6
Durley Cres. Tot 6D 26
Durlston Rd. Sotn 2B 28
Durnford Rd. Sotn 5D 30
Dutton La. Eastl 3B 16
Dutton's Rd. Roms 4B 6
    (in two parts)
Dyer Rd. Sotn 4G 29
Dymott Clo. Sotn 6H 29
Dyneley Grn. Sotn 2A 32
Dyram Clo. Eastl 2H 15
Dyserth Clo. Sotn 4B 42

E

Eagle Clo. Chan F 3D 14
Earls Clo. Eastl 5G 17
Earl's Rd. Sotn 3C 30
E. Bargate.
  Sotn 1C 40 (4E 5)
Eastbourne Av. Sotn 3H 29
Eastbrook Clo. Park G 2E 49
Eastchurch Clo. Sotn 5D 20
Eastcot Clo. Holb 5C 54
East Dri. Eastl 3D 16
Eastern Rd. W End 2D 32
Eastfield Rd. Sotn 3E 31
Eastgate St.
  Sotn 2C 40 (5E 5)
Eastleigh Rd. F Oak 3F 17
Eastmeare Ct. Tot 5C 26
East Pk. Ter.
  Sotn 6C 30 (1E 5)
East Rd. Hythe 6H 53
East St. Sotn 1C 40 (4E 5)
East St. Cen.
  Sotn 1C 40 (4F 5)
Eastville Rd. Eastl 3F 17
Eastwood Ct. Roms 5B 6
Eddystone Rd. Tot 1D 26
Edelvale Rd. Sotn 2B 32
Eden Rd. W End 1B 32
Eden Wlk. Chan F 2D 14
Edge Hill Rd. Sotn 2H 31
Edinburgh Ct. Sotn 5E 29
    (off Regents Pk. Rd.)
Edith Haisman Clo.
  Sotn 6H 29
Edmunds Clo. Bot 6B 34
Edney Path. Sar G 1B 48
Edward Av. Eastl 3D 16
Edward Clo. Black 4E 55
Edward Rd. Hythe 2E 53
Edward Rd. Sotn 4G 29
Edwina Clo. N Bad 3F 13
Edwina Clo. Sotn 5H 31
Edwina Ho. Sotn 5G 23
Edwina Mountbatten Ho.
  Roms 5B 6
    (off Palmerston St.)
Edwin Jones Grn.
  Sotn 3A 30
Effingham Gdns. Sotn 1C 42
Eight Acres. Roms 5D 6
Elan Clo. W End 2B 32
Elderberry Clo. F Oak 5G 17
Elder Clo. L Hth 5D 48
Elder Clo. March 4E 39
Elder Grn. Col C 5G 11
Eldon Ho. Sotn 2C 40 (5F 5)
Eldridge Gdns. Roms 4C 6

Electron Way. Chan F 1E 15
Elgar Clo. Sotn 2C 42
Elgar Rd. Sotn 2C 42
Elgin Clo. Hythe 3E 53
Elgin Rd. Sotn 6H 29
Elingfield Ct. Tot 4G 27
Eling Hill. Tot 6H 27
Eling La. Tot 4G 27
Eling Vw. Sotn 4B 28
Eling Wharf. Tot 4H 27
Elizabeth Clo. W End 2D 32
Elizabeth Ct. Sotn 2E 31
Elizabeth Ct. W End 2D 32
Elizabeth Gdns. Dib P 5E 53
Elizabeth Ho. Cal 1C 26
Elizabeth Way. Eastl 2B 16
Elland Clo. F Oak 3F 17
Elldene Ct. Tot 6E 27
Ellen Gdns. Chan F 2C 14
Elliot Clo. Tot 4D 26
Elliot Ri. H End 1A 34
Ellis Rd. Sotn 6E 33
Ellwood Av. Sotn 6E 33
Ellwood Clo. Sotn 5E 33
Elm Clo. Sotn 5B 22
Elm Ct. Sotn 2H 41
Elm Cres. Hythe 1A 54
Elmdale Clo. Wars 6B 48
Elmes Dri. Sotn 4D 28
Elmfield N. Block.
  Sotn 6H 29
Elmfield W. Block.
  Sotn 6H 29
Elm Gdns. W End 6D 24
Elm Gro. Eastl 5H 15
Elmsleigh Ct. Sotn 5C 22
Elmsleigh Gdns. Sotn 5C 22
Elmslie Gdns. Burs 4F 43
Elm St. Sotn 1D 40 (4H 5)
Elm Ter. Sotn 2D 40 (5H 5)
Elm Tree Clo. Asht 3B 36
Elmtree Gdns. Eastl 5A 16
Elmtree Gdns. Roms 6F 7
Elmwood Ct. Sotn 1F 29
Elstree Rd. Sotn 6G 31
Elver Ct. Tot 5G 27
Embley Clo. Cal 1D 26
Embsay Rd. Swanw 5B 44
Emerald Clo. Sotn 5B 32
Emer Clo. N Bad 2E 13
Emily Davis Halls. Sotn 2C 4
Emmanuel Clo. Fare 5G 49
Emmett Rd. Rown 4D 20
Emmons Clo. Hamb 6G 47
Empress Pk. Ind. Est.
  Sotn 4D 30
Empress Rd. Sotn 4C 40
    (Central Rd.)
Empress Rd. Sotn 4D 30
    (Imperial Rd.)
Emsworth Rd. Sotn 3F 29
Endeavour Clo. Sotn 4F 29
Endeavour Way. Hythe 1D 52
Enderwood Clo. Tot 3B 26
Endle St. Sotn 2E 41 (5H 5)
Enfield Gro. Sotn 2G 41
Englefield Rd. Sotn 4F 31
Ennel Copse. N Bad 3E 13
Ennerdale Gdns.
  W End 2B 32
Ennerdale Rd. Sotn 1C 28
Ensign Pk. Hamb 5E 47
Ensign Way. Hamb 5E 47
Enterprise Clo. Wars 6C 48
Enterprise Rd. Chilw 6G 13
Enterprise Way. Sotn 3D 40
Epping Clo. Sotn 2B 32

Epsilon Ho. *Sotn* 6H **13**
Epsom Ct. *White* 5G **45**
   (off Timor Clo.)
Erica Clo. *L Hth* 4D **48**
Erskine Ct. *Sotn* 4E **21**
Escombe Rd. *Eastl* 4D **16**
Essex Grn. *Chan F* 5E **15**
Estridge Clo. *Burs* 4G **43**
Ethelburt Av. *Sotn* 4E **23**
Ethelred Gdns. *Tot* 5C **26**
European Way. *Sotn* 3D **40**
Evans St. *Sotn* 1C **40** (4F **5**)
Evelyn Cres. *Sotn* 3H **29**
Evenlode Rd. *Sotn* 2C **28**
Evergreen Clo.
   March 4D **38**
Evergreens. *Tot* 5G **27**
Evesham Clo. *Sotn* 4D **22**
Ewart Clo. *Hythe* 1E **53**
Ewell Way. *Tot* 2D **26**
Exbury Clo. *Eastl* 5F **17**
Exbury Rd. *Black* 4E **55**
Exeter Clo. *L Hth* 4D **48**
Exeter Clo. *Sotn* 2A **32**
Exeter Rd. *Sotn* 3A **32**
Exford Av. *Sotn* 4C **32**
Exford Dri. *Sotn* 4C **32**
Exleigh Clo. *Sotn* 5B **32**
Exmoor Clo. *Tot* 4B **26**
Exmoor Clo. *White* 6F **45**
Exmoor Rd. *Sotn* 5D **30**
Exmouth St.
   Sotn 6C **30** (2E **5**)
Eyeworth Wlk. *Dib* 2A **52**
Eynham Av. *Sotn* 5C **32**
Eynham Clo. *Sotn* 5C **32**
Eyre Clo. *Tot* 5D **26**

F

Faber M. *Roms* 4E **7**
Factory Rd. *Eastl* 5A **16**
Fairbairn Wlk. *Chan F* 1B **14**
Faircross Clo. *Holb* 5C **54**
Fairfax Ct. *Sotn* 5E **33**
Fairfax M. *Sotn* 5E **33**
Fairfield. *Roms* 3D **6**
Fairfield Clo. *Hythe* 2D **52**
Fairfield Lodge. *Sotn* 5G **21**
Fairfield Rd. *Shaw* 1D **10**
Fair Grn. *Sotn* 6B **32**
Fairisle Rd. *Sotn* 5C **20**
Fairlawn Clo. *Rown* 3D **20**
Fairlea Grange. *Sotn* 5B **22**
Fairlie Clo. *H End* 6H **25**
Fairmead Way. *Tot* 6E **27**
Fair Oak Ct. *F Oak* 2F **17**
Fair Oak Rd. *Eastl* 4D **16**
Fairview Clo. *Hythe* 3E **53**
Fairview Clo. *Roms* 3E **7**
Fairview Dri. *Hythe* 4D **52**
Fairview Dri. *Roms* 3E **7**
Fairview Pde. *Hythe* 4E **53**
Fairway Gdns. *Rown* 4C **20**
Fairway Rd. *Hythe* 2D **52**
Fairway, The. *Wars* 6D **48**
Falaise Clo. *Sotn* 5G **21**
Falconer Ct. *Holb* 2C **54**
Falcon Fields. *Fawl* 2H **55**
Falcon Sq. *Eastl* 6F **15**
Falcon Way. *Bot* 2D **34**
Falkland Ct. *Chan F* 4E **15**
   (off Falkland Rd.)
Falkland Rd. *Chan F* 5E **15**
Falkland Rd. *Sotn* 3E **29**
Falstaff Way. *Tot* 6D **26**
Fanshawe St. *Sotn* 5C **30**

Faringdon Rd. *Sotn* 4D **32**
Farley Clo. *F Oak* 3G **17**
Farley Ct. *Sotn* 1H **29**
Farm Clo. *Hamb* 5G **47**
Farmery Clo. *Sotn* 5F **23**
Farm La. *Asht* 3B **36**
Farm Rd. *Fare* 5H **49**
Farringford Rd. *Sotn* 5D **32**
Fastnet Clo. *Sotn* 4C **20**
Fawley Bus. Cen.
   Black 2G **55**
Fawley By-Pass. *Fawl* 2H **55**
Fawley Rd. *Holb* 2E **55**
Fawley Rd. *Hythe* 4E **53**
Fawley Rd. *Sotn* 5E **29**
Fell Clo. *L Hth* 3E **49**
Feltham Clo. *Roms* 4F **7**
Ferndale. *H End* 6B **34**
Ferndale Rd. *March* 4D **38**
Ferndene Way. *Sotn* 3H **31**
Fernhills Rd. *Hythe* 5F **53**
Fernlea Gdns. *Sotn* 6A **22**
Fernlea Way. *Dib P* 3B **52**
Fern Rd. *Hythe* 3D **52**
Fern Rd. *Sotn* 3H **41**
Fernside Clo. *Holb* 5C **54**
Fernside Clo. *Sotn* 3D **28**
Fernside Ct. *Sotn* 5A **22**
Fernside Wlk. *F Oak* 2G **17**
Fernside Way. *Eastl* 2G **17**
Fern Way. *Fare* 4H **49**
Fernwood Cres.
   Sotn 3H **31**
Fernyhurst Av. *Rown* 4D **20**
Ferry Bri. Grn. *H End* 5A **34**
Ferrymans Quay.
   Net A 2B **46**
Ferry Rd. *Hythe* 3D **52**
Field Clo. *L Hth* 5E **49**
Field Clo. *Roms* 5D **6**
Field Clo. *Sotn* 4E **23**
Fielden Clo. *N Bad* 3D **12**
Fieldfare Ct. *Tot* 3C **26**
Fields Clo. *Black* 4E **55**
Field Vw. *Chan F* 1B **14**
Filton Clo. *Cal* 2C **26**
Finches, The. *Sotn* 3F **29**
   (SO16)
Finches, The. *Sotn* 1D **30**
   (SO17)
Finlay Clo. *Sotn* 1C **42**
Finzi Clo. *Sotn* 2C **42**
Fircroft Dri. *Chan F* 2F **15**
Fircrest Clo. *Sotn* 4F **21**
Firgrove Clo. *N Bad* 3D **12**
Firgrove Ct. *Sotn* 4G **29**
Firgrove Rd. *N Bad* 3D **12**
Firgrove Rd. *Sotn* 4G **29**
Fir Rd. *Asht* 3B **36**
Firs Dri. *H End* 6G **33**
First Av. *Sotn* 4B **28**
Firs, The. *Sotn* 5B **22**
First St. *Hythe* 6H **53**
Fir Tree Ct. *Sotn* 3B **32**
Firtree Gro. *Hythe* 6E **53**
Firtree La. *H Hth* 1G **25**
Firtree Way. *Sotn* 6B **32**
Firwood Cvn. Pk. *Chan F* . .5E **9**
Firwood Clo. *Chan F* 5E **9**
Fisher's Rd. *Tot* 5G **27**
Fishlake Meadows.
   Roms 3B **6**
Fitzgerald Clo. *White* 5G **45**
Fitzhugh Pl. *Sotn* 4B **30**
Fitzhugh St.
   Sotn 6B **30** (2C **4**)
Fitzroy Clo. *Sotn* 2B **22**
Five Elms Dri. *Roms* 6E **7**

Flamborough Clo.
   Sotn 1B **28**
Flanders Ind. Pk. *H End* . . .3H **33**
Flanders Rd. *H End* 3H **33**
Fleet End Bottom.
   Wars 1D **50**
Fleet End Rd. *Wars* 6D **48**
Fleming Av. *N Bad* 3F **13**
Fleming Clo. *Fare* 3H **49**
Fleming Ct. *N Bad* 3F **13**
Fleming Pl. *Col C* 4F **11**
Fleming Pl. *Roms* 4C **6**
Fleming Rd. *Sotn* 5F **23**
Fletcher Clo. *Dib* 3B **52**
Fletchwood La. *Asht* 3A **36**
   (in two parts)
Fletchwood Rd. *Tot* 5B **26**
Fleuret Clo. *Hythe* 5E **53**
Flexford Clo. *Chan F* 4C **8**
Flexford Rd. *N Bad* 1G **13**
Flint Clo. *Sotn* 1E **43**
Floating Bri. Rd. *Sotn* 2E **41**
Florence Rd. *Sotn* 3F **41**
Florins, The. *Fare* 6E **49**
Flowerdown Clo. *Cal* 3C **26**
Flowers Clo. *Hamb* 4E **47**
Font Clo. *Fare* 4G **49**
Fontley Clo. *Sotn* 1E **43**
Fontwell Clo. *Cal* 2C **26**
   (in two parts)
Foord Rd. *H End* 6G **33**
Footner Clo. *Roms* 2F **7**
Forbes Clo. *Sotn* 3D **20**
Ford Av. *Chan F* 3F **15**
Fordington Vs. *Chan F* 1E **15**
Forest Clo. *Chan F* 5E **9**
Forest Clo. *N Bad* 2C **12**
Forest Edge. *Fawl* 2G **55**
Foresters Ga. *Black* 6E **55**
Foresters Rd. *Fawl* 3F **55**
Forest Front. *Hythe* 6D **52**
   (in two parts)
Forest Ga. *Black* 6F **55**
Forest Hills Dri. *Sotn* 6G **23**
Forest Hill Way. *Dib P* 4D **52**
Forest La. *Hythe* 2B **54**
Forest Mdw. *Dib P* 6E **53**
Forest Rd. *Chan F* 5F **9**
Forest Vw.
   Sotn 1B **40** (5D **4**)
Forge Clo. *Burs* 4G **43**
Forge La. *Fawl* 2H **55**
Forge Rd. *Black* 6F **55**
Forster Rd. *Sotn* 4C **30**
Forsythia Clo. *H End* 3H **33**
Forsythia Pl. *Sotn* 6H **31**
Forth Clo. *Chan F* 2D **14**
Forth Ho. *Sotn* 5E **31**
Fort Rd. *Sotn* 2G **41**
Fortune Ct. *Chan F* 1E **15**
Foundry Cres. *Burs* 5F **43**
Foundry La. *Sotn* 3F **29**
Fountain Ct. *Col C* 4G **11**
Fountain Ct. *H End* 5H **33**
Four Acres. *Bot* 5E **35**
Fourposts Hill.
   Sotn 6A **30** (1A **4**)
Fourshells Clo. *Fawl* 3F **55**
Fowey Clo. *Chan F* 6D **8**
Fowey, The. *Black* 3E **55**
Fowlers Rd. *H End* 3H **33**
Fowlers Wlk. *Chilw* 5H **13**
Foxbury Clo. *Hythe* 4E **53**
Fox Clo. *Eastl* 5F **17**
Foxcott Clo. *Sotn* 5H **41**
Foxcroft Dri. *Holb* 5B **54**
Foxglade. *Black* 6F **55**
Foxgloves, The. *H End* 6B **34**
Foxhayes La. *Black* 6F **55**

Foxhills. *Asht* 1C **36**
Foxhills Clo. *Asht* 2C **36**
Foxlands. *Black* 6F **55**
Fox's Wlk. *Black* 6F **55**
Foxtail Dri. *Dib P* 5D **52**
Foxy Paddock. *Black* 6F **55**
Foyes Ct. *Sotn* 4H **29**
Foy Gdns. *Wars* 6A **48**
Foyle Rd. *Chan F* 1D **14**
Frampton Clo. *Col C* 4F **11**
Frampton Way. *Tot* 5F **27**
Franconia Dri. *Nurs* 6H **19**
Franklyn Av. *Sotn* 1A **42**
Fraser Clo. *Sotn* 3D **20**
Fratton Way. *F Oak* 3F **17**
Frayslea. *Dib P* 4E **53**
Freda Routh Gdns.
   F Oak 2G **17**
Frederick St. *Sotn* 5D **30**
Freegrounds Clo.
   H End 5A **34**
Freegrounds Rd.
   H End 5A **34**
Freemantle Bus. Cen.
   Sotn 6G **29**
Freemantle Clo. *Sotn* 6H **31**
Freemantle Comn. Rd.
   Sotn 6H **31**
French St. *Sotn* . . .2B **40** (6D **4**)
Frensham Clo. *H End* 5A **34**
Frensham Ct. *H End* 5A **34**
Freshfield Rd. *Sotn* 4F **29**
Freshfield Sq. *Sotn* 4F **29**
Freshwater Ct. *Chan F* 4G **9**
Friars Cft. *Cal* 1C **26**
Friars Cft. *Net A* 6B **42**
Friars Rd. *Eastl* 6H **15**
Friars Way. *Sotn* 5F **23**
Fritham Clo. *Tot* 4C **26**
Fritham Rd. *Sotn* 3D **32**
Frobisher Ct. *March* 2E **39**
Frobisher Gdns. *Sotn* 1C **42**
Frobisher Ind. Cen.
   Roms 3B **6**
Froghall. *Dib P* 5E **53**
Frogmore La. *Nurs* 6B **20**
Frome Clo. *March* 4E **39**
Frome Rd. *W End* 6A **24**
Frost La. *Hythe* 5E **53**
Fry Clo. *Fawl* 3F **55**
Fry Clo. *Hamb* 3G **47**
Fryern Arc. *Chan F* 6F **9**
Fryern Clo. *Chan F* 1G **15**
Fuchsia Gdns. *Sotn* 1H **29**
Fullerton Clo. *Sotn* 5H **41**
Fulmar Clo. *Sotn* 4F **21**
Fulmar Dri. *Hythe* 4F **53**
Furze Clo. *Sotn* 6A **32**
Furzedale Gdns. *Hythe* . . .5F **53**
Furzedale Pk. *Hythe* 5F **53**
Furzedown M. *Hythe* 5F **53**
Furzedown Rd. *Sotn* 1C **30**
Furze Rd. *Sotn* 6A **32**
Furzey Av. *Hythe* 4F **53**
Furzey Clo. *Fawl* 4F **55**
Fyeford Clo. *Rown* 3D **20**
Fyfield Clo. *White* 5G **45**

G

Gables Ct. *Sotn* 4B **22**
Gage Clo. *March* 3E **39**
Gainsborough Clo.
   Sotn 3C **42**
Gainsborough Ct.
   N Bad 3F **13**
Gainsford Rd. *Sotn* 6F **31**
Galleon Clo. *Wars* 6D **48**

Gallops, The. *Fare* 5H **49**
Galsworthy Rd. *Tot* 4D **26**
Gamble Clo. *Sotn* 1H **41**
Gamble Rd. *Ports* 4F **5**
Gamma Ho. *Sotn* 6G **13**
Ganger Farm Rd. *Roms* . . .2F **7**
Gannet Clo. *Hythe* 4F **53**
Gannet Clo. *Sotn* 4F **21**
Garden M. *Wars* 6A **48**
Gardiner Clo. *March* 3E **39**
Garfield Rd. *Net A* 1A **46**
Garfield Rd. *Sotn* 4G **31**
Garland Way. *Tot* 3B **26**
Garnock Rd. *Sotn* 3F **41**
Garratt Clo. *H End* 1A **34**
Garretts Clo. *Sotn* 4A **42**
Garrick Gdns. *Sotn* 3A **42**
Garton Rd. *Sotn* 2G **41**
Gashouse Hill. *Net A* 2C **46**
Gaston Gdns. *Roms* 4C **6**
Gatcombe. *Net A* 6C **42**
Gatcombe Gdns.
    W End 1A **32**
Gatehouse, The.
    W End 1C **32**
Gaters Hill. *Sotn* 5A **24**
Gatwick Clo. *Sotn* 5E **21**
Gavan St. *Sotn* 6D **32**
Gemini Clo. *Sotn* 5D **20**
Gento Clo. *Bot* 5C **34**
George Curl Way.
    Sotn I 3H **23**
George Perrett Way.
    Chan F 3B **14**
George St. *Eastl* 4B **16**
Gerard Cres. *Sotn* 5D **32**
Gibbs Rd. *Sotn* 6B **30** (2D **4**)
Gilbury Clo. *Sotn* 5G **23**
Gilchrist Gdns. *Wars* 2A **50**
Giles Clo. *H End* 2B **34**
Gillcrest. *Fare* 3G **49**
Gilpin Clo. *Sotn* 6E **33**
Gipsy Gro. *Sotn* 4G **29**
Girton Clo. *Fare* 6G **49**
Glades, The. *L Hth* 3E **49**
Glade, The. *Black* 6E **55**
Glade, The. *Chan F* 4H **9**
Gladstone Rd. *Sotn* 6B **32**
Glasslaw Rd. *Sotn* 3A **32**
Glebe Ct. *Bot* 3E **35**
Glebe Ct. *F Oak* 2G **17**
Glebe Ct. *Sotn* 1C **30**
Glencarron Way. *Sotn* 6A **22**
Glencoyne Gdns. *Sotn* 1D **28**
Glenda Clo. *Wars* 1B **50**
Glendale. *L Hth* 5E **49**
Glendowan Rd. *Chan F* . . .6C **8**
Glen Eyre Clo. *Sotn* 5C **22**
Glen Eyre Dri. *Sotn* 4C **22**
Glen Eyre Rd. *Sotn* 4B **22**
Glen Eyre Way. *Sotn* 5C **22**
Glenfield Av. *Sotn* 4H **31**
Glenfield Cres. *Sotn* 4H **31**
Glenfield Way. *Sotn* 4H **31**
Glenlea Clo. *W End* 2D **32**
Glenlea Dri. *W End* 2D **32**
Glenmore Ct. *Sotn* 3C **30**
Glenn Rd. *W End* 1D **32**
Glen Pk. *Col C* 4H **11**
Glen Rd. *Sotn* 4F **41**
Glen Rd. *Swanw* 6D **44**
    (in two parts)
Glenside. *Hythe* 3D **52**
Glenside. *W End* 2D **32**
Glenside Av. *Sotn* 1D **42**
Glenwood Av. *Sotn* 4C **22**
Glenwood Ct. *F Oak* 2H **17**
Gloster Ct. *Seg W* 2G **49**

Gloucester Sq. *Sotn* 6E **5**
Glyn Jones Clo. *Fawl* 3F **55**
Godfrey Olson Ho.
    Eastl 4B **16**
Goldcrest Gdns. *Sotn* 4E **21**
Goldcrest La. *Tot* 3C **26**
Golden Ct. *W End* 6F **25**
Golden Gro.
    Sotn 6D **30** (2G **5**)
Golden Hind Pk.
    Hythe 4D **52**
Goldsmith Clo. *Tot* 4D **26**
Goldsmith Rd. *Eastl* 6H **15**
Goldwire Dri. *Chan F* 2B **14**
Golf Course Rd. *Sotn* 4A **22**
Goodacre Dri. *Chan F* 2B **14**
Goodhalls La. *H End* 4G **33**
    (in two parts)
Goodison Clo. *F Oak* 6H **17**
Goodlands Va. *H End* 4G **33**
Goodwin Clo. *Sotn* 1B **28**
Goodwood Clo. *Fare* 5H **49**
Goodwood Gdns. *Tot* 3C **26**
Goodwood Rd. *Eastl* 2H **15**
Gordon Av. *Sotn* 3C **30**
Gordon Rd. *Chan F* 4F **9**
Gordon Ter. *Sotn* 3A **42**
Gorse Clo. *L Hth* 5D **48**
Gorselands Rd. *Sotn* 2B **32**
Gort Cres. *Sotn* 1B **42**
Gover Rd. *Sotn* 2A **28**
Grace Dieu Gdns. *Burs* . . .4F **43**
Graddidge Way. *Tot* 4D **26**
Grafton Gdns. *Sotn* 4G **21**
Graham Ct. *Sotn* 5A **32**
Graham Ho. *Sotn* 5E **31**
Graham Rd. *Sotn* 5C **30**
Graham St. *Sotn* 5E **31**
Grainger Gdns. *Sotn* 2C **42**
Granada Rd. *H End* 6G **33**
Granby Gro. *Sotn* 6D **22**
Grange Clo. *Sotn* 5G **23**
Grange Ct. *Net A* 1B **46**
Grange Ct. *Sotn* 4G **23**
Grange Dri. *H End* 3B **34**
Grange La. *Gos* 4F **5**
    (in two parts)
Grange M. *Roms* 3F **7**
Grange Pk. *H End* 2A **34**
Grange Rd. *H End* 3A **34**
Grange Rd. *Net A* 1A **46**
Grange Rd. *Sotn* 2F **29**
Grangewood Ct. *F Oak* . . .5H **17**
Grangewood Gdns.
    F Oak 5H **17**
Grantham Av. *Hamb* 4E **47**
Grantham Ct. *Eastl* 5A **16**
Grantham Rd. *Eastl* 5H **15**
    (in two parts)
Grantham Rd. *Sotn* 5H **31**
Granville St.
    Sotn 1D **40** (4H **5**)
Grasdean Clo. *Sotn* 2A **32**
Grasmere. *Eastl* 5H **15**
Grasmere Clo. *W End* 2B **32**
Grasmere Ct. *Sotn* 1C **28**
Grassymead. *Fare* 3G **49**
Grateley Clo. *Sotn* 5H **41**
Gravel Wlk. *Black* 3F **55**
Grayling Mead. *Roms* 3C **6**
Graylings. *Sotn* 3E **29**
Grays Av. *Hythe* 3F **53**
Grays Clo. *Col C* 5F **11**
Grays Clo. *Roms* 5D **6**
Greatbridge Rd. *Roms* 1B **6**
Gt. Elms Clo. *Holb* 5B **54**
Gt. Well Dri. *Roms* 4D **6**

Greatwood Clo. *Hythe* 4E **53**
Greenacres Dri. *Ott* 2C **10**
Greenaway La. *Wars* 5B **48**
Greenbank Cres. *Sotn* 4B **22**
Green Clo. *Hythe* 2E **53**
Greendale Clo. *Chan F* 1G **15**
Green Fld. Clo. *H End* 1H **43**
Greenfields Av. *Tot* 2E **27**
Greenfields Clo. *Tot* 2E **27**
Greenfinch Clo. *Eastl* 6F **15**
Greenhill La. *Rown* 1C **20**
Greenhill Ter. *Roms* 6A **6**
Greenhill Vw. *Roms* 6A **6**
Green La. *Amp* 4H **7**
Green La. *Black* 5F **55**
Green La. *Bur* 4F **45**
Green La. *Burs* 3F **43**
Green La. *Cal* 5B **18**
Green La. *Chilw* 6B **14**
Green La. *Hamb* 5G **47**
Green La. *Holb* 6B **54**
Green La. *Lwr S* 5B **44**
Green La. *Sotn* 1C **28**
Green La. *Wars* 6D **48**
Greenlea Cres. *Sotn* 4F **23**
Green Pk. Rd. *Sotn* 4C **28**
Greens Clo. *Eastl* 6G **17**
Green, The. *Roms* 3F **7**
Grenadier Clo. *L Hth* 5F **49**
Grendon Clo. *Sotn* 4D **22**
Grenville Ct. *Sotn* 4A **30**
Grenville Gdns. *Dib P* 5E **53**
Gresley Gdns. *H End* 1A **34**
Greville Rd. *Sotn* 4H **29**
Greyhound Clo. *H End* 6H **25**
Greywell Av. *Sotn* 5G **21**
Greywell Ct. *Sotn* 5G **21**
Griffen Clo. *Eastl* 5E **17**
Griffin Ct. *Sotn* 3E **31**
Griffin Ind. Pk. *Tot* 6E **19**
Griffon Clo. *Burs* 4G **43**
Grosvenor Clo. *Sotn* 1E **31**
Grosvenor Ct. *Roms* 5F **7**
Grosvenor Ct. Sotn 2E **31**
    (off Grosvenor Clo.)
Grosvenor Gdns. *Sotn* 1E **31**
Grosvenor Gdns.
    W End 3D **32**
Grosvenor Mans. Sotn . . .5B **30**
    (off Grosvenor Sq.)
Grosvenor M. *Sotn* 1E **31**
Grosvenor Rd. *Chan F* 4G **9**
Grosvenor Rd. *Sotn* 1E **31**
Grosvenor Sq.
    Sotn 5B **30** (1D **4**)
Grovebury. *L Hth* 5E **49**
Grove Copse. *Sotn* 4C **42**
Grove Gdns. *Sotn* 4B **42**
Grovely Way. *Cram* 3H **7**
Grove M. *Sotn* 3B **42**
Grove Pl. *Sotn* 3B **42**
Grove Rd. *Shaw* 1C **10**
Grove Rd. *Sotn* 4G **29**
Grove St. *Sotn* 1D **40** (4G **5**)
Grove, The. *Burs* 4G **43**
Grove, The. *Net A* 6D **42**
Grove, The. *Sotn* 4B **42**
Guardian Ct. *Sotn* 2C **30**
Guernsey Clo. *Sotn* 6C **20**
Guest Rd. *Eastl* 4D **16**

Guildford Dri. *Chan F* 4D **14**
Guildford St.
    Sotn 6D **30** (1H **5**)
Guillemot Clo. *Hythe* 3F **53**
Gull Coppice. *White* 6G **45**
Gulls, The. *March* 3D **38**
Gullycroft Mead.
    H End 4H **33**
Gurney Rd. *Sotn* 3G **29**

H

Hack Dri. *Col C* 5F **11**
Hackworth Gdns.
    H End 1A **34**
Haddon Dri. *Eastl* 2A **16**
Hadleigh Gdns. *Eastl* 2A **16**
Hadley Fld. *Holb* 3B **54**
Hadrians Clo. *Chan F* 6G **9**
Hadrian Way. *Chilw* 2A **22**
Haflinger Dri. *White* 5F **45**
Haig Rd. *Eastl* 5G **17**
Haileybury Gdns.
    H End 2A **34**
Halden Clo. *Roms* 3E **7**
Hales Dri. *H End* 6G **33**
Halifax Ct. *W End* 1C **32**
Hallett Clo. *Sotn* 1A **32**
Hall Lands La. *F Oak* 2G **17**
Halstead Rd. *Sotn* 1H **31**
Halterworth Clo. *Roms* 5E **7**
Halterworth La.
    Roms & Cram 5F **7**
Haltons Clo. *Tot* 2D **26**
Halyards. *Hamb* 3G **47**
Hambert Way. *Tot* 6E **27**
Hamblecliff Ho. *Hamb* 4D **46**
Hamble Cliff Stables.
    Hamb 4D **46**
Hamble Clo. *Wars* 6A **48**
Hamble Ct. *Chan F* 2F **15**
Hamble Ho. Gdns.
    Hamb 5G **47**
Hamble La. *Burs* 5F **43**
Hamble La. *Hamb* 4E **47**
Hamble Mnr. Ct.
    Hamb 5G **47**
Hamble Pk. Cvn. Site.
    Wars 6D **48**
Hambleside Ct. *Hamb* 5F **47**
Hamble Wood. *Bot* 5E **35**
Hamblewood Ct. *Bot* 5E **35**
Hameldon Clo. *Sotn* 4D **28**
Hamilton M. *Hythe* 5F **53**
Hamilton Rd. *Eastl* 4D **16**
Hamilton Rd. *Hythe* 6F **53**
Hamlet Ct. *Fawl* 2H **55**
Hammonds Clo. *Tot* 3E **27**
Hammond's Grn. *Tot* 3D **26**
Hammonds La. *Tot* 3E **27**
Hammonds Way. *Tot* 3E **27**
Hampshire Corporate Pk.
    Chan F 4D **14**
Hampshire Ct. *Chan F* 4E **15**
Hampton Clo. *Black* 5E **55**
Hampton Gdns. *Black* 5E **55**
Hampton La. *Black* 3E **55**
Hampton Towers.
    Sotn 5G **41**
Hamtun Cres. *Tot* 2E **27**
Hamtun Gdns. *Tot* 2E **27**
Hamtun Rd. *Sotn* 2C **42**
Hamtun St.
    Sotn 2B **40** (5D **4**)
Handel Rd.
    Sotn 5B **30** (1C **4**)
Handel Ter.
    Sotn 6A **30** (1B **4**)

Handford Pl. *Sotn* 5B 30
Hanley Rd. *Sotn* 3H 29
Hannay Ri. *Sotn* 6D 32
Hann Rd. *Rown* 3C 20
Hanns Way. *Eastl* 4A 16
Hanover Bldgs.
　　Sotn 1C 40 (4E 5)
Hanover Clo. *Roms* 5B 6
Hanover Ct. *Hythe* 2E 53
Hanover Ho. *Tot* 3G 27
Hanoverian Way.
　　White 6G 45
Harborough Rd. *Sotn* . . .5B 30
Harbourne Gdns.
　　W End 1B 32
Harbour Pde.
　　Sotn 1A 40 (3B 4)
Harcourt Rd. *Sotn* 3F 31
Harding La. *F Oak* 4H 17
　　(in two parts)
Hardley Ind. Est.
　　Hythe 2A 54
Hardley La. *Hythe* 1B 54
Hardwicke Clo. *Sotn* 1D 28
Hardwicke Way. *Hamb* . .5D 46
Hardwick Rd. *Chan F* 1F 15
Hardy Clo. *L Hth* 3F 49
Hardy Clo. *Sotn* 5F 29
Hardy Dri. *Hythe* 4F 53
Hardy Rd. *Eastl* 6A 16
Harefield Ct. *Roms* 4E 7
Harefield Rd. *Sotn* 5E 23
Hare La. *Twy* 1G 11
Harewood Clo. *Eastl* 1A 16
Harland Cres. *Sotn* 2H 29
Harlaxton Clo. *Eastl* 2H 15
Harlech Dri. *Chan F* 3C 14
Harley Ct. *Wars* 6B 48
Harlyn Rd. *Sotn* 2D 28
Harold Clo. *Tot* 5D 26
Harold Rd. *Sotn* 4G 29
Harrage, The. *Roms* 5C 6
Harrier Clo. *Sotn* 3F 21
Harrier Way. *Hythe* 2B 54
Harris Av. *H End* 3A 34
Harrison Rd. *Sotn* 6E 23
Harrison's Cut.
　　Sotn 1D 40 (4F 5)
　　(SO14)
Harrison's Cut. *Sotn* 2F 29
　　(SO15)
Hart Ct. *Sotn* 2H 41
Hart Hill. *Hythe* 5G 53
Hartington Rd.
　　Sotn 6D 30 (1H 5)
Hartley Av. *Sotn* 1D 30
Hartley Clo. *Dib P* 5E 53
Hartley Clo. *Eastl* 6G 17
Hartley Rd. *Eastl* 6G 17
Hartley Wlk. *Dib P* 5E 53
Hartsgrove Av. *Black* 5E 55
Hartsgrove Clo. *Black* 4E 55
Harvest Rd. *Chan F* 1B 14
Harvey Ct. *Black* 3E 55
Harvey Cres. *Wars* 6D 48
Harvey Gdns. *Hythe* 3F 53
Harvey Rd. *Eastl* 4E 17
Harwood Clo. *Tot* 3E 27
Haselbury Rd. *Tot* 4F 27
Haselfoot Gdns. 4E 33
Hatch Mead. *W End* 1C 32
Hathaway Clo. *Eastl* 3B 16
Hatherell Clo. *W End* 2D 32
Hatherley Mans. *Sotn* . . .4G 29
Hatley Rd. *Sotn* 3A 32
Havelock Ct. *Wars* 6A 48
Havelock Rd.
　　Sotn 6B 30 (1C 4)

Havelock Rd. *Wars* 6A 48
Havendale. *H End* 6B 34
　　(in two parts)
Havenstone Way. *Sotn* . . .5G 23
Haven, The. *Eastl* 1B 16
Haven, The. *H End* 1H 43
Haven, The. *L Hth* 3G 49
Havre Towers. *Sotn* 5G 41
Haweswater Clo. *Sotn* . . .2D 28
Hawkeswood Rd. *Sotn* . . .4E 31
Hawkhill. *Dib* 3A 52
Hawkhurst Clo. *Sotn* 4A 42
Hawkins Ct. *March* 2D 38
Hawkley Grn. *Sotn* 4H 41
Hawthorn Clo. *Col C* 5G 11
Hawthorn Clo. *F Oak* 2F 17
Hawthorn Clo. *H End* 5B 34
Hawthorne Rd. *Tot* 3D 26
Hawthorn La. *Sar G* 2C 48
Hawthorn Rd. *Hythe* 3D 52
Hawthorn Rd. *Sotn* 1C 30
Hawthorns, The. *Eastl* 6G 15
Hawthorns, The.
　　March 4E 39
　　(Limes, The)
Hawthorns, The.
　　March 4D 38
　　(Main Rd.)
Hayburn Rd. *Sotn* 1B 28
Haydock Clo. *Tot* 3C 26
Hayes Mead. *Holb* 3B 54
Hayle Rd. *W End* 1B 32
Hayley Clo. *Hythe* 6D 52
Haynes Way. *Dib P* 5C 52
Hayter Gdns. *Roms* 4D 6
Hayward Clo. *Tot* 4D 26
Hayward Ct. *Holb* 4C 54
Hazel Clo. *Chan F* 3E 9
Hazel Clo. *Col C* 4G 11
Hazeldown Rd. *Rown* 4C 20
Hazeleigh Av. *Sotn* 3G 41
Hazel Farm Rd. *Tot* 4C 26
Hazel Gro. *Asht* 2A 36
Hazel Gro. *L Hth* 5F 49
Hazel Rd. *Sotn* 1F 41
Hazelwood Rd. *Sotn* 2A 32
Headland Dri. *L Hth* 3E 49
Heath Clo. *F Oak* 3G 17
Heathcote Rd. *Chan F* 1F 15
Heatherbrae Gdns.
　　N Bad 3D 12
Heather Chase. *Eastl* 5G 17
Heather Clo. *Tot* 4E 27
Heather Ct. *Sotn* 4C 32
Heatherdeane Rd.
　　Sotn 1C 30
Heatherdene Rd.
　　Chan F 4G 9
Heatherlands Rd.
　　Chilw 1B 22
Heather Rd. *Fawl* 3F 55
Heatherstone Av.
　　Dib P 6D 52
Heatherview Clo.
　　N Bad 2D 12
Heathfield. *Hythe* 4D 52
Heathfield Clo. *Chan F* 3E 9
Heathfield Clo. *Sotn* 2C 42
Heathfield Rd. *Chan F* 3E 9
Heathfield Rd. *Sotn* 2B 42
Heath Gdns. *Net A* 6D 42
Heath Ho. Clo. *H End* 1H 43
Heath Ho. Gdns. *H End* 1H 43
Heath Ho. La. *H End* 1H 43
Heathlands Clo. *Chan F* 5E 9
Heathlands Rd. *Chan F* 5E 9
Heath Rd. *L Hth* 4D 48

Heath Rd. *N Bad* 4E 13
Heath Rd. *Sotn* 6A 32
Heath Rd. N. *L Hth* 3D 48
Heath Rd. S. *L Hth* 4D 48
Hedera Rd. *L Hth* 4D 48
Hedge End Bus. Cen.
　　H End 2H 33
Hedge End Retail Pk.
　　H End 4G 33
　　(in two parts)
Hedgerow Clo. *Rown* 2C 20
Hedgerow Dri. *Sotn* 2B 32
Hedley Clo. *Fawl* 4F 55
Hedley Gdns. *H End* 1H 33
Hedley Wlk. *Black* 4F 55
Heights, The. *H End* 5G 33
Helford Gdns. *W End* 1B 32
Helvellyn Rd. *Sotn* 3D 28
Hemdean Gdns.
　　W End 2D 32
Hemlock Way. *Chan F* 2B 14
Hemming Clo. *Tot* 5E 27
Hemmingway Gdns.
　　White 5G 45
Henry Clo. *Holb* 2B 54
Henry Rd. *Eastl* 3D 16
Henry Rd. *Sotn* 4F 29
Henry St. *Sotn* 5B 30
Henstead Ct. *Sotn* 5B 30
Henstead Rd. *Sotn* 5B 30
Hensting La. *Fish P* 6H 11
Henty Rd. *Sotn* 3F 29
Hepworth Clo. *Sotn* 3C 42
Herald Ind. Est. *H End* 2H 33
Herald Rd. *H End* 2H 33
Herbert Walker Av.
　　Sotn 6E 29 (4A 4)
　　(in two parts)
Hereward Clo. *Roms* 5E 7
Heron Sq. *Eastl* 5G 15
Herons Wood. *Cal* 1D 26
Herrick Clo. *Sotn* 1D 42
Hertsfield. *Fare* 4G 49
Hesketh Ho. *Sotn* 5G 29
Hestia Clo. *Roms* 4F 7
Hewetts Ri. *Wars* 1A 50
Hewitt's Rd. *Sotn* 6H 29
Hexagon Cen., The.
　　Chan F 5E 15
Heye's Dri. *Sotn* 2C 42
Heysham Rd. *Sotn* 3F 29
Heywood Grn. *Sotn* 6E 33
Hickory Gdns. *W End* 6C 24
Highbridge Rd.
　　Highb & Col C 6C 10
Highbury Clo. *F Oak* 3F 17
Highclere Rd. *Sotn* 6H 21
Highclere Way. *Chan F* 4C 14
Highcliff Av. *Sotn* 3C 30
Highcliffe Dri. *Eastl* 6A 10
Highcrown M. *Sotn* 1C 30
Highcrown St. *Sotn* 1C 30
Highfield Av. *Sotn* 6B 22
Highfield Clo. *Chan F* 1G 15
Highfield Clo. *Sotn* 1C 30
Highfield Cres. *Sotn* 1D 30
Highfield La. *Sotn* 1C 30
Highfield Rd. *Chan F* 1G 15
Highfield Rd. *Sotn* 2B 30
Highfields. *Wars* 6D 48
High Firs Gdns. *Roms* 5F 7
High Firs Rd. *Roms* 4F 7
High Firs Rd. *Sotn* 6B 32
Highgrove Clo. *Tot* 6D 26
Highlands Clo. *Dib P* 4E 53
Highlands Clo. *N Bad* 2C 12
Highlands Ho. *Sotn* 2F 41
Highlands Way. *Dib P* 4D 52

Highmeadow. *Sotn* 5C 32
Highnam Gdns. *Sar G* 3D 48
High Oaks Clo. *L Hth* 4E 49
High Rd. *Sotn* 6F 23
High St. *Bot* 4D 34
High St. *Burs* 6G 43
High St. *Eastl* 6A 16
High St. *Hamb* 5G 47
High St. *Hythe* 1E 53
High St. *Sotn* 1C 40 (4D 4)
High St. *Tot* 4G 27
High St. *Twy* 1G 11
High St. *W End* 1C 32
Hightown Towers.
　　Sotn 1E 43
High Trees. *F Oak* 2H 17
High Vw. Way. *Sotn* 3H 31
Highwood La. *Roms* 4F 7
Hilda Pl. *Sotn* 6E 31
　　(off Kent St.)
Hill Cft. *Fare* 4H 49
Hilldene Way. *W End* 2D 32
Hilldown Rd. *Sotn* 1D 30
Hill Farm Rd. *Sotn* 5A 30
Hillgrove Rd. *Sotn* 6H 23
Hill La. *Col C* 4F 11
Hill La. *Sotn* 1A 4
Hill Pl. *Burs* 5H 43
Hillside Av. *Roms* 5D 6
Hillside Av. *Sotn* 2G 31
Hillside Clo. *Chan F* 1F 15
Hillsons Rd. *Bot* 4F 35
Hill St. *Cal* 3C 18
Hilltop Dri. *Sotn* 1D 42
Hillview Rd. *Hythe* 3D 52
Hillway, The. *Chan F* 6F 9
Hillyfields. *Nurs* 5B 20
Hiltingbury Clo. *Chan F* 4F 9
Hiltingbury Ct. *Chan F* 4D 8
Hiltingbury Rd. *Chan F* 4D 8
Hilton Rd. *H End* 4A 34
Hinkler Ct. *Sotn* 1D 42
Hinkler Rd. *Sotn* 5E 33
Hinton Cres. *Sotn* 6E 33
Hirst Rd. *Hythe* 3F 53
Hispano Av. *White* 6G 45
Hobart Dri. *Hythe* 3E 53
Hobb La. *H End* 6B 34
Hobson Way. *Holb* 5D 54
Hocombe Dri. *Chan F* 3D 8
Hocombe Pk. Clo.
　　Chan F 3D 8
Hocombe Rd. *Chan F* 3D 8
Hocombe Wood Rd.
　　Chan F 3C 8
Hodder Clo. *Chan F* 2D 14
Hoe La. *N Bad* 5A 12
Hogarth Clo. *Roms* 3E 7
Hogarth Clo. *Sotn* 3C 42
Hogwood La. *W End* 3E 25
Holbury Drove. *Holb* 5B 54
Holcroft Ho. *Sotn* 5E 33
Holcroft Rd. *Sotn* 6E 33
Holkham Clo. *Sotn* 6C 20
Holland Clo. *Chan F* 4E 15
Holland Pk. *Sar G* 4D 48
Holland Pl. *Sotn* 2F 29
Holland Rd. *Sotn* 3F 41
Holland Rd. *Tot* 4C 26
Hollingbourne Clo.
　　Sotn 3F 31
Hollman Dri. *Roms* 4A 6
Hollybank Clo. *Hythe* 3E 53
Hollybank Cres. *Hythe* 2D 52
Hollybank Rd. *Hythe* 2D 52

Hollybrook Av. *Sotn* 6G **21**
Hollybrook Clo. *Sotn* 1F **29**
Hollybrook Gdns.
  L Hth 2E **49**
Hollybrook Rd. *Sotn* 1G **29**
Holly Clo. *Hythe* 1A **54**
Holly Clo. *Sar G* 4C **48**
Holly Dell. *Sotn* 4A **22**
Holly Gdns. *W End* 6D **24**
Holly Hatch Rd. *Tot* 5E **27**
Holly Hill. *Sotn* 4A **22**
Holly Hill Clo. *Sotn* 4A **22**
Holly Hill La. *Sar G* 3A **48**
Holly Hill Mans. *L Hth* 3C **48**
Holly Lodge. *Chan F* 4E **15**
Holly Lodge. *Sotn* 2D **48**
Holly M. *Sotn* 5B **22**
Holly Oak Ct. *Sotn* 5E **21**
Holly Oak Rd. *Sotn* 6E **21**
  (in two parts)
Holly Rd. *Asht* 3B **36**
Holly Rd. *Black* 5E **55**
Hollywood Clo. *N Bad* 3D **12**
Holmes Clo. *Net A* 1B **46**
Holmesland Dri. *Bot* 4D **34**
Holmesland La. *Bot* 4D **34**
Holmesland Wlk. *Bot* 4D **34**
Holmgrove. *Fare* 4G **49**
Holmsley Clo. *Sotn* 4C **32**
Holmsley Ct. *Tot* 3B **26**
Holt Ct. *Sotn* 5G **41**
Holt Rd. *Sotn* 4B **30**
Holt Vw. *Eastl* 5F **17**
Holybourne Rd. *Roms* 5E **7**
Holyrood Av. *Sotn* 1D **30**
Holyrood Ho.
  Sotn 2C **40** (5E **5**)
Holyrood Pl.
  Sotn 2C **40** (5E **5**)
Homeborough Ho.
  Hythe 1E **53**
Home Farm Clo. *Hythe* . . .3F **53**
Homefield. *Roms* 3D **6**
Home Fld. Dri. *Nurs* 4A **20**
Homemead Ho. *Roms* 6B **6**
Homepoint Ho. *Sotn* 4A **32**
Homer Farm La. *Black* . . .6E **55**
Homer Mobile Home Pk.
  Black 6E **55**
Home Rule Rd. *L Hth* 3F **49**
Homespinney Ho.
  Sotn 1F **31**
Honeysuckle Clo.
  L Hth 2E **49**
Honeysuckle Cotts.
  Sotn 5E **23**
Honeysuckle Rd. *Sotn* 5C **22**
Honeysuckle Way.
  Chan F 1C **14**
Honeywood Clo. *Tot* 2D **26**
Honister Clo. *Sotn* 3C **28**
Hood Clo. *L Hth* 3F **49**
Hood Rd. *Sotn* 3A **32**
Hook Clo. *Amp* 3C **8**
Hook Cres. *Amp* 3C **8**
Hook La. *Wars & Fare* 2E **51**
Hook Pk. Rd. *Wars* 2A **50**
Hook Rd. *Amp* 2A **8**
Hook Water Clo. *Chan F* . . .3D **8**
Hook Water Rd. *Chan F* . . .3C **8**
Hookwood La. *Amp* 3B **8**
Hope Rd. *W End* 1E **33**
Hornbeam Clo. *H End* 5B **34**
Hornbeam Gdns.
  W End 6D **24**
Hornbeam Rd. *Chan F* 1A **14**
Hornby Clo. *Wars* 1B **50**
Hornchurch Rd. *Sotn* 5D **20**

Horns Drove. *Rown* 4B **20**
Horns Hill. *Sotn* 3B **20**
Horsebridge Way.
  Rown 4C **20**
Horsecroft. *Roms* 4C **6**
Horsefair Ct. *Roms* 5B **6**
Horsefair M. *Roms* 5B **6**
Horsefair, The. *Roms* 5B **6**
Horseshoe Bri. *Sotn* 3D **30**
Horseshoe Clo. *Fare* 5H **49**
Horseshoe Dri. *Roms* 2E **7**
Horseshoe Lodge.
  Wars 6C **48**
Horton Way. *Eastl* 5F **17**
Hotspur Clo. *Hythe* 1D **52**
Hound Clo. *Net A* 2D **46**
Hound Rd. *Net A* 2C **46**
Hound Rd. Gdns.
  Net A 1D **46**
Hound Way. *Net A* 1C **46**
Houndwell Pl.
  Sotn 1C **40** (4F **5**)
Hounsdown Av. *Tot* 6F **27**
Hounsdown Clo. *Tot* 6F **27**
House Clo. *Col C* 4G **11**
Hoveton Gro. *Chan F* 5D **8**
Howard Clo. *Chan F* 3F **15**
Howard Clo. *F Oak* 2F **17**
Howard Clo. *Sotn* 5G **23**
Howard Oliver Ho.
  Hythe 3F **53**
Howard Rd. *Sotn* 5H **29**
Howard's Gro. *Sotn* 3G **29**
Howerts Clo. *Wars* 2B **50**
Hudson Ct. *Tot* 5D **26**
Hughes Clo. *Black* 4E **55**
Hulles Way. *N Bad* 3D **12**
Hulse Lodge. *Sotn* 3B **30**
Hulse Rd. *Sotn* 3B **30**
Hulton Clo. *Sotn* 4F **41**
Humber Gdns. *Burs* 4G **43**
Hundred, The. *Roms* 5B **6**
Hungerford. *Burs* 6F **43**
Hunt Av. *Net A* 1C **46**
Hunter Clo. *Holb* 2B **54**
Hunter Ct. *Sotn* 2F **29**
Hunters Ct. *Burs* 1H **43**
Hunters Cres. *Roms* 2F **7**
Hunters Cres. *Tot* 5B **26**
Hunters Hill. *Tot* 2D **36**
Hunter's Ride. *Win* 1A **8**
Hunters Way. *Eastl* 5G **17**
Huntingdon Clo. *Fare* 6G **49**
Huntingdon Clo. *Tot* 2E **27**
Huntly Way. *Sotn* 4H **31**
Hunton Clo. *Sotn* 6H **21**
Hunts Pond Rd.
  Park G & Fare 2F **49**
Hurdles, The. *Fare* 5H **49**
Hurlingham Gdns.
  Sotn 4C **22**
Hurricane Dri. *Rown* 3C **20**
Hursley Ct. *Chan F* 4D **8**
Hursley Dri. *Black* 6E **55**
Hursley Rd. *Chan F* 2D **8**
Hurstbourne Pl. *Sotn* 5H **41**
Hurst Clo. *Chan F* 3C **14**
Hurst Clo. *Tot* 3F **27**
Hurst Grn. Clo. *Sotn* 4A **42**
Hutwood Rd. *Chilw* 1C **22**
Huxley Clo. *L Hth* 5G **49**
Huxley Ct. *Dib P* 4A **52**
Hyde Clo. *Sotn* 2G **29**
Hyde Clo. *Tot* 4B **26**
Hymans Way. *Tot* 4H **29**
Hyssop Clo. *White* 6H **45**
Hythe By-Pass. *Dib* 3A **52**
Hythe Rd. *March* 5C **38**

I
Ibbotson Way. *Tot* 6D **26**
Ibsen Clo. *White* 5G **45**
Ida Ct. *Sotn* 3H **41**
Iddesleigh Rd. *Bourn* 3G **5**
Ideal Pk. Homes Cvn. Site.
  Bram 6F **11**
Ilex Cres. *L Hth* 4D **48**
Imber Way. *Sotn* 1C **42**
Imperial Av. *Sotn* 3F **29**
Imperial Pk. Ind. Est.
  Sotn 4D **30**
Imperial Rd. *Sotn* 4D **30**
Imperial Way. *W Dock* 6G **29**
Ingersley Ri. *W End* 2E **33**
Ingle Glen. *Dib P* 5E **53**
Ingle Grn. *Cal* 2B **26**
Ingleside. *Net A* 6C **42**
Ingleton Rd. *Sotn* 2B **28**
Inglewood. *F Oak* 1F **17**
Ingram Ct. *Sotn* 3E **31**
Inkerman Rd. *Sotn* 2F **41**
International Way.
  Sotn 5G **41**
Ionic Clo. *Chan F* 6H **9**
Ipley Way. *Hythe* 4E **53**
Iris Rd. *Sotn* 5D **22**
Ironbridge Cres.
  Park G 1E **49**
Ironside Ct. *Sotn* 5D **4**
Irving Rd. *Sotn* 2D **28**
Irwell Clo. *Chan F* 2C **14**
Isis Clo. *Sotn* 3C **28**
Itchen Av. *Eastl* 5F **17**
Itchen Bri., The.
  Sotn 2E **41** (6H **5**)
Itchen Grange. *Eastl* 4D **16**
Itchenside Clo. *Sotn* 5H **23**
Itchen Vw. *Sotn* 5H **23**
Itchin Clo. *Tot* 5D **26**
Ivanhoe Rd. *Sotn* 2H **29**
Ivor Clo. *Holb* 4C **54**
Ivy Clo. *Tot* 1E **27**
Ivy Dene. *Sotn* 1D **42**
Ivy La. *W End* 1B **32**
Ivy Rd. *Sotn* 3E **31**
Ivy Ter. *H End* 5H **33**

J
Jacaranda Clo. *Fare* 3H **49**
Jack Clo. *Chan F* 1A **14**
Jackdaw Ri. *Eastl* 6F **15**
Jackie Wigg Gdns. *Tot* 4G **27**
Jackman's Clo. *Sotn* 2F **41**
Jacobs Clo. *Roms* 5D **6**
Jacob's Gutter La. *Tot* 6F **27**
  (in two parts)
Jacob's Wlk. *Tot* 1E **37**
James Ct. *Roms* 6D **6**
James Grieve Av.
  L Hth 5E **49**
Jameson Rd. *Sotn* 2H **41**
James St. *Sotn* 1D **40** (3G **5**)
Janaway Gdns. *Sotn* 3F **31**
Janes Clo. *Black* 5E **55**
Janson Rd. *Sotn* 4G **29**
Jarvis Fields. *Burs* 5H **43**
Jasmine Rd. *H End* 3H **33**
Java Dri. *White* 6G **45**
Jeffries Clo. *Rown* 4C **20**
Jellicoe Ho. *H End* 3B **34**
Jenkyns Clo. *Bot* 4E **35**
Jenner Way. *Roms* 4F **7**
Jennings Rd. *Tot* 3G **27**
Jermyns La. *Amp* 1F **7**
Jerome Ct. *Sotn* 5D **32**

Jerrett's La. *Nurs* 6B **20**
Jersey Clo. *Sotn* 6C **20**
Jesmond Gro. *L Hth* 6E **49**
Jessamine Rd. *Sotn* 1F **29**
Jessie Ter. *Sotn* 2C **40** (6F **5**)
Jessop Clo. *Hythe* 1D **52**
Jessop Wlk. *Hythe* 1D **52**
  (off Jessop Clo.)
Jetty Rd. *Hythe* 1H **55**
Jex Blake Clo. *Sotn* 5F **21**
Jockey La. *Eastl* 2E **17**
John Bunyan Clo.
  White 5G **45**
John Darling Mall.
  Eastl 3A **16**
Johnson St.
  Sotn 1C **40** (3F **5**)
  (in two parts)
John's Rd. *Sotn* 3F **41**
John St. *Sotn* 2C **40** (6F **5**)
Jonas Nichols Sq. *Sotn* 3G **5**
Jones La. *Hythe* 2D **52**
Jordan Ho. *Sotn* 6G **29**
Josian Wlk.
  Sotn 6D **30** (2G **5**)
Jubilee Clo. *Eastl* 6H **15**
Jubilee Ct. *H End* 6H **33**
Jubilee Gdns.
  Sotn 4B **32**
Jubilee M. *Net A* 1A **46**
Jubilee Rd. *Roms* 4B **6**
Julian Clo. *Chilw* 3A **22**
Julian Ct. *Sotn* 1G **31**
Julian Rd. *Sotn* 2B **42**
Julius Clo. *Chan F* 1G **15**
Jumar Clo. *Wars* 2B **50**
Junction Rd. *Tot* 4G **27**
Juniper Clo. *N Bad* 2D **12**
Juniper Ct. *Sotn* 4G **31**
Juniper Rd. *Sotn* 4H **31**
Jupiter Clo. *Sotn* 6D **20**
Jurds Lake Way. *Sotn* 4F **41**
Jurd Way. *Burs* 4F **43**
Justinian Clo. *Chan F* 6H **9**
Jutland Clo. *White* 6F **45**

K
Kanes Hill. *Sotn* 5E **33**
Kanes Hill Cvn. Site.
  H End 1F **43**
Kathleen Rd. *Sotn* 2A **42**
Katrine Cres. *Chan F* 5C **8**
Kayak Clo. *Wars* 6C **48**
Kayleigh Clo. *Tot* 5D **26**
Keats Clo. *White* 4F **45**
Keats Rd. *Sotn* 5C **32**
Keble Clo. *Chan F* 2E **15**
Keble Rd. *Chan F* 3E **15**
Keepers Clo. *Chan F* 1D **14**
Kelburn Clo. *Chan F* 6D **8**
Kellett Rd. *Sotn* 3A **30**
Kelly Ho. *Sotn* 5G **23**
Kelmscott Gdns.
  Chan F 4C **8**
Kelsey Clo. *Fare* 6F **49**
Kelston Clo. *Sotn* 4E **29**
Kelvin Clo. *Hythe* 3E **53**
Kelvin Gro. *Net A* 1C **46**
Kelvin Rd. *Eastl* 5H **15**
Kemps Quay Ind. Pk.
  Sotn 4F **31**
Kempton Ct. *White* 5G **45**
  (off Timor Clo.)
Kendal Av. *Sotn* 2B **28**
Kendal Clo. *Chan F* 6G **9**
Kendal Ct. *Sotn* 2B **28**
Kenilworth Dri. *Eastl* 1A **16**

Kenilworth Gdns.—Lincoln Clo.

Kenilworth Gdns. *W End* 2E **33**
Kenilworth Ho. Sotn 5E 31
(off Princes Ct.)
Kenilworth Rd. *Sotn* 5B **30**
Kenmore Clo. *Tot* 1E **37**
Kennedy Rd. *Sotn* 6D **20**
Kennet Clo. *W End* 6B **24**
Kennett Clo. *Roms* 4F **7**
Kennett Rd. *Roms* 4F **7**
Kensington Clo. *Eastl* 2D **16**
Kensington Fields. *Dib P* 4B **52**
Kensington Gdns. *Fare* 5G **49**
Kenson Gdns. *Sotn* 1A **42**
Kent Gdns. *Tot* 6D **26**
Kent Ho. *Sotn* 5E **31**
Kentish Rd. *Sotn* 4G **29**
Kent Rd. *Chan F* 4E **15**
Kent Rd. *Sotn* 2E **31**
Kent St. *Sotn* 6E **31**
Kenwyn Clo. *W End* 1B **32**
Kern Clo. *Sotn* 6D **20**
Kerrigan Ct. *Sotn* 3C **30**
Kerry Clo. *Chan F* 1E **15**
Kesteven Way. *Sotn* 3A **32**
Kestrel Clo. *Bot* 2D **34**
Kestrel Clo. *March* 4C **38**
Kestrel Clo. *Sotn* 4F **21**
Kestrel Rd. *Eastl* 5F **15**
Kestrels, The. *Burs* 5F **43**
Keswick Rd. *Sotn* 2F **41**
Kevlyn Cres. *Burs* 4E **43**
Kew La. *Burs* 6G **43**
Keynsham Rd. *Sotn* 5B **32**
Khartoum Rd. *Sotn* 1C **30**
Kielder Clo. *Chan F* 6C **8**
Kilford Ct. *Bot* 5E **35**
Killarney Clo. *Sotn* 2E **43**
Kiln Clo. *Dib P* 3C **52**
Kiln Grn. *Col C* 5G **11**
Kiln La. *Ott & Bram* 3B **10**
(in two parts)
Kilnyard Clo. *Tot* 2D **26**
Kimberley Clo. *F Oak* 2G **17**
Kimberley Ct. *Sotn* 3G **41**
Kimbridge Clo. *Sotn* 4C **20**
Kineton Rd. *Sotn* 2A **30**
King Cup Av. *L Hth* 4D **48**
Kingdom Clo. *Fare* 2H **49**
King Edward Av. *Sotn* 3E **29**
King Edward Pk. Cvn. Pk. *Chan F* 4B **8**
Kingfisher Clo. *Hamb* 3G **47**
Kingfisher Copse. *L Hth* 4F **49**
Kingfisher Rd. *Eastl* 5F **15**
Kingfisher Way. *March* 4C **38**
Kingfisher Way. *Roms* 4C **6**
King George's Av. *Sotn* 5D **28**
Kingland Mkt. *Sotn* 1C **40** (3F **5**)
Kings Av. *Hamb* 4E **47**
Kingsbridge La. *Sotn* 6B **30** (2C **4**)
Kingsbury Rd. *Sotn* 4D **30**
Kingsclere Av. *Sotn* 4H **41**
Kingsclere Clo. *Sotn* 4H **41**
Kings Clo. *Chan F* 6F **9**
Kings Copse Av. *H End* 1B **44**
Kings Copse Rd. *H End* 1B **44**
Kingsdown Way. *Sotn* 1H **31**
Kings Fld. *Burs* 4G **43**
Kings Fld. Gdns. *Burs* 4G **43**
Kingsfold Av. *Sotn* 6H **23**
Kings Ho. *Sotn* 2C **40** (5F **5**)
Kingsland Ct. *Sotn* 1C **40** (3F **5**)
Kingsland Ho. *Sotn* 2E **5**
Kingsland Mkt. *Sotn* 1C **40** (3F **5**)
Kingsland Sq. *Sotn* 1C **40** (3F **5**)
Kingsley Gdns. *Tot* 4B **26**
Kingsley Rd. *Sotn* 4F **29**
Kingsmead Ct. *Sotn* 2F **29**
King's Pk. Rd. *Sotn* 5C **30**
Kings Ride. *Black* 6E **55**
King's Rd. *Chan F* 1E **15**
Kingston. *Net A* 6C **42**
Kingston Rd. *Sotn* 5H **29**
King St. *Sotn* 2C **40** (5F **5**)
Kingsway. *Chan F* 6F **9**
Kingsway. *Sotn* 6C **30** (2F **5**)
Kingsway Ct. *Chan F* 5G **9**
Kingsway Gdns. *Chan F* 5G **9**
Kingswood. *March* 4E **39**
Kinloss Ct. *Sotn* 4E **21**
Kinross Rd. *Tot* 4F **27**
Kinsbourne Clo. *Sotn* 5E **33**
Kinsbourne Ri. *Sotn* 5F **33**
Kinsbourne Way. *Sotn* 5E **33**
Kinver Clo. *Roms* 3E **7**
Kipling Clo. *White* 4F **45**
Kipling Ct. *Sotn* 4H **41**
Kipling Rd. *Eastl* 4H **15**
Kirk Gdns. *Tot* 6F **27**
Kitchener Rd. *Sotn* 6E **23**
Kites Cft. Clo. *Fare* 6G **49**
Kleves Ct. *Sotn* 5B **32**
Knatchbull Clo. *Roms* 5C **6**
Knellers La. *Tot* 1D **36**
Knighton Rd. *Sotn* 1H **41**
Knights Clo. *Wars* 6C **48**
Knightstone Grange. *Hythe* 4E **53**
Knightwood Clo. *Asht* 3B **36**
Knightwood Rd. *Chan F* 5B **8**
Knightwood Rd. *Hythe* 4F **53**
Knightwood Vw. *Chan F* 1E **15**
Knotgrass Rd. *L Hth* 5C **48**
Knowle Hill. *Eastl* 6B **10**
Knyght Clo. *Roms* 6D **6**
Kootenay Av. *Sotn* 4E **33**

L

Laburnum Clo. *N Bad* 2E **13**
Laburnum Ct. *Sotn* 2F **41**
Laburnum Cres. *Hythe* 1A **54**
Laburnum Gro. *Eastl* 4A **16**
Laburnum Ho. *H End* 5B **34**
Laburnum Rd. *H End* 5B **34**
Laburnum Rd. *Sotn* 5E **23**
Lackford Av. *Tot* 5E **27**
Lackford Way. *Tot* 5F **27**
Lacon Clo. *Sotn* 3G **31**
Lady Betty's Dri. *Fare* 1H **49**
Ladycross Rd. *Hythe* 4E **53**
Ladywood. *Eastl* 1H **15**
Lake Ct. *Hurs* 2B **8**
Lake Farm Clo. *H End* 3A **34**
Lake Ho. *Sotn* 5G **29**
Lakeland Gdns. *March* 4C **38**
Lakelands Dri. *Sotn* 5G **29**
Lake Rd. *Chan F* 5G **9**
Lake Rd. *Sotn* 3F **41**
Lakeside Av. *Rown* 4C **20**
Lakewood Clo. *Chan F* 5F **9**
Lakewood Rd. *Asht* 2C **36**
Lakewood Rd. *Chan F* 6F **9**
Lamberhurst Clo. *Sotn* 5A **42**
Lambourne Clo. *Dib P* 5D **52**
Lambourne Dri. *L Hth* 4E **49**
Lambourne Ho. *H End* 5H **33**
Lambourne Rd. *W End* 1B **32**
Lambourn Sq. *Chan F* 1D **14**
Lammas Rd. *Hythe* 4E **53**
Lancaster Clo. *Burs* 4G **43**
Lancaster Ct. *W End* 1C **32**
Lancaster Rd. *Sotn* 6D **20**
Lancelot Clo. *Chan F* 1B **14**
Lance's Hill. *Sotn* 4H **31**
Landguard Rd. *Sotn* 5H **29**
Landseer Rd. *Sotn* 2C **42**
Lands End Rd. *Burs* 6H **43**
Lanehays Rd. *Hythe* 3D **52**
Lane, The. *Fawl* 2H **55**
Langbar Clo. *Sotn* 5G **31**
Langdale Clo. *Sotn* 3D **28**
Langdown Firs. *Hythe* 3E **53**
Langdown Lawn. *Hythe* 4E **53**
Langdown Lawn Clo. *Hythe* 4E **53**
Langdown Rd. *Hythe* 3E **53**
Langham Clo. *N Bad* 3D **12**
Langhorn Rd. *Sotn* 5E **23**
Langley Lodge Gdns. *Black* 6F **55**
Langley Rd. *Sotn* 5E **29**
Langrish Rd. *Sotn* 5F **21**
Lansdowne Clo. *Roms* 4B **6**
Lansdowne Ct. *Roms* 4B **6**
Lansdowne Gdns. *Roms* 4B **6**
Lansdowne Hill. *Sotn* 2B **40** (5D **4**)
Lansdowne Rd. *Sotn* 4E **29**
Lapwing Dri. *Tot* 3C **26**
Larch Av. *Holb* 3C **54**
Larch Clo. *W End* 6D **24**
Larchdale Clo. *Wars* 1B **50**
Larch Rd. *Sotn* 6E **21**
Larch Way. *Burs* 5F **43**
Larchwood Ct. *Sotn* 6H **29**
Larchwood Rd. *Tot* 5C **26**
Lark Rd. *Eastl* 6F **15**
Larkspur Chase. *Sotn* 6E **33**
Larkspur Clo. *L Hth* 5C **48**
Larkspur Dri. *Chan F* 1B **14**
Larkspur Dri. *March* 5C **38**
Larkspur Gdns. *H End* 5A **34**
Larkspur Gdns. *Holb* 4B **54**
Laser Clo. *Wars* 6C **48**
Latchmore Dri. *Dib* 2A **52**
Latelie Clo. *Net A* 2C **46**
Latham Clo. *F Oak* 5H **17**
Latham Ct. *Sotn* 4F **29**
Latham Rd. *F Oak* 5H **17**
Latham Rd. *Roms* 4C **6**
Latimer Ga. *Sotn* 6F **5**
Latimer St. *Roms* 5B **6**
Latimer St. *Sotn* 2C **40** (6F **5**)
Launcelyn Clo. *N Bad* 4D **12**
Launceston Dri. *Eastl* 2H **15**
Laundry Rd. *Sotn* 6E **21**
Laurel Clo. *Hythe* 3D **52**
Laurel Clo. *L Hth* 3F **49**
Laurel Clo. *Sotn* 2F **41**
Laurel Gdns. *L Hth* 3F **49**
Laurel Rd. *L Hth* 3F **49**
Laurence Ct. *F Oak* 2F **17**
Laurie Wlk. *Black* 4F **55**
Lauriston Dri. *Chan F* 4D **8**
Lavender Clo. *Sotn* 6H **31**
Laverstoke Clo. *Rown* 4C **20**
Lavington Gdns. *N Bad* 4D **12**
Lawford Way. *Tot* 4E **27**
Lawn Dri. *L Hth* 5E **49**
Lawn Rd. *Eastl* 3B **16**
Lawn Rd. *Sotn* 3D **30**
Lawnside Rd. *Sotn* 3E **29**
Lawnswood. *F Oak* 3G **17**
Lawrence Ct. *Sotn* 3H **41**
Lawrence Gro. *Sotn* 3H **41**
Lawrence Ho. *Hythe* 2F **53**
Lawson Clo. *Swanw* 5B **44**
Laxton Clo. *L Hth* 4F **49**
Laxton Clo. *Sotn* 3A **42**
Leabrook. *Sar G* 2E **49**
Leafy La. *White* 1H **49**
Leander Clo. *Eastl* 2A **16**
Lea Rd. *Black* 6E **55**
Leaside Way. *Sotn* 4E **23**
Leatherhead Gdns. *H End* 1B **34**
Lebanon Rd. *Sotn* 4B **28**
Leckford Clo. *Sotn* 3D **32**
Lee Chu. La. *Lee* 1F **19**
Lee Drove. *Roms* 6A **12**
Legion Clo. *Sotn* 5E **23**
Leicester Rd. *Sotn* 1H **29**
Leigh Ct. *F Oak* 4G **15**
Leigh Rd. *Chan F & Eastl* 3E **15**
Leigh Rd. *Sotn* 2C **30**
Leighton Av. *Sotn* 3F **29**
Leighton Rd. *Sotn* 2G **41**
Lemon Rd. *Sotn* 4F **29**
Lennox Clo. *Chan F* 5G **9**
Lennox Clo. *Sotn* 4D **20**
Leonards Ct. *Sotn* 3A **28**
Lepe Rd. *Black* 6E **55**
Leslie Loader Ct. *Eastl* 2A **16**
Leslie Loader M. *Sotn* 6G **31**
Leven Clo. *Chan F* 5C **8**
Lewes Clo. *Eastl* 1A **16**
Lewin Clo. *Col C* 5F **11**
Lewins Wlk. *Burs* 4F **43**
Lewis Clo. *Dib P* 4A **52**
Lewis Ho. *Sotn* 6C **30** (2F **5**)
Lewis Silkin Way. *Sotn* 5E **21**
Lewry Clo. *H End* 4A **34**
Lexby Rd. *Tot* 5G **27**
Leybourne Av. *Sotn* 3H **31**
Leyton Rd. *Sotn* 5E **31**
Liberty Row. Hamb 5G 47
(off Farm Clo.)
Library Rd. *Fern* 3F **5**
Library Rd. *Tot* 4G **27**
Lichen Way. *March* 3D **38**
Lichfield Rd. *Fare* 4G **49**
Liddel Way. *Chan F* 2D **14**
Lightning Clo. *Fawl* 3F **55**
Lilac Rd. *Sotn* 5D **22**
Lilley Clo. *March* 3D **38**
Lime Av. *Sotn* 6A **32**
Lime Clo. *Col C* 5G **11**
Lime Clo. *Dib P* 4C **52**
Lime Clo. *Sotn* 6A **32**
Lime Gdns. *W End* 6D **24**
Limekiln La. *Holb* 3B **54**
(in two parts)
Lime Kiln La. Est. *Holb* 3B **54**
Limes, The. *March* 4E **39**
Lime St. *Sotn* 2C **40** (5F **5**)
Lime Wlk. *Bot* 4D **34**
Lime Wlk. *Dib P* 4C **52**
Linacre Rd. *Sotn* 6D **32**
Lincoln Clo. *Fare* 4G **49**
Lincoln Clo. *Roms* 3E **7**

Lincoln Ct. *Sotn* 1A **30**
Lincoln Ct. *W End* 1C **32**
Lincolns Ri. *Eastl* 4B **10**
Linda Rd. *Fawl* 2H **55**
Linden Ct. *Park G* 3F **49**
Linden Ct. *Roms* 5B **6**
Linden Ct. *Sotn* 6B **24**
Linden Gdns. *H End* 6B **34**
Linden Gro. *Chan F* 5E **9**
Linden Rd. *Roms* 5C **6**
Linden Rd. *Sotn* 5E **21**
Linden Wlk. *N Bad* 2D **12**
Lindsay Rd. *Sotn* 5E **33**
Lindway. *Park G* 1E **49**
Liners Ind. Est. *Sotn* 5G **29**
Linford Ct. *F Oak* 2F **17**
Linford Cres. *Sotn* 6H **21**
Ling Dale. *Sotn* 2B **22**
Lingdale Pl. *Sotn* 3C **30**
Lingfield Gdns. *Sotn* 1H **31**
Lingwood Clo. *Sotn* 2B **22**
Lingwood Wlk. *Sotn* 2B **22**
Link Rd. *Sotn* 6D **20**
Links Vw. Way. *Sotn* 3B **22**
Linnet Sq. *Eastl* 6F **15**
Linnets, The. *Tot* 3C **26**
Linwood Clo. *Hythe* 4E **53**
Lionheart Way. *Burs* 4F **43**
Lipizzaner Fields.
  White 5F **45**
Lisbon Rd. *Sotn* 5H **29**
Litchfield Cres. *Sotn* 2H **31**
Litchfield Rd. *Sotn* 2H **31**
Lit Holbury Pk. Homes.
  Holb 3B **54**
Lit. Abshot Rd. *Fare* 1F **51**
Littlefield Cres. *Chan F* . . .1A **14**
Lit. Kimble Wlk. *H End* . . .5A **34**
Lit. Lance's Hill. *Sotn* 4H **31**
Lit. Meads. *Roms* 5A **6**
Lit. Oak Rd. *Sotn* 5B **22**
Lit. Park Clo. *H End* 5H **33**
Lit. Park Farm Rd.
  Fare 2G **49**
Lit. Quob La. *W End* 1E **33**
Lit. Reynolds. *Tot* 6D **26**
Littlewood Gdns.
  L Hth 4C **48**
Littlewood Gdns.
  W End 2D **32**
Liverpool St. *Sotn* 4C **30**
Livingstone Rd. *Sotn* 3C **30**
Lloyd Av. *March* 4C **38**
Loane Rd. *Sotn* 2H **41**
Lobelia Rd. *Sotn* 5E **23**
Lockerley Cres. *Sotn* 2D **28**
Locke Rd. *H End* 3A **34**
Locks Heath Cen.
  L Hth 4E **49**
Locks Heath Pk. Rd.
  L Hth 6F **49**
Locksley Ct. *Sotn* 4B **30**
Locksley Rd. *Eastl* 6G **15**
Locks Rd. *L Hth* 5E **49**
Lockswood Keep.
  L Hth 3E **49**
Lockswood Rd. *L Hth* 4D **48**
Lodge Dri. *Dib P* 5D **52**
Lodge Rd. *L Hth* 4F **49**
Lodge Rd. *Sotn* 4C **30**
Lodge, The. *Sotn* 4B **30**
Lofting Clo. *Eastl* 5E **17**
Logan Clo. *Sotn* 4D **20**
Lomax Clo. *H End* 2A **34**
London Rd. *Sotn* 5B **30**
Longacres. *Fare* 3G **49**
Long Beech Dri. *Tot* 5D **26**
Longbridge Clo. *Cal* 1D **26**

Longbridge Ct. *Cal* 1D **26**
Longbridge Ind. Pk.
  Sotn 2E **41**
Longclose Rd. *H End* 4B **34**
Long Copse. *Holb* 5D **54**
Long Dri. *W End* 1E **33**
Longfield Rd. *F Oak* 3G **17**
Long La. *Burs* 5G **43**
Long La. *Holb* 2B **54**
Long La. *March* 4B **38**
Long La. Clo. *Holb* 5D **54**
Longleat Gdns. *Sotn* 5F **21**
Longmead Av. *Eastl* 3D **16**
Longmeadow Gdns.
  Hythe 2E **53**
Longmead Rd. *Sotn* 1A **32**
Longmore Av. *Sotn* 3F **41**
Longmore Cres. *Sotn* 3F **41**
Longridge Rd. *H End* 5A **34**
Longstock Clo. *Sotn* 5A **42**
Longstock Cres. *Tot* 4D **26**
Loperwood La. *Cal* 1A **26**
                (in two parts)
Lord Mountbatten Clo.
  Sotn 5G **23**
Lords Hill Cen. E.
  Sotn 5D **20**
Lords Hill Cen. W.
  Sotn 5D **20**
Lord's Hill District Cen.
  Sotn 5D **20**
Lords Hill Way. *Sotn* 5C **20**
Lordswood. *Highb* 6E **11**
Lordswood Clo. *Sotn* 5H **21**
Lordswood Ct. *Sotn* 5G **21**
Lordswood Gdns.
  Sotn 5H **21**
Lordswood La. *Chilw* 1H **21**
Lordswood Rd. *Sotn* 5G **21**
Loreille Gdns. *Rown* 2C **20**
Lorne Pl. *Sotn* 4A **32**
Lortemore Pl. *Roms* 5B **6**
Loughwood Clo. *Eastl* 1A **16**
Lovage Gdns. *Tot* 4C **26**
Lovage Rd. *White* 6H **45**
Love La. *Roms* 5B **6**
Lwr. Alfred St. *Sotn* 5D **30**
Lwr. Banister St. *Sotn* 5B **30**
Lwr. Brownhill Rd.
  Sotn 1A **28**
Lwr. Canal Wlk.
  Sotn 3C **40** (6E **5**)
Lwr. Church Rd. *Fare* 4G **49**
Lwr. Duncan Rd.
  Park G 2F **49**
Lwr. Moors Rd. *Col C* . . .4F **11**
Lwr. Mortimer Rd.
  Sotn 2F **41**
Lwr. Mullins La. *Hythe* . . .3C **52**
Lwr. New Rd. *W End* 2D **32**
Lwr. Northam Rd.
  H End 5A **34**
Lwr. St Helens Rd.
  H End 6A **34**
Lwr. Spinney. *Wars* 2A **50**
Lwr. Swanwick Rd.
  Swanw 5B **44**
Lwr. Vicarage Rd. *Sotn* . . .2F **41**
Lwr. William St. *Sotn* 5F **31**
Lwr. York St. *Sotn* 5F **31**
Lowford Hill. *Burs* 4F **43**
Lowry Gdns. *Sotn* 3C **42**
Lucas Clo. *Rown* 4D **20**
Luccombe Pl. *Sotn* 1H **29**
Luccombe Rd. *Sotn* 1H **29**
Lucerne Gdns. *H End* 4G **33**
Ludlow Rd. *Sotn* 1G **41**
Lukes Clo. *Hamb* 5G **47**

Lukin Dri. *Nurs* 3A **20**
Lulworth Bus. Cen. *Tot* . . .1E **27**
Lulworth Clo. *Chan F* 4D **14**
Lulworth Clo. *Sotn* 1C **28**
Lulworth Grn. *Sotn* 1C **28**
Lumsden Av. *Sotn* 4G **29**
Lumsden Mans. *Sotn* 4G **29**
Lundy Clo. *Sotn* 4C **20**
Lunedale Rd. *Dib P* 6C **52**
Lupin Rd. *Sotn* 4E **23**
Luton Rd. *Sotn* 1B **42**
Luxton Clo. *Bot* 3D **34**
Lyburn Clo. *Sotn* 5G **21**
Lyburn Ct. *Sotn* 5G **21**
Lydgate. *Tot* 4D **26**
Lydgate Clo. *Sotn* 1D **42**
Lydgate Grn. *Sotn* 1D **42**
Lydgate Rd. *Sotn* 1D **42**
Lydiard Clo. *Eastl* 2A **16**
Lydlynch Rd. *Tot* 4E **27**
Lydney Rd. *L Hth* 4D **48**
Lyme Clo. *Eastl* 2H **15**
Lymer La. *Sotn* 3A **20**
Lymer Vs. *Nurs* 3A **20**
Lyndale Rd. *Park G* 3F **49**
Lynden Ga. *Sotn* 2A **42**
Lyndhurst Rd. *Asht* 5A **36**
Lyndock Clo. *Sotn* 3G **41**
Lyndock Pl. *Sotn* 3G **41**
Lynn Clo. *W End* 6B **24**
Lynton Ct. *Tot* 5E **27**
Lynton Rd. *H End* 4A **34**
Lynx Clo. *Eastl* 5F **17**
Lyon St. *Sotn* 5C **30**
Lytham Rd. *Sotn* 2A **32**
Lytton Rd. *Hythe* 4F **53**

M

MacArthur Cres. *Sotn* 3A **32**
Macnaghten Rd. *Sotn* 4F **31**
Maddison St.
  Sotn 1B **40** (4D **4**)
Maddoxford La. *Bot* 1D **34**
Maddoxford Way. *Bot* 2D **34**
Madeira Rd. *Ports* 3F **5**
Maffey Ct. *Bot* 4E **35**
Magazine La. *March* 3D **38**
Magdalene Way. *Fare* 5G **49**
Magnolia Clo. *Dib* 2A **52**
Magnolia Gro. *F Oak* 2H **17**
Magnolia Rd. *Sotn* 6H **31**
Magpie Dri. *Tot* 4C **26**
Magpie Gdns. *Sotn* 1C **42**
Magpie La. *Eastl* 5G **15**
Main Rd.
  Col C & Fish P 4G **11**
Main Rd. *Dib* 1A **52**
                (Bramshott Hill)
Main Rd. *Dib* 2C **54**
                (Long La.)
Main Rd. *March* 4D **38**
Main Rd. *Ott & Comp* . . .3B **10**
Main Rd. *Tot* 1E **37**
Mainstone. *Roms* 6A **6**
Mainstream Ct. *Eastl* 4D **16**
Majestic Rd. *Nurs* 6H **19**
Malcolm Clo. *Chan F* 4G **9**
Malcolm Clo. *L Hth* 4F **49**
Malcolm Rd. *Chan F* 4G **9**
Malcroft M. *March* 4E **39**
Maldon Clo. *Eastl* 4D **16**
Maldon Rd. *Sotn* 6G **31**
Malibres Rd. *Chan F* 5H **9**
Malin Clo. *Sotn* 5C **20**
Mallard Clo. *Roms* 4C **6**
Mallard Gdns. *H End* 1A **34**
Mallards Rd. *Burs* 6F **43**

Mallett Clo. *H End* 1C **34**
Mallow Clo. *L Hth* 5D **48**
Mallow Rd. *H End* 5G **33**
Mall, The. *Chan F* 6G **9**
Malmesbury Clo.
  F Oak 2F **17**
Malmesbury Ct. *Net A* 2B **46**
Malmesbury Pl. *Sotn* 4H **29**
Malmesbury Rd. *Roms* 4B **6**
Malmesbury Rd. *Sotn* 4H **29**
Malory Clo. *Sotn* 5D **32**
Malthouse Clo. *Roms* 4B **6**
Malthouse Gdns.
  March 4D **38**
Malvern Dri. *Dib P* 3B **52**
Malvern Gdns. *H End* 1B **34**
Malvern Rd. *Sotn* 1G **29**
Malwood Av. *Sotn* 6H **21**
Malwood Gdns. *Tot* 3C **26**
Malwood Rd. *Hythe* 2D **52**
Malwood Rd. W.
  Hythe 2D **52**
Manaton Way. *H End* 2H **33**
Manchester Rd. *Net A* 2A **46**
Mandela Way.
  Sotn 6A **30** (1A **4**)
Manley Rd. *Burs* 4F **43**
Manns Clo. *W End* 1C **32**
Manor Clo. *Burs* 4F **43**
Manor Clo. *Tot* 5E **27**
Manor Ct. *Fare* 3H **49**
Manor Cres. *Burs* 4F **43**
Mnr. Farm Clo. *Eastl* 5E **17**
Mnr. Farm Grn. *Twy* 1F **11**
Mnr. Farm Gro. *Eastl* 5E **17**
Mnr. Farm Rd. *Sotn* 2F **31**
Manor Ho. Av. *Sotn* 5C **28**
Manor Rd. *Chilw* 1H **21**
Manor Rd. *Eastl* 5E **17**
Manor Rd. *Holb* 4C **54**
Manor Rd. N. *Sotn* 1G **41**
Manor Rd. S. *Sotn* 2G **41**
Manor Ter. *Burs* 4E **43**
Mansbridge Cotts.
  Sotn 5H **23**
Mansbridge Rd. *Eastl* 6A **16**
Mansbridge Rd.
  Sotn & W End 5G **23**
Mansel Ct. *Sotn* 1C **28**
Mansell Clo. *Dib P* 5C **52**
Mansel Rd. E. *Sotn* 2C **28**
Mansel Rd. W. *Sotn* 1B **28**
Mansergh Wlk. *Tot* 3B **26**
Mansion Rd. *Sotn* 5G **29**
Manston Ct. *Sotn* 5D **20**
Maple Clo. *Burs* 5F **43**
Maple Clo. *Roms* 6F **7**
Maple Gdns. *Tot* 5C **26**
Maple Leaf Gdns.
  Eastl 5A **16**
Maple Rd. *Hythe* 6F **53**
Maple Rd. *Sotn* 4G **31**
Maple Sq. *Eastl* 6G **15**
Maples, The. *Chan F* 5E **9**
Mapleton Rd. *H End* 5A **34**
Maplewood Clo.
  Tot 5C **26**
Maplin Rd. *Sotn* 1B **28**
Marathon Pl. *Eastl* 4H **17**
Marchwood By-Pass.
  March 5F **27**
Marchwood Ind. Est.
  March 2E **39**
Marchwood Rd. *Sotn* 5F **29**
Marchwood Rd. *Tot* 1H **37**
Marchwood Ter.
  March 3D **38**
                (off Main Rd.)

Marcus Clo. *Eastl* 5H **17**
Mardale Rd. *Sotn* 3B **28**
Mardale Wlk. *Sotn* 3B **28**
Mardon Clo. *Sotn* 4G **23**
Margam Av. *Sotn* 6H **31**
Marianne Clo. *Sotn* 5D **28**
Marie Rd. *Sotn* 2C **42**
Marina Clo. *Hamb* 5G **47**
Marine Pde.
  Sotn 1D **40** (4H **5**)
Mariners Clo. *Hamb* 3G **47**
Mariners M. *Hythe* 2E **53**
Mariners Way. *Wars* 6A **48**
Maritime Av. *March* 2E **39**
Maritime Wlk. *Sotn* 3D **40**
Maritime Way. *E Dock* ..3C **40**
    (in two parts)
Marjoram Way. *White* ...6H **45**
Mark Clo. *Sotn* 4F **29**
Marken Clo. *L Hth* 4D **48**
Market Bldgs. *Sotn* 5F **23**
Market Pl. *Roms* 5B **6**
Market Pl. *Sotn* ...2C **40** (5E **5**)
Market St. *Eastl* 6B **16**
    (in two parts)
Marland Ho.
  Sotn 6B **30** (2D **4**)
Marlands Shop. Cen.
  Sotn 1B **40** (2D **4**)
Marlborough Ct.
  Chan F 3C **14**
Marlborough Ct. *Dib P* ...4C **52**
Marlborough Gdns.
  H End 6H **25**
Marlborough Ho. *Sotn* ...3B **30**
Marlborough Rd.
  Chan F 4G **9**
Marlborough Rd. *Sotn* ...3F **29**
Marlhill Clo. *Sotn* 1H **31**
Marlowe Ct. *Sotn* 4H **41**
Marls Rd. *Bot* 4C **34**
Marne Rd. *Sotn* 4A **32**
Marshfield Clo. *March* ...4B **38**
Marsh Gdns. *H End* 1A **34**
Marsh Ho. *Sotn* ...2C **40** (5F **5**)
Marsh La. *Fawl* 1H **55**
Marsh La. *Sotn* ...1C **40** (5G **5**)
Marsh Pde. Hythe 2E **53**
    (off Marsh, The)
Marsh, The. *Hythe* 1E **53**
Marston Rd. *Sotn* 6D **32**
Martindale Ter. Sotn 3C **28**
    (off Kendal Av.)
Martins, The. *F Oak* 3G **17**
Martley Gdns. *H End* 1A **34**
Marvin Clo. *Bot* 4C **34**
Marvin Rd. *Bot* 4C **34**
Marvin Way. *Sotn* 5C **32**
Marybridge Clo. *Tot* 5E **27**
Maryfield. *Sotn* ...1D **40** (4G **5**)
Maryland Clo. *Sotn* 6H **23**
Masefield Clo. *Eastl* 4H **15**
Masefield Grn. *Sotn* 5D **32**
Matheson Rd. *Sotn* 3D **20**
Matley Gdns. *Tot* 4B **26**
Maunsell Way. *H End* ...2B **34**
Mauretania Ho. *Sotn* 5E **31**
Mauretania Rd. *Nurs* 5H **19**
Maxwell Rd. *Sotn* 2A **42**
Maybray King Way.
  Sotn 4H **31**
Maybush Ct. *Sotn* 2E **29**
Maybush Rd. *Sotn* 1C **28**
May Clo. *Holb* 5D **54**
May Copse. *Holb* 5D **54**
May Cres. *Holb* 5D **54**
Maycroft Ct. *Sotn* 3B **30**
Mayfair Ct. *Bot* 4E **35**

Mayfair Gdns. *Sotn* 4B **30**
Mayfield Av. *Tot* 3E **27**
Mayfield Rd. *Sotn* 6D **22**
Mayflower Clo. *Chan F* ...2D **14**
Mayflower Rd. *Sotn* 3F **29**
Mayflowers, The. *Sotn* ...5C **22**
Maynard Rd. *Tot* 4F **27**
Maypole Vs. *Eastl* 5B **10**
Mayridge. *Fare* 4G **49**
May Rd. *Sotn* 4G **29**
Maytree Clo. *F Oak* 2G **17**
Maytree Clo. *L Hth* 4E **49**
Maytree Rd. *Chan F* 3E **9**
Maytree Rd. *Sotn* 5A **32**
Mayvale Clo. *March* 4D **38**
Meacher Clo. *Tot* 3E **27**
Meadbrook Gdns.
  Chan F............1E **15**
Mead Clo. *Roms* 5E **7**
Mead Ct. *Chan F* 1E **15**
Mead Cres. *Sotn* 6F **23**
Meadcroft Clo. *Wars* 1B **50**
Meadow Av. *L Hth* 3E **49**
Meadow Clo. *N Bad* 4E **13**
Meadow Clo. *Tot* 6F **27**
Meadow Clo. *W End* 1E **33**
Meadowcroft Clo. *Ott* ...2C **10**
Meadow Gro. *Chan F* 3E **15**
Meadowhead Rd.
  Sotn 6B **22**
Meadow La. *Hamb* 5G **47**
Meadowmead Av.
  Sotn 4E **29**
Meadowside Clo. *Sotn* ...5G **23**
Meadows, The. *Sar G* ...2E **49**
Meadow, The. *Roms* 3C **6**
Meadow Way. *Fawl* 2G **55**
Mead Rd. *Chan F* 1E **15**
Meads, The. *Chan F* 2C **14**
Meads, The. *Roms* 5A **6**
Mead, The. *Hythe* 3C **52**
Mears Rd. *F Oak* 2G **17**
Medina Chambers.
  Sotn 3B **40**
Medina Clo. *Chan F* 2G **15**
Medina Rd. *Sotn* 2F **29**
Medlar Clo. *H End* 5B **34**
Medley Pl. *Sotn* 4E **29**
Medwall Grn. *Sotn* 6D **32**
Medway Dri. *Chan F* 5C **8**
Megan Rd. *W End* 1D **32**
Meggeson Av. *Sotn* 1H **31**
Melbourne Gdns.
  H End 5A **34**
Melbourne Rd. *H End* ...5A **34**
Melbourne St.
  Sotn 1D **40** (4H **5**)
Melbury Ct. *Sotn* 2B **30**
Melchet Rd. *Sotn* 3C **32**
Melick Clo. *March* 3D **38**
Melrose Ct. *Cal* 2C **26**
    (in two parts)
Melrose Rd. *Sotn* 1H **29**
Melville Clo. *Sotn* 4G **21**
Mendip Gdns. *Dib P* 4B **52**
Mendip Rd. *Sotn* 3D **28**
Menzies Clo. *Sotn* 4D **20**
Meon Clo. *Roms* 5F **7**
Meon Ct. *Sotn* 3D **32**
Meon Cres. *Chan F* 2F **15**
Meon Rd. *Fare* 5H **51**
Meon Rd. *Roms* 5F **7**
Mercer Way. *Roms* 4D **6**
Merchants Wlk. *Sotn* ...6D **4**
Mercury Clo. *Sotn* 5D **20**
Mercury Gdns. *Hamb* ...3G **47**
Merdon Av. *Chan F* 5E **9**
Merdon Clo. *Chan F* 5F **9**

Mere Cft. *Fare* 4H **49**
Meredith Gdns. *Tot* 5D **26**
Meredith Towers.
  Sotn 1E **43**
Meridan Point. Sotn 5C **30**
    (off St Mary's Rd.)
Meridians Cross. *Sotn* ...3D **40**
Merlin Ct. *Sotn* 2F **41**
Merlin Gdns. *H End* 4H **33**
Merlin Quay. *Sotn* 1E **41**
Merlin Way. *Chan F* 6B **8**
Mermaid Way. *Sotn* 3D **40**
Merrick Way. *Chan F* 5C **8**
Merridale Rd. *Sotn* 1G **41**
Merrieleas Clo. *Chan F* ..6E **9**
Merrieleas Dri. *Chan F* ..6E **9**
Merriemeade Clo.
  Dib P 5C **52**
Merriemeade Pde.
  Dib P 5C **52**
Merritt Ct. *Chan F* 4F **15**
Merrivale Clo. *Hythe* 3C **52**
Merryfield. *Fare* 3G **49**
Merry Gdns. *N Bad* 2E **13**
Merryoak Grn. *Sotn* 6H **31**
Merryoak Rd. *Sotn* 1H **41**
Mersea Gdns. *Sotn* 1A **42**
Mersham Gdns. *Sotn* ...4A **32**
Merton Rd. *Sotn* 6D **22**
Methuen St. *Sotn* 4C **30**
Metuchen Way. *H End* ...1A **44**
Mews Ct. *Ott* 2B **10**
Mews, The. *Black* 6F **55**
Mews, The. *Chan F* 4E **15**
Mews, The. *Rown* 3D **20**
Meynell Clo. *Eastl* 4H **15**
Michaels Way. *F Oak* 2G **17**
Michael's Way. *Hythe* ...2D **52**
Michelmersh Clo.
  Rown 4C **20**
Michigan Way. *Tot* 3B **26**
Midanbury B'way.
  Sotn 2H **31**
Midanbury Ct. *Sotn* 3G **31**
Midanbury Cres. *Sotn* ..2H **31**
Midanbury La. *Sotn* 4G **31**
Midanbury Wlk. *Sotn* ...3H **31**
Middlebridge St.
  Roms 6B **6**
Middle Rd. *N Bad* 2E **13**
Middle Rd. *Park G* 2F **49**
Middle Rd. *Sotn* 2A **42**
Middle St. *Sotn* 4C **30**
Middleton Clo. *Sotn* 1A **32**
Midlands Est. *W End* ...1C **32**
Midway. *Hythe* 3D **52**
Milbury Cres. *Sotn* 5A **32**
Milford Gdns. *Chan F* ...1G **15**
Milkwood Ct. *Tot* 4C **26**
Millais Rd. *Sotn* 2G **41**
Millbank Ho. *Sotn* 5E **31**
Millbank St. *Sotn* 6E **31**
Millbank Wharf. *Sotn* ...6E **31**
Millbridge Gdns. *Sotn* ..1B **42**
Millbrook Clo. *Chan F* ...2D **14**
Millbrook Flyover.
  Sotn 4C **28**
Millbrook Point Rd.
  Sotn 6D **28**
Millbrook Rd. *Sotn* 4C **28**
Millbrook Rd. E.
  Sotn 5G **29** (1A **4**)
Millbrook Rd. W. *Sotn* ..5F **29**
Millbrook Towers.
  Sotn 1C **28**
Millbrook Trad. Est.
  Sotn 4C **28**
    (Manor Ho. Av.)

Millbrook Trad. Est.
  Sotn 5D **28**
    (Tanner's Brook Way)
Mill Clo. *Nurs* 4B **20**
Millcourt. *F Oak* 2G **17**
Millers Way. *Dib P* 4D **52**
Mill Est. Yd. *Sotn* 4A **20**
Mill Hill. *Bot* 5E **35**
Mill Ho Cen. *Tot* 4G **27**
Mill Ho. Bus. Cen.
  Sotn 1E **41**
Milliken Clo. *Fawl* 3F **55**
Mill La. *Nurs* 5E **19**
Mill La. *Roms* 5A **6**
Mill Pond, The. *Holb* 2B **54**
Mill Rd. *Sotn* 4D **28**
Mill Rd. *Tot* 4G **27**
Millstream Ri. *Roms* 5A **6**
Mill St. *Eastl* 3B **16**
Mill Way. *Tot* 6E **27**
Milne Clo. *Dib P* 4A **52**
Milner Ct. *Sotn* 3G **29**
Milton Gro. *L Hth* 5F **49**
Milton Rd. *Eastl* 2B **16**
Milton Rd. *Sotn* 5A **30**
Milverton Clo. *Tot* 6G **27**
Milverton Ct. *Sotn* 4B **32**
Milverton Rd. *Tot* 5G **27**
Mimosa Dri. *F Oak* 2H **17**
Minden Ho. Roms 5D **6**
    (off Chambers Av.)
Minstead Av. *Sotn* 3G **31**
Minster Ct. *Sotn* 5G **29**
Mintern Clo. *Eastl* 2D **16**
Mirror Clo. *Wars* 6D **48**
Misselbrook La.
  N Bad 3H **13**
Missenden Acres.
  H End 3A **34**
Mistletoe Gdns. *Sar G* ..2C **48**
Mitchell Clo. *Fare* 2H **49**
Mitchell Dri. *F Oak* 1F **17**
Mitchell Point. *Hamb* ...5E **47**
Mitchell Rd. *Eastl* 5B **16**
Mitchells Clo. *Roms* 5C **6**
Mitchell Way. *Sotn* 3H **23**
Mitre Copse. *Eastl* 5F **17**
Moat Clo. *Holb* 5B **54**
Moat Hill. *Sotn* 6H **23**
Moir Ho. *Dib P* 5C **52**
Monarch Clo. *L Hth* 5E **49**
Monarch Way. *W End* ...1F **33**
Monastery Rd. *Sotn* 4G **31**
Mon Cres. *Sotn* 4C **32**
Monks Brook Clo.
  Eastl 6G **23**
Monks Path. *Sotn* 6G **23**
Monks Pl. *Tot* 5D **26**
Monks Rd. *Net A* 1B **46**
Monks Wlk. *Dib P* 6C **52**
Monks Way. *Eastl* 6G **15**
Monks Way. *Sotn* 5G **23**
Monks Wood Clo.
  Sotn 3D **22**
Monkton La. *Tot* 5C **26**
Monmouth Clo.
  Chan F 1D **14**
Monmouth Gdns. *Tot* ...6D **26**
Monnow Gdns. *W End* ..2B **32**
Montague Av. *Sotn* 2D **42**
Montague Clo. *Sotn* 2D **42**
Montague Clo. *Dib P* ...6C **52**
Montague Rd. *Eastl* 4D **16**
Monterey Dri. *L Hth* 5E **49**
Montfort Clo. *Roms* 5F **7**
Montfort Heights. *Roms* .5F **7**
Montfort Rd. *Roms* 6F **7**
Montgomery Av. *Tot* ...3D **26**

Montgomery Rd. *Sotn* 4A **32**
Montgomery Way.
　Chan F 4D **14**
Montpelier Clo.
　Park G 4G **49**
Montrose Clo. *Bot* 5C **34**
Monument Ct. *Sotn* 3C **40**
　(off Winkle St.)
Moonscross Av. *Tot* 1F **37**
Moore Cres. *Net A* 1C **46**
Moorgreen Pk. Cvn. Site.
　W End 1F **33**
Moorgreen Rd. *W End* 2E **33**
Moorhead Ct. *Ocn V* 3E **41**
Moorhill Gdns. *Sotn* 4E **33**
Moorhill Rd. *W End* 3D **32**
Moorland Clo. *Dib P* 3B **52**
Moorland Clo. *L Hth* 3E **49**
Moorlands Cres. *Sotn* 3B **32**
Moors Clo. *Col C* 4F **11**
　(in two parts)
Mopley. *Black* 6F **55**
Mopley Clo. *Black* 6F **55**
Mordaunt Rd. *Sotn* 4C **30**
Morgan Le Fay Dri.
　N Bad 6B **8**
Morgan Rd. *H End* 6A **34**
Morland Rd. *Sotn* 2G **29**
Morley Clo. *Sotn* 5H **31**
Morpeth Av. *Tot* 3F **27**
Morris Clo. *Dib* 2B **52**
Morris Rd.
　Sotn 6A **30** (1B **4**)
Morse Ct. *Net A* 1A **46**
Mortimer Clo. *Net A* 1B **46**
Mortimer Clo. *Tot* 2D **26**
Mortimer Rd. *Bot* 5E **35**
Mortimer Rd. *Sotn* 1G **41**
Mortimers Dri. *F Oak* 2G **17**
Mortimers La. *F Oak* 2F **17**
Mortimer Way. *N Bad* 4D **12**
Mosaic Clo. *Sotn* 1F **43**
Mosedale Wlk. *Sotn* 3C **28**
Moselle Ct. *Sotn* 6G **29**
Moss Dri. *March* 3D **38**
Mossleigh Av. *Rown* 4D **20**
Mottisfont Clo. *Sotn* 5E **29**
Mottisfont Rd. *Eastl* 3A **16**
Mountain Ash Clo.
　Sotn 4C **32**
Mountbatten Av. *Roms* . . .5C **6**
Mountbatten Bus. Cen.
　Sotn 6H **29**
Mountbatten Ho. *Sotn* 5B **30**
　(off Grosvenor Sq.)
Mountbatten Retail Pk.
　Sotn 1A **40** (2B **4**)
Mountbatten Rd. *Eastl* 2A **16**
Mountbatten Rd. *Tot* 4D **26**
Mountbatten Way.
　Sotn 6G **29** (2A **4**)
Mount Dri. *Chan F* 3G **15**
Mountfield. *Hythe* 2C **52**
Mounthouse Clo.
　Hythe 1E **53**
Mt. Pleasant. *Roms* 6B **6**
Mt. Pleasant Ind. Est.
　Sotn 4D **30**
Mt. Pleasant Rd. *Sotn* 4D **30**
Mt. Temple. *Roms* 5D **6**
Mount, The. *Sotn* 2E **29**
　(Romsey Rd.)
Mount, The. *Sotn* 5B **22**
　(Winchester Rd.)
Mount Vw. *Eastl* 3B **16**
Mousehole La. *Hythe* 3E **53**
Mousehole La. *Sotn* 3H **31**
Mowbray Rd. *Sotn* 1B **42**

Mulberry Corner.
　Chan F 3C **14**
Mulberry La. *Sar G* 2C **48**
Mulberry Rd. *March* 4D **38**
Mulberry Wlk. *Sotn* 3G **29**
Mullen Clo. *Sotn* 1G **41**
Munro Cres. *Sotn* 4D **28**
Muria Est. *Sotn* 6E **31**
Murray Clo. *Sotn* 5E **33**
Mussett Clo. *Tot* 4E **27**
Mustang Av. *White* 6F **45**
Myrtle Av. *Tot* 5D **26**
Myrtle Rd. *Sotn* 5F **21**
Myvern Clo. *Holb* 5D **54**

N

Napier Rd. *Sotn* 6E **33**
Narrow La. *Roms* 5B **6**
Nash Clo. *Dib P* 5B **52**
Nash Rd. *Dib P* 5B **52**
Navigators Way.
　H End 2A **34**
Neath Way. *Chan F* 1C **14**
Neilson Clo. *Chan F* 6E **9**
Nelson Clo. *Holb* 5C **54**
Nelson Clo. *Roms* 4C **6**
Nelson Ct. *Hythe* 5F **53**
Nelson Ga.
　Sotn 6A **30** (1B **4**)
Nelson Hill.
　Sotn 6A **30** (2A **4**)
Nelson Ind. Pk. *H End* 2H **33**
Nelson Rd. *Eastl* 3D **16**
Nelson Rd. *Sotn* 5G **29**
Nelsons Gdns. *H End* 6H **25**
Neptune Ct. *Sotn* 5D **20**
Neptune Way. *Sotn* 3D **40**
Nerquis Clo. *Roms* 4E **7**
Netherhill La. *Bot* 2F **35**
Netley Cliff. *Net A* 2B **46**
Netley Clo. *Chan F* 4D **14**
Netley Firs Clo. *Sotn* 1F **43**
Netley Firs Rd. *H End* 6G **33**
Netley Hill Est. *H End* 1F **43**
Netley Lodge Clo.
　Net A 2C **46**
Netley Rd. *Fare* 6G **49**
Nettlestone. *Net A* 6C **42**
Neva Rd. *Sotn* 3H **31**
Neville Dri. *Roms* 3C **6**
Newbridge. *Net A* 1C **46**
Newbury Clo. *F Oak* 5H **17**
Newbury Pl. *Wars* 5D **48**
Newbury Rd. *Sotn* 2G **29**
Newcliffe Gdns.
　H End 6H **33**
New Cliff Ho. *Sotn* 4G **41**
Newcombe Rd. *Sotn* 5A **30**
New Cotts. *Sotn* 1A **28**
New Ct. *Fare* 2H **49**
New Forest Enterprise Cen.
　Tot 6E **27**
Newlands Av. *Sotn* 4G **29**
Newlands Clo. *Black* 4E **55**
Newlands Clo. *Chan F* 2A **14**
Newlands Copse.
　Black 4F **55**
Newlands Rd. *Fawl* 3E **55**
Newlyn Wlk. *Roms* 3D **6**
Newman St. *Sotn* 3F **29**
Newport Clo. *Chan F* 3C **14**
New Rd. *Asht* 2B **36**
New Rd. *Black* 4E **55**
New Rd. *Col C* 4F **11**
New Rd. *Eastl* 5H **17**
New Rd. *Hythe* 6F **53**
　(Hardley La., in two parts)

New Rd. *Hythe* 2E **53**
　(Marsh, The)
New Rd. *Net A* 1A **46**
New Rd. *Roms* 4D **6**
New Rd. *Sotn* 6C **30** (2E **5**)
New Rd. *Swanw* 5D **44**
New Rd. *Wars* 1B **50**
Newton La. *Roms* 5B **6**
Newton Rd. *Sotn* 2G **31**
Newtown Ct. *Wars* 6A **48**
Newtown Rd. *Eastl* 3A **16**
Newtown Rd. *Sotn* 3A **42**
Newtown Rd. *Wars* 2A **50**
Nicholas Rd. *Black* 6E **55**
Nichol Rd. *Chan F* 4F **9**
Nicholson Wlk.
　Rown 3B **20**
Nichols Rd.
　Sotn 6D **30** (1G **5**)
Nickleby Gdns. *Tot* 4B **26**
Nickson Clo. *Chan F* 5D **8**
Nightingale Av. *Eastl* 6E **15**
Nightingale Clo. *Burs* 5F **43**
Nightingale Clo. *Roms* 5D **6**
Nightingale Ct. *Sotn* 5G **29**
Nightingale Dri. *Tot* 3C **26**
Nightingale Gro. *Sotn* 4G **29**
Nightingale Ho. *Net A* 3C **46**
Nightingale Ho. *Roms* 4D **6**
Nightingale M. *L Hth* 3C **46**
　(Nightingale Wlk.)
Nightingale M. *L Hth* 4F **49**
　(Woodpecker Copse)
Nightingale Rd. *Sotn* 4G **29**
Nightingale Wlk. *Net A* 3C **46**
Nile Rd. *Sotn* 1C **30**
Ninian Clo. *F Oak* 3F **17**
Noads Clo. *Dib P* 4D **52**
Noads Way. *Dib P* 5C **52**
Noble Rd. *H End* 5B **34**
Nob's Crook. *Col C* 5G **11**
Nomad Clo. *Sotn* 2B **32**
Nook, The. *Eastl* 2B **16**
Norbury Clo. *Chan F* 6D **8**
Norbury Gdns. *Hamb* 5E **47**
Norcliffe Rd. *Sotn* 3C **30**
Norcroft Ct. *Sotn* 1G **29**
Norfolk Gdns. *H End* 6A **34**
Norfolk Clo. *Chan F* 4E **15**
Norfolk Ct. *Sotn* 3H **29**
Norham Av. *Sotn* 1G **29**
Norham Clo. *Sotn* 1G **29**
Norham Bri. *Sotn* 5E **31**
Norlands Dri. *Ott* 1C **10**
Normandy Clo. *Rown* 3C **20**
Normandy Ct. *Wars* 6A **48**
Normandy Ho. *Roms* 5D **6**
　(off Chambers Av.)
Normandy Way.
　March 2D **38**
Norman Gdns. *H End* 6G **33**
Norman Ho. *Sotn* 5E **31**
Norman Rd. *Black* 5F **55**
Norman Rd. *Sotn* 6H **29**
Norris Clo. *Roms* 2F **7**
Norris Hill. *Sotn* 2G **31**
Northam Bri. *Sotn* 5E **31**
Northam Bus. Cen.
　Sotn 5E **31**
Northam Cen. *Sotn* 6E **31**
　(off Kent St.)
Northampton La.
　Black 5E **55**
Northam Rd.
　Sotn 6D **30** (2F **5**)
Northbourne Clo.
　Dib P 5E **53**
Northbrook Ind. Est.
　Sotn 1G **29**

Northbrook Rd.
　Sotn 6D **30** (1G **5**)
North Clo. *Roms* 3F **7**
Northcote Rd. *Sotn* 1E **31**
North Ct. *Sotn* 3F **29**
Northdene Rd. *Chan F* 2E **15**
N. East Clo. *Sotn* 6C **32**
N. East Rd. *Sotn* 1A **42**
N. End Clo. *Chan F* 3E **15**
Northern Anchorage.
　Sotn 2F **41**
Northerwood Clo.
　N Bad 3D **12**
Northfield Rd. *Sotn* 6H **23**
North Front.
　Sotn 6C **30** (2E **5**)
　(in two parts)
Northlands Clo. *Tot* 3D **26**
Northlands Gdns. *Sotn* 4A **30**
Northlands Rd. *Eastl* 4A **16**
Northlands Rd. *Roms* 6F **7**
Northlands Rd. *Sotn* 4A **30**
Northlands Rd. *Tot* 3E **27**
Northleigh Corner.
　Sotn 4G **23**
N. Millers Dale. *Chan F* 4C **8**
Northmore Clo. *L Hth* 2F **49**
Northmore Rd. *L Hth* 2F **49**
Northolt Gdns. *Sotn* 4E **21**
North Rd. *Dib P* 4B **52**
North Rd. *Sotn* 2E **31**
Northwood Clo. *Sotn* 3C **22**
Norton Clo. *Sotn* 2G **41**
Norton Welch Clo.
　N Bad 3F **13**
Norwich Clo. *Sar G* 3C **48**
Norwich Rd. *Sotn* 1H **31**
Noyce Dri. *F Oak* 3G **17**
Nursery Gdns. *Chan F* 4E **15**
Nursery Gdns. *Roms* 5D **6**
Nursery Gdns. *Sotn* 5B **32**
Nursery Gro. *H End* 6A **34**
Nursery Rd. *Sotn* 2F **31**
Nursling Ind. Est.
　Nurs 5H **19**
Nursling St. *Nurs* 4A **20**
Nutash. *Fare* 3G **49**
Nutbeem Rd. *Eastl* 5A **16**
Nutburn Rd. *N Bad* 2F **13**
Nutfield Ct. *Sotn* 6C **20**
Nutfield Rd. *Rown* 3B **20**
Nutsey Av. *Tot* 1D **26**
Nutsey Clo. *Tot* 6E **19**
Nutsey La. *Tot* 1E **27**
Nutshalling Av. *Rown* 4B **20**
Nutshalling Clo. *Cal* 1C **26**
Nutwood Way. *Tot* 1E **27**

O

Oakbank Rd. *Eastl* 3C **16**
Oakbank Rd. *Sotn* 2F **41**
Oak Clo. *Dib P* 5C **52**
Oak Clo. *Sotn* 3A **28**
Oak Coppice Clo. *Eastl* 5G **17**
Oakdene. *Sotn* 1D **30**
Oakdene. *Tot* 4C **26**
Oakdene Ct. *F Oak* 2F **17**
Oak Dri. *F Oak* 2F **17**
Oakenbrow. *Dib P* 4B **52**
Oakfield Rd. *Tot* 4F **27**
Oakfields. *Eastl* 6A **10**
Oak Grn. Way. *Sotn* 3A **32**
Oakgrove Gdns. *Eastl* 5E **17**
Oakgrove Rd. *Eastl* 5E **17**
Oakhill. *Burs* 4H **43**

Oakhill Clo. *Burs* 4H **43**
Oakhill Clo. *Chan F* 2G **15**
Oakhill Ct. *Chan F* 2G **15**
Oakhill Ter. *Burs* 4H **43**
Oakhurst Clo. *Net A* 1C **46**
Oakhurst Rd. *Sotn* 6C **22**
Oakhurst Way. *Net A* 1C **46**
Oakland Dri. *March* 4C **38**
Oaklands Av. *Tot* 4F **27**
Oaklands Gdns. *Fare* 6G **49**
Oaklands, The. *Chan F* 4E **15**
Oaklands Way. *Dib P* 4A **52**
Oaklands Way. *Fare* 6G **49**
Oaklands Way. *Sotn* 5B **22**
Oak Leaf Clo. *March* 5C **38**
Oakleigh Cres. *Tot* 5E **27**
Oakleigh Gdns. *Roms* 5D **6**
Oakley Clo. *Holb* 4C **54**
Oakley Ho. *Sotn* 4B **30**
Oakley John Wlk.
   Sotn 5H **31**
Oakley Rd. *Sotn* 2D **28**
Oakmount Av. *Chan F* 3F **15**
Oakmount Av. *Sotn* 2C **30**
Oakmount Av. *Tot* 3F **27**
Oakmount Rd. *Chan F* 6G **9**
Oakridge Rd. *Sotn* 3B **28**
Oak Rd. *Burs* 5F **43**
Oak Rd. *Dib P* 5B **52**
Oak Rd. *Sotn* 3F **41**
Oaks, The. *Burs* 5F **43**
Oaks, The. *Sotn* 6H **31**
Oaktree. *Sotn* 6A **22**
Oaktree Cvn. Pk.
   W End 5D **24**
Oaktree Gdns. *H End* 5H **33**
Oak Tree Rd. *Sotn* 2F **31**
Oak Tree Way. *Eastl* 2A **16**
Oak Va. *W End* 6B **24**
Oakville Mans. *Sotn* 1C **4**
Oak Wlk. *F Oak* 2F **17**
Oakwood Av. *Ott* 2C **10**
Oakwood Clo. *Chan F* 4F **9**
Oakwood Clo. *Ott* 1C **10**
Oakwood Clo. *Roms* 3E **7**
Oakwood Clo. *Wars* 1B **50**
Oakwood Ct. *Chan F* 4E **25**
Oakwood Ct. *W End* 6E **25**
Oakwood Dri. *Sotn* 4G **21**
Oakwood Rd. *Chan F* 5F **9**
Oakwood Way.
   Hamb 4G **47**
Oatfield Gdns. *Cal* 2C **26**
Oatlands. *Roms* 4C **6**
Oatlands Clo. *Bot* 2D **34**
Oatlands Rd. *Bot* 2D **34**
Oatley Wlk. *Black* 3F **55**
Obelisk Rd. *Sotn* 3F **41**
Occupation La. *Fare* 1H **51**
Ocean Quay. *Sotn* 6E **31**
Ocean Rd. *E Dock* 4C **40**
Ocean Way. *Sotn* 3D **40**
Ocknell Gro. *Dib* 3A **52**
O'Connell Rd. *Eastl* 5G **15**
Octavia Gdns. *Chan F* 6H **9**
Octavia Rd. *Sotn* 5G **23**
Odiham Clo. *Chan F* 4D **14**
Odiham Clo. *Sotn* 5D **20**
Ogle Rd. *Sotn* 1B **40** (3D **4**)
Okement Clo. *W End* 1B **32**
Old Barn Clo. *Cal* 1C **26**
Old Bitumen Rd.
   Hythe 1H **55**
Old Bri. Clo. *Burs* 4H **43**
Old Bri. Ho. Rd. *Burs* 4H **43**
Oldbury Ct. *Sotn* 1B **28**
Old Common. *L Hth* 3E **49**

Old Comn. Gdns.
   L Hth 3E **49**
Old Cracknore Clo.
   March 3D **38**
Oldenburg. *White* 5F **45**
Old Farm Dri. *Sotn* 6H **23**
Old Garden Clo. *L Hth* 5G **49**
Old Ivy La. *W End* 1B **32**
Old Magazine Clo.
   March 3D **38**
Old Mill Way. *Sotn* 2E **29**
Old Parsonage Ct. *Ott* 2C **10**
Old Priory Clo. *Hamb* 5G **47**
Old Rectory Ct. *Tot* 6H **27**
Old Redbridge Rd.
   Sotn 3A **28**
Old Rd. *Roms* 3D **6**
Old Salisbury La. *E Wel* 1A **6**
          (in two parts)
Old School Clo. *Holb* 2B **54**
Old School Clo. *Net A* 6C **42**
Old School Gdns.
   W End 1E **33**
Old Shambehurst La.
   H End 1A **34**
Old Swanwick La.
   Lwr S 5B **44**
Old Well Clo., The.
   Sotn 2C **42**
Oleander Clo. *L Hth* 2E **49**
Oleander Dri. *Tot* 3B **26**
Olive Rd. *Sotn* 5E **21**
Oliver Rd. *Sotn* 6F **23**
Olivers Clo. *Tot* 4B **26**
Olympic Way. *Eastl* 4G **17**
Omdurman Rd. *Sotn* 1C **30**
Omega Enterprise Pk.
   Chan F 1E **15**
Onibury Clo. *Sotn* 2A **32**
Onibury Rd. *Sotn* 2A **32**
Onslow Rd. *Sotn* 5C **30**
Orchard Av. *Eastl* 6F **17**
Orchard Clo. *Col C* 4F **11**
Orchard Clo. *Fawl* 2H **55**
Orchard Clo. *N Bad* 2D **12**
Orchard Clo. *Tot* 6F **27**
Orchard Ct. *Bot* 4C **34**
Orchard Ho.
   Sotn 2C **40** (5E **5**)
Orchard La. *Roms* 5B **6**
Orchard La.
   Sotn 2C **40** (5F **5**)
Orchard Pl. *Sotn* . . .2C **40** (6E **5**)
Orchard Rd. *F Oak* 2F **17**
Orchard Rd. *L Hth* 5D **48**
Orchards Way. *Sotn* 1C **30**
Orchards Way. *W End* 2D **32**
Orchard, The. *Chilw* 6A **14**
Orchard, The. *Sotn* 4D **22**
Orchard Way. *Dib P* 4C **52**
Ordnance Rd. *Sotn* 5C **30**
Ordnance Way. *March* 2E **39**
Oregon Clo. *Sotn* 1A **42**
Oriana Way. *Nurs* 5H **19**
Oriel Dri. *Fare* 6G **49**
Oriental Ter.
   Sotn 2C **40** (6E **5**)
Orion Clo. *Sotn* 5D **20**
Orion Ind. Cen. *Sotn* 4G **23**
Orkney Clo. *Sotn* 5C **20**
Ormesby Dri. *Chan F* 4D **8**
Ormond Clo. *F Oak* 4H **17**
Orpen Rd. *Sotn* 2C **42**
Orwell Clo. *Sotn* 2C **28**
Orwell Cres. *Fare* 5G **49**
Osborne Clo. *Net A* 2D **46**
Osborne Dri. *Chan F* 2G **15**
Osborne Gdns. *F Oak* 3G **17**

Osborne Gdns. *Sotn* 2E **31**
Osborne Rd. *Tot* 4G **27**
Osborne Rd. *Wars* 1A **50**
Osborne Rd. N. *Sotn* 2E **31**
Osborne Rd. S. *Sotn* 3D **30**
Oslands La. *Swanw* 6B **44**
Oslo Towers. *Sotn* 5G **41**
Osprey Clo. *March* 4C **38**
Osprey Clo. *Sotn* 4F **21**
Osterley Clo. *Bot* 5C **34**
Osterley Rd. *Sotn* 6G **31**
Otterbourne Ho. *Ott* 3B **10**
Otterbourne Ho. Gdns.
   Ott 3B **10**
Otter Clo. *Eastl* 5F **17**
Ouse Clo. *Chan F* 5C **8**
Outer Circ. *Sotn* 5E **21**
Outlands La. *Curd* 5H **35**
Overbrook. *Hythe* 4D **52**
Overbrook Way. *N Bad* 2C **12**
Overcliff Ri. *Sotn* 5A **22**
Overdell Ct. *Sotn* 4A **30**
Oviat Clo. *Tot* 4B **26**
Ovington Ct. *Sotn* 3D **32**
Ovington Rd. *Eastl* 6A **16**
Owen Rd. *Eastl* 5H **15**
Oxburgh Clo. *Eastl* 2H **15**
Oxford Av. *Sotn* 5C **30** (1F **5**)
Oxford M. *Sotn* 2C **40** (6F **5**)
Oxford Rd. *Sotn* 4C **30**
Oxford St. *Sotn* 2C **40** (6F **5**)
Oxlease Clo. *Roms* 3D **6**
Ozier Rd. *Sotn* 1A **32**

P

Pacific Clo. *Sotn* 3D **40**
Packridge La. *Roms* 6C **12**
Paddocks, The. *Fawl* 2H **55**
Paddock, The. *Cal* 1C **26**
Paddock, The. *Eastl* 1B **16**
Padwell Rd. *Sotn* 4C **30**
Page Clo. *Holb* 6D **54**
Paget St. *Sotn* 2D **40** (5H **5**)
Paignton Rd. *Sotn* 2D **28**
Paimpol Pl. *Roms* 6B **6**
Painswick Clo. *Sar G* 1D **48**
Paling Bus. Pk. *H End* 1H **43**
Pallet Clo. *Col C* 5F **11**
Pallot Clo. *Burs* 4F **43**
Palmers Clo. *F Oak* 2G **17**
Palmerston Ho. *Sotn* 5E **5**
Palmerston Rd.
   Sotn 6C **30** (2E **5**)
Palmerston St. *Roms* 5B **6**
Palm Rd. *Sotn* 6E **21**
Palomino Dri. *White* 6F **45**
Pangbourne Clo. *Sotn* 1A **42**
Pansy Rd. *Sotn* 5C **22**
Pantheon Rd. *Chan F* 6H **9**
Panwell Rd. *Sotn* 4A **32**
Pardoe Clo. *H End* 6A **34**
Parham Dri. *Eastl* 3H **15**
Park Clo. *Hythe* 2F **53**
Park Clo. *March* 4B **38**
Park Ct. *Roms* 2A **12**
Park Ga. Bus. Cen.
   Swanw 1F **49**
Park Glen. *Park G* 3G **49**
Pk. Hill Clo. *Holb* 5C **54**
Parklands. *Sar G* 3E **49**
Parklands. *Sotn* 2G **31**
Parklands. *Tot* 3F **27**
Parklands Clo. *Chan F* 6E **9**
Park La. *Holb* 4B **54**
Park La. *March* 3A **38**
Park La. *Ott & Eastl* 4B **10**
Park La. *Sotn* 6B **30** (1C **4**)

Park Rd. *Chan F* 5E **9**
Park Rd. *Sotn* 5G **29**
Parkside. *Tot* 6F **27**
Parkside Av. *Sotn* 3B **28**
Park St. *Sotn* 3F **29**
Park Vw. *Bot* 4E **35**
Park Vw. *H End* 4H **33**
Parkville Rd. *Sotn* 5F **23**
Park Wlk. *Sotn* 6C **30** (2E **5**)
Park Way. *F Oak* 2H **17**
Parkway Ct. *Chan F* 6F **9**
Parkway Gdns. *Chan F* 6E **9**
Parkway, The. *Sotn* 4C **22**
Pk. Wood Clo. *H End* 4B **34**
Parnell Rd. *Eastl* 5H **15**
Parry Rd. *Sotn* 1D **42**
Parsonage Rd. *Sotn* 5D **30**
Partridge Rd. *Dib P* 5D **52**
Partry Clo. *Chan F* 5C **8**
Passage La. *Wars* 6H **47**
Passfield Av. *Eastl* 6G **15**
Passfield Clo. *Eastl* 5G **15**
Pastures, The. *Fare* 3G **49**
Pat Bear Clo. *Sotn* 3A **28**
Patricia Clo. *W End* 1D **32**
Patricia Dri. *H End* 4B **34**
Paulet Clo. *Sotn* 2A **32**
Paulet Lacave Av. *Sotn* 3B **20**
Pauletts La. *Cal* 1B **26**
Paulson Clo. *Chan F* 5E **9**
Pavilion Rd. *H End* 3C **34**
Pavillion Ct. *Sotn* 4A **30**
Paxton Clo. *H End* 6B **34**
Paynes La. *F Oak* 1F **17**
Payne's Rd. *Sotn* 5G **29**
Paynes Rd. *Sotn* 5G **29**
Peach Rd. *Sotn* 5E **21**
Peak Clo. *Sotn* 3D **28**
Peartree Av. *Sotn* 1G **43**
Pear Tree Clo. *Bot* 1D **34**
Peartree Clo. *Sotn* 1F **41**
Peartree Gdns. *Sotn* 5A **32**
Peartree Rd. *Dib P* 4C **52**
Peartree Rd. *Sotn* 1F **41**
Pebble Ct. *March* 3D **38**
Peel Clo. *Roms* 3F **7**
Peel St. *Sotn* 6E **31**
Peewit Hill Clo. *Burs* 2G **43**
Pegasus Clo. *Hamb* 5F **47**
Pegasus Clo. *Sotn* 5D **20**
Pembers Clo. *F Oak* 2G **17**
Pembrey Clo. *Sotn* 4D **20**
Pembroke Clo. *Eastl* 2H **15**
Pembroke Clo. *Roms* 5C **6**
Pembroke Clo. *Tot* 3G **27**
Pembroke Ct. *Sotn* 2C **30**
Pembroke Rd. *Sotn* 1B **42**
Pendle Clo. *Sotn* 3D **28**
Pendleton Gdns. *Black* 4E **55**
Pendula Way. *Eastl* 2E **17**
Penelope Gdns. *Burs* 4F **43**
Penhale Gdns. *Fare* 6F **49**
Penhale Way. *Tot* 6E **27**
Penistone Clo. *Sotn* 3A **42**
Pennard Way. *Chan F* 3C **14**
Pennine Gdns. *Dib P* 4B **52**
Pennine Ho. *Sotn* 4D **28**
Pennine Rd. *Sotn* 4C **28**
Pennine Way. *Chan F* 3F **15**
Pennington Clo. *Col C* 5F **11**
Pennycress. *L Hth* 5C **48**
Penrhyn Clo. *Eastl* 2H **15**
Penshurst Way. *Eastl* 1A **16**
Pentagon, The. *Black* 3G **55**
Pentire Av. *Sotn* 2H **29**
Pentire Way. *Sotn* 1H **29**
Pentland Clo. *Dib P* 4B **52**
Pentridge Way. *Tot* 6D **26**

Peppard Clo. *Sotn* 4A **32**
Peppercorn Way.
  H End 6H **25**
Pepys Av. *Sotn* 6D **32**
Percivale Rd. *Chan F* 3B **14**
Percy Clo. *Hythe* 1D **52**
Percy Rd. *Sotn* 3E **29**
Peregrine Clo. *Tot* 5C **26**
Pern Dri. *Bot* 4E **35**
Perran Rd. *Sotn* 2B **28**
Perrywood Clo. *Holb* 5C **54**
Perrywood Gdns. *Tot* 3C **26**
Pershore Clo. *L Hth* 4E **49**
Persian Dri. *White* 6F **45**
Peterborough Rd.
  Sotn 4C **30**
Peters Clo. *L Hth* 4C **48**
Peterscroft Av. *Asht* 4A **36**
Peters Rd. *L Hth* 4C **48**
Pettinger Gdns. *Sotn* 3F **31**
Petty Clo. *Holb* 6D **6**
Petworth Gdns. *Eastl* 2A **16**
Petworth Gdns. *Sotn* 4F **21**
Pevensey Clo. *Sotn* 2B **28**
Peverells Rd. *Chan F* 6G **9**
Peverells Wood Av.
  Chan F 6G **9**
Peverells Wood Clo.
  Chan F 6H **9**
Peveril Rd. *Sotn* 1G **41**
Pewitt Hill. *Burs* 2G **43**
  (in two parts)
Pewsey Pl. *Sotn* 1H **29**
Phi Ho. *Sotn* 6G **13**
Phillimore Rd. *Sotn* 5F **23**
Phillips Clo. *Rown* 3C **20**
Philpott Dri. *March* 4D **38**
Phoenix Clo. *Burs* 4G **43**
Phoenix Ind. Pk. *Eastl* . . .5C **16**
Pickwick Clo. *Tot* 4B **26**
Pilands Wood Rd.
  Burs 5F **43**
Pilgrim Pl. *Sotn* 5G **23**
Pilgrims Clo. *Chan F* 2B **14**
Pimpernel Clo. *L Hth* 5C **48**
Pine Clo. *Asht* 2C **36**
Pine Clo. *Dib P* 4D **52**
Pine Clo. *N Bad* 2D **12**
Pine Cres. *Chan F* 4E **9**
Pine Dri. *Sotn* 4D **32**
Pine Dri. E. *Sotn* 4E **33**
Pinefield Rd. *Sotn* 1H **31**
Pinegrove Rd. *Sotn* 2H **41**
Pinehurst Rd. *Sotn* 2B **22**
Pinelands Ct. *Sotn* 5G **21**
Pinelands Rd. *Chilw* 1B **22**
Pine Rd. *Chan F* 4D **8**
Pine Rd. *Roms* 6F **7**
Pines, The. *Sotn* 6F **21**
Pine Vw. Clo. *Burs* 4G **43**
Pine Wlk. *Chilw* 2A **22**
  (in two parts)
Pine Wlk. *Sar G* 2E **49**
Pine Way. *Sotn* 2B **22**
Pinewood. *Sotn* 3B **22**
Pinewood Clo. *Roms* 3F **7**
Pinewood Cres. *Hythe* 4F **53**
Pinewood Dri. *Hythe* 5F **53**
Pinewood Pk. *Sotn* 6F **33**
Pinto Clo. *White* 6G **45**
Pipers Clo. *Tot* 5D **26**
Piping Clo. *Col C* 5F **11**
Piping Grn. *Col C* 5F **11**
Piping Rd. *Col C* 5F **11**
Pirelli St. *Sotn* 1B **40** (3C **4**)
Pirrie Clo. *Sotn* 2H **29**
Pitchponds Rd. *Wars* 1A **50**

Pitmore Clo. *Eastl* 5B **10**
Pitmore Rd. *Eastl* 5B **10**
Pitt Rd. *Sotn* 5G **29**
Plaitford Wlk. *Sotn* 2D **28**
Plantation Dri. *March* 4C **38**
Platform Rd.
  Sotn 3C **40** (6F **5**)
Players Cres. *Tot* 6E **27**
Plaza Pde. *Roms* 5C **6**
Plover Clo. *Sotn* 4F **21**
Ploverfield. *Burs* 5H **43**
Plover Rd. *Tot* 4C **26**
Pointout Clo. *Sotn* 6A **22**
Pointout Rd. *Sotn* 6A **22**
Polesden Clo. *Chan F* 5D **8**
Poles La. *Ott* 1A **10**
Polygon, The.
  Sotn 6A **30** (1B **4**)
Pond Clo. *March* 3D **38**
Pondhead Clo. *Holb* 5C **54**
Pond Rd. *Sar G* 1D **48**
Pooksgreen. *March* 3A **38**
Poole Rd. *Sotn* 1G **41**
Popes La. *Tot* 4F **27**
Poplar Dri. *March* 4B **38**
Poplar Rd. *Sotn* 5H **31**
Poplar Way. *H End* 4B **34**
Poplar Way. *N Bad* 2D **12**
Poppy Clo. *L Hth* 5D **48**
Poppyfields. *Chan F* 1C **14**
Poppy Rd. *Sotn* 4E **23**
Porchester Rd. *Sotn* 2G **41**
Porlock Rd. *Sotn* 1B **28**
Portal Rd. *Eastl* 4D **16**
Portal Rd. *Sotn* 1B **42**
Portal Rd. *Tot* 4D **26**
Portchester Ri. *Eastl* 6A **10**
Portcullis Ho. *Sotn* 3C **40**
  (off Central Rd.)
Portelet Ho. *Sotn* 6B **20**
Portelet Pl. *H End* 6A **34**
Porteous Cres. *Chan F* . . .1H **15**
Portersbridge M. *Roms* . . .5B **6**
Portersbridge St. *Roms* . . .5B **6**
Porter's La.
  Sotn 2B **40** (6D **4**)
Port Hamble. *Hamb* 4G **47**
Portland St.
  Sotn 1B **40** (3D **4**)
Portland Ter.
  Sotn 1B **40** (2D **4**)
Portside Clo. *March* 2E **39**
Portsmouth Rd. *Burs* 4G **43**
Portsmouth Rd. *Fish P* . . .6H **11**
Portsmouth Rd.
  Sotn & Burs 2F **41**
Portswood Av. *Sotn* 3D **30**
Portswood Cen. *Sotn* 2D **30**
Portswood Pk. *Sotn* 3D **30**
Portswood Rd. *Sotn* 3D **30**
Portview Rd. *Sotn* 1H **31**
Portway Clo. *Sotn* 4B **32**
Posbrook La. *Fare* 4H **51**
Postern Ct. *Sotn* . . .2B **40** (5D **4**)
Potters Heron Clo. *Amp* . . .2A **8**
Potters Heron La. *Amp* 2A **8**
Poulner Clo. *Sotn* 4A **42**
Pound Ga. Dri. *Fare* 6G **49**
Pound La. *Amp* 1G **13**
Pound La. *Tot* 2E **37**
Pound Rd. *Burs* 4E **43**
Pound St. *Sotn* 4A **32**
Pound Tree Rd.
  Sotn 1C **40** (3E **5**)
Powell Cres. *Tot* 6F **27**
Precinct, The. *H End* 5A **34**
Precinct, The. *Holb* 4C **54**
Precosa Rd. *Bot* 6C **34**

Prelate Way. *Titch* 5G **49**
Premier Cen., The.
  Roms 6G **7**
Premier Pde. *Sotn* 6H **23**
Premier Way. *Roms* 2B **12**
Preshaw Clo. *Sotn* 5G **21**
Prestwood Rd. *H End* 5A **34**
Pretoria Rd. *H End* 6H **33**
Priest Cft. *Black* 3E **55**
Priestcroft Dri. *Black* 3E **55**
Priestfields. *Fare* 5G **49**
Priestlands. *Roms* 4B **6**
Priestlands Clo.
  W'Inds 5A **26**
Priestley Clo. *Tot* 4D **26**
Priestwood Clo. *Sotn* 4D **32**
Primate Rd. *Fare* 4H **49**
Primrose Clo. *Chan F* 3B **14**
Primrose Clo. *H End* 6A **34**
Primrose Rd. *Sotn* 5C **22**
Primrose Way. *L Hth* 5D **48**
Primrose Way. *Roms* 4F **7**
Prince of Wales Av.
  Sotn 4E **29**
Prince Rd. *Rown* 3C **20**
Princes Ct. *Sotn* 5E **31**
Princes Ho. Sotn 5E **31**
  (off Princes Ct.)
Prince's Rd. *Roms* 4B **6**
Princes Rd. *Sotn* 5H **29**
Princess Clo. *W End* 1E **33**
Princess Rd. *Asht* 3B **36**
Princes St. *Sotn* 5E **31**
Prince William Ct.
  Eastl 5F **17**
Priors Hill La. *Burs* 5E **43**
Priory Av. *Sotn* 2F **31**
Priory Clo. *Sotn* 2F **31**
Priory Ho. Sotn . . .6C **30** (2F **5**)
Priory Rd. *Eastl* 6H **15**
Priory Rd. *Net A* 1B **46**
Priory Rd. *Sotn* 2E **31**
Proctor Clo. *Sotn* 6D **32**
Proctor Dri. *N Bad* 4D **12**
Promenade, The.
  Hythe 1E **53**
Prospect Ho. *Sotn* 6H **31**
Prospect Pl. *Chan F* 1E **15**
Prospect Pl. *Hythe* 1E **53**
Providence Hill. *Burs* 3G **43**
Prunus Clo. *Sotn* 4G **21**
Pudbrooke Gdns.
  H End 3H **33**
Pudbrook Ho. *Bot* 5D **34**
Puffin Clo. *Sotn* 4F **21**
Purbrook Clo. *Sotn* 5G **21**
Purcell Rd. *Sotn* 2D **42**
Purkess Clo. *Chan F* 6F **9**
Purlieu Dri. *Dib P* 4B **52**
Purvis Gdns. *Sotn* 3B **42**
Pycroft Clo. *Sotn* 6A **32**
Pyland's La. *Burs* 2H **43**
Pylewell Rd. *Hythe* 1E **53**

Q

Quadrangle, The.
  Eastl 3A **16**
Quadrangle, The. *Roms* . . .6G **7**
Quantock Rd. *Sotn* 3C **28**
Quantocks, The. *Dib P* 4B **52**
Quay Haven. *Swanw* 6B **44**
Quay La. *Lwr S* 6B **44**
Quayside. *Bot* 6E **35**
Quayside Rd. *Sotn* 4E **31**
Quayside Wlk. *March* 2D **38**
Quay, The. *Hamb* 5G **47**
Quebec Gdns. *Burs* 4F **43**

Queen Elizabeth Ct.
  Sotn 6E **23**
Queens Bldgs.
  Sotn 1C **40** (4F **5**)
Queens Clo. *Hythe* 3F **53**
Queen's Clo. *Roms* 5D **6**
Queen's Ct.
  Sotn 6A **30** (1B **4**)
Queens Ho.
  Sotn 2C **40** (5E **5**)
Queens Ride. *N Bad* 3C **12**
Queens Rd. *Chan F* 4F **9**
Queen's Rd. *Sotn* 1G **29**
Queens Rd. *Wars* 1A **50**
Queens Ter.
  Sotn 2C **40** (6F **5**)
Queenstown Rd. *Sotn* 5H **29**
Queens Vw. *Net A* 1B **46**
Queen's Way.
  Sotn 2C **40** (6E **5**)
Querida Clo. *Lwr S* 5B **44**
Quilter Clo. *Sotn* 1D **42**
Quob Farm Clo.
  W End 6E **25**
Quob La. *W End* 5E **25**

R

Rachel Clo. *Eastl* 5H **17**
Radcliffe Ct. *Sotn* 5D **30**
Radcliffe Rd.
  Sotn 6D **30** (1H **5**)
Radleigh Gdns. *Tot* 3B **26**
Radley Clo. *H End* 2A **34**
Radstock Rd. *Sotn* 2F **41**
Radway Cres. *Sotn* 3H **29**
Radway Rd. *Sotn* 3H **29**
Raeburn Dri. *H End* 4A **34**
Raglan Clo. *Chan F* 3B **14**
Raglan Ct. *Eastl* 1A **16**
Raglan Ct. *Park G* 2E **49**
Railway Cotts. *Sotn* 3A **28**
  (in two parts)
Railway Vw. Rd. *Sotn* 3E **31**
Rainbow Pl. *Sotn* 5G **29**
Raley Rd. *L Hth* 5E **49**
Ralph La. *Roms* 3D **6**
Ramalley La. *Chan F* 5D **8**
  (in two parts)
Rampart Rd. *Sotn* 4F **31**
Randall Clo. *Cal* 1C **26**
Randall Rd. *Chan F* 3F **9**
Randolph St. *Sotn* 4G **29**
  (in two parts)
Ranelagh Gdns. *Sotn* 4A **30**
Ranfurly Gdns. *Dib P* 5C **52**
Range Gdns. *Sotn* 2B **42**
Ranmore Ct. *Dib* 3A **52**
  (off Hawkhill)
Ratcliffe Rd. *Dib P* 5D **52**
Ratcliffe Rd. *H End* 4A **34**
Ratlake La. *Win* 1B **8**
Rattigan Gdns. *White* 5G **45**
Raven Rd. *Sotn* 5D **30**
Ravenscroft Clo. *Burs* 4F **43**
Ravenscroft Way. *Bot* 2D **34**
Raven Sq. *Eastl* 5F **15**
Ravenswood. *Fare* 4G **49**
Raymond Clo. *Holb* 5D **54**
Raymond Clo. *W End* 6F **25**
Raymond Rd. *Sotn* 3H **29**
Rayners Gdns. *Sotn* 5F **23**
Reading Room La.
  Curd 3H **35**
Recess, The. *Eastl* 2B **16**
Rectory Ct. *Bot* 4D **34**
Redbridge Causeway.
  Sotn 3H **27**

Radbridge Flyover—St Agathas Rd.

Redbridge Flyover. Sotn . . . 3A 28
Redbridge Hill. Sotn . . . 2D 28
Redbridge La. Sotn & Nurs . . . 1A 28
Redbridge Rd. Sotn . . . 3A 28
Redbridge Towers. Sotn . . . 3A 28
Redcar St. Sotn . . . 3F 29
Redcote Clo. Sotn . . . 4B 32
Redcourt. Sotn . . . 5B 22
Redcroft La. Burs . . . 4G 43
Redfords, The. Tot . . . 2E 27
Redhill. Sotn . . . 5A 22
Redhill Clo. Sotn . . . 5A 22
Redhill Cres. Sotn . . . 5A 22
Redhill Way. Sotn . . . 5A 22
Redlands Dri. Sotn . . . 5H 31
Red Lodge. Chan F . . . 4D 14
Redmoor Clo. Sotn . . . 5H 31
Red Oaks Dri. Park G . . . 2G 49
Redrise Clo. Holb . . . 5B 54
Redward Rd. Rown . . . 4D 20
Redwing Gdns. Tot . . . 3C 26
Redwood Clo. Dib P . . . 3A 52
Redwood Clo. W End . . . 1C 32
Redwood Gdns. Tot . . . 5C 26
Redwood Way. Sotn . . . 3C 22
Reed Dri. March . . . 3D 38
Reeves Way. Burs . . . 4F 43
Regent Clo. Ott . . . 1C 10
Regent Ct. Sotn . . . 2C 30
Regent Ho. H End . . . 1A 34
Regent Rd. Chan F . . . 1F 15
Regents Ct. Sotn . . . 3F 29
Regents Ga. Sar G . . . 2C 48
Regents Gro. Sotn . . . 2F 29
Regent's Pk. Gdns. Sotn . . . 4F 29
Regent's Pk. Rd. Sotn . . . 5E 29
Regent St. Sotn . . . 1B 40 (3D 4)
Reginald Mitchell Ct. Eastl . . . 3H 15
Reliant Clo. Chan F . . . 2D 14
Renda Rd. Holb . . . 4C 54
Renown Clo. Chan F . . . 2D 14
Repton Gdns. H End . . . 1B 34 (in two parts)
Reservoir La. H End . . . 5G 33
Retreat, The. Eastl . . . 3B 16
Retreat, The. Tot . . . 6G 27
Rex Est. Chan F . . . 2F 15
Reynolds Ct. Roms . . . 6D 6
Reynolds Dale. Asht . . . 6D 26
Reynolds Rd. F Oak . . . 3G 17
Reynolds Rd. Sotn . . . 3G 29
Rhinefield Clo. Eastl . . . 5F 17
Rhyme Hall M. Fawl . . . 2H 55
Ribble Clo. Chan F . . . 2F 15
Ribble Ct. Sotn . . . 2C 28
Richards Clo. Black . . . 3F 55
Richards Clo. L Hth . . . 4E 49
Richards Ct. Sotn . . . 2F 29
Richards Ct. W End . . . 1C 32
Richard Taunton Pl. Sotn . . . 1C 30
Richlans Rd. H End . . . 5A 34
Richmond Clo. Cal . . . 2B 26
Richmond Clo. Chan F . . . 4E 9
Richmond Gdns. Sotn . . . 2D 30
Richmond La. Roms . . . 3D 6
Richmond Pk. Ott . . . 1D 10
Richmond Rd. Sotn . . . 5G 29
Richmond St. Sotn . . . 2C 40 (5F 5)
Richville Rd. Sotn . . . 3E 29
Ridding Clo. Sotn . . . 2F 29
Ridge La. Bot . . . 2H 45
Ridgemount Av. Sotn . . . 4B 22
Ridgemount La. Sotn . . . 4B 22
Ridgeway Clo. Chan F . . . 2G 15
Ridgeway Clo. F Oak . . . 1F 17
Ridgeway Wlk. Chan F . . . 2G 15
Ridgewood Clo. Dib . . . 2A 52
Ridings, The. Eastl . . . 5G 17
Ridley Clo. Holb . . . 4C 54
Rigby Rd. Sotn . . . 3D 30
Rimington Gdns. Roms . . . 2E 7
Ring, The. Chilw . . . 2A 22
Ringwood Dri. N Bad . . . 2C 12
Ringwood Rd. Tot . . . 4A 26
Ripplewood. March . . . 4E 39
Ripstone Gdns. Sotn . . . 6D 22
Ritchie Ct. Sotn . . . 1B 42
Riverdene Pl. Sotn . . . 3F 31
River Grn. Hamb . . . 5G 47
Rivermead Clo. Roms . . . 5A 6
Rivermead Ho. Roms . . . 5A 6
River M. Eastl . . . 4D 16
Riversdale Clo. Sotn . . . 5G 41
Riverside. Eastl . . . 4D 16
Riverside Cvn. Pk. Hamb . . . 2G 47
Riverside Ct. Sotn . . . 3F 31
Riverside Gdns. Roms . . . 6A 6
River Vw. Tot . . . 6F 27
River Vw. Ho. Sotn . . . 2F 41
River Vw. Rd. Sotn . . . 1F 31
Riverview Ter. Swanw . . . 5B 44
River Wlk. Sotn . . . 6G 23
R. J. Mitchell Cen, The. Sotn . . . 1E 41
Robard Ho. Burs . . . 4F 43
Robere Ho. Sotn . . . 2G 41
Robert Cecil Av. Sotn . . . 5G 23
Robert Ho. Roms . . . 4C 6
Roberts Rd. Hythe . . . 2D 52
Roberts Rd. Sotn . . . 6H 29 (1A 4)
Roberts Rd. Tot . . . 5F 27
Robert Whitworth Dri. Roms . . . 3C 6
Robin Gdns. Tot . . . 3C 26
Robinia Grn. Sotn . . . 4G 21
Robin's Mdw. Fare . . . 6G 49
Robin Sq. Eastl . . . 5E 15
Rochester St. Sotn . . . 6E 31 (1H 5)
Rockall Clo. Sotn . . . 4C 20
Rockery Clo. Dib . . . 2A 52
Rockleigh Dri. Tot . . . 1D 36
Rockleigh Rd. Sotn . . . 6H 21
Rockram Gdns. Dib . . . 3A 52
Rockstone Ct. Sotn . . . 5C 30
Rockstone La. Sotn . . . 5C 30
Rockstone Pl. Sotn . . . 5B 30
Rodney Ct. Sotn . . . 1C 42
Roewood Clo. Holb . . . 5C 54
Roewood Rd. Holb . . . 5C 54
Rogers Clo. Eastl . . . 3E 17
Rogers Rd. Eastl . . . 3E 17
Roker Way. F Oak . . . 6H 17
Rollestone Rd. Holb . . . 5B 54
Roman Clo. Chan F . . . 6G 9
Roman Dri. Chilw . . . 2A 22
Roman Gdns. Dib P . . . 5B 52
Roman Rd. Chilw & Sotn . . . 1B 22
Roman Rd. Dib P . . . 3A 52
Roman Rd. Hythe . . . 2B 54
Roman Way. Dib P . . . 5B 52
Romford Rd. Wars . . . 1B 50
Romill Clo. W End . . . 6B 24
Romsey By-Pass. Roms . . . 6A 6
Romsey Clo. Eastl . . . 4A 16
Romsey Ct. Sotn . . . 5H 29
Romsey Ind. Est. Roms . . . 4B 6
Romsey Rd. Eastl . . . 4A 16
Romsey Rd. Nurs & Sotn . . . 2A 20
Romsey Rd. Ower & Roms . . . 2A 18
Ronald Pugh Ct. Sotn . . . 5G 23
Rookery Av. White . . . 6F 45
Rookley. Net A . . . 6C 42
Rooksbridge. Dib . . . 3A 52
Rookwood Clo. Eastl . . . 1B 16
Rope Wlk. Hamb . . . 5G 47
Ropley Clo. Sotn . . . 5A 42
Rosebank Clo. Rown . . . 4C 20
Rosebank Lodge. Rown . . . 4C 20
Rosebery Av. Hythe . . . 4E 53
Rosebery Cres. Eastl . . . 1B 16
Rosebrook Ct. Sotn . . . 4G 31
Rose Clo. H End . . . 3A 34
Rose Clo. Hythe . . . 4E 53
Rosedale Av. Roms . . . 5D 6
Rosehip Clo. F Oak . . . 6G 17
Roselands. Sotn . . . 3D 32
Roselands Clo. F Oak . . . 4H 17
Roselands Gdns. Sotn . . . 1C 30
Roseleigh Dri. Tot . . . 5E 27
Rosemary Ct. Tot . . . 4B 26
Rosemary Gdns. H End . . . 6A 34
Rosemary Gdns. White . . . 5H 45
Rosemary Price Ct. H End . . . 3A 34
Rosemoor Gro. Chan F . . . 4D 8
Rosendale Rd. Chan F . . . 3F 15
Rose Rd. Sotn . . . 3C 30
Rose Rd. Tot . . . 5G 27
Rosewall Rd. Sotn . . . 6D 20
Rosewood Gdns. March . . . 4E 39
Rosoman Ct. Sotn . . . 1H 41
Rosoman Rd. Sotn . . . 1H 41
Rossan Av. Wars . . . 1B 50
Ross Gdns. Sotn . . . 1E 29
Rossington Av. Sotn . . . 4H 31
Rossington Way. Sotn . . . 4H 31
Rosslyn Clo. N Bad . . . 3E 13
Ross M. Net A . . . 2A 46
Roston Clo. Sotn . . . 6A 24
Rosyth Rd. Sotn . . . 4H 31
Rotary Ct. Net A . . . 1B 46
Rotary Ho. Sotn . . . 2H 29
Rothbury Clo. Sotn . . . 1A 42
Rothbury Clo. Tot . . . 2D 26
Rother Clo. W End . . . 2B 32
Rother Dale. Sotn . . . 2E 43
Rothsbury Dri. Chan F . . . 1D 14
Rothschild Clo. Sotn . . . 4G 41
Rothville Pl. Chan F . . . 3D 8
Rotterdam Towers. Sotn . . . 5H 41
Roughdown La. Holb . . . 6C 54
Round Copse. Dib . . . 3A 52
Roundhill Clo. Sotn . . . 2A 32
Roundhouse Dri. Tot . . . 5B 26
Routs Way. Rown . . . 2C 20
Rowan Clo. Burs . . . 5F 43
Rowan Clo. Roms . . . 6F 7
Rowan Clo. Sotn . . . 6E 21
Rowan Clo. Tot . . . 5D 26
Rowan Ct. Sotn . . . 1G 29 (SO16)
Rowan Ct. Sotn . . . 2H 41 (SO19)
Rowan Gdns. H End . . . 5B 34
Rowans, The. March . . . 4D 38
Rowborough Rd. Sotn . . . 3H 31
Rowe Asheway. L Hth . . . 4D 48
Rowhill Dri. Dib . . . 3A 52
Rowlands Clo. Chan F . . . 3C 14
Rowlands Wlk. Sotn . . . 1A 32
Rowley Clo. Bot . . . 3D 34
Rowley Ct. Bot . . . 3D 34
Rowley Dri. Bot . . . 3D 34
Rownhams Clo. Rown . . . 3C 20
Rownhams Ct. Sotn . . . 6D 20
Rownhams Ho. Sotn . . . 3C 20
Rownhams La. N Bad & Rown . . . 2D 12
Rownhams La. Rown . . . 4D 20 (in two parts)
Rownhams Pk. Rown . . . 1C 20
Rownhams Rd. N Bad . . . 4E 13
Rownhams Rd. Sotn . . . 1D 28
Rownhams Rd. N. Sotn . . . 3D 20
Rownhams Way. Rown . . . 3C 20
Rowse Clo. Roms . . . 3C 6
Roxburgh Ho. L Hth . . . 4E 49
Royal Ct. Sotn . . . 1D 30
Royal Cres. Rd. Sotn . . . 2D 40 (6G 5)
Royal London Pk. H End . . . 3H 33
Roy's Copse. Dib . . . 2A 52
Royston Av. Eastl . . . 2A 16
Royston Clo. Sotn . . . 1D 30
Royston Ct. Tot . . . 2E 27
Rozel Ct. Sotn . . . 6C 20
Ruby Rd. Sotn . . . 5A 32
Rufford Clo. Eastl . . . 1A 16
Rufus Clo. Chan F . . . 5G 9
Rufus Clo. Rown . . . 3B 20
Rufus Gdns. Tot . . . 4C 26
Rumbridge Gdns. Tot . . . 5G 27
Rumbridge St. Tot . . . 5F 27
Runnymede. W End . . . 2D 32
Runnymede Ct. W End . . . 2D 32
Rushes, The. March . . . 3D 38
Rushington Av. Tot . . . 5F 27
Rushington Bus. Pk. Tot . . . 6E 27
Rushington La. Tot . . . 6E 27
Rushpole Ct. Dib . . . 3A 52
Ruskin Rd. Eastl . . . 3A 16
Rusland Clo. Chan F . . . 6D 8
Russell Ct. March . . . 3D 38
Russell Pl. Sotn . . . 2D 30
Russell St. Sotn . . . 2C 40 (5F 5)
Russet Ho. H End . . . 5H 33
Rustan Clo. F Oak . . . 2G 17
Rustan Clo. H End . . . 5A 34
Rutland Ct. Sotn . . . 4A 32
Rutland Gdns. Burs . . . 4G 43
Rutland Way. Sotn . . . 2A 32
Ruxley Clo. Holb . . . 4C 54
Ryde Ter. Sotn . . . 2D 40 (5H 5)
Rye Clo. Chan F . . . 1B 14
Ryecroft. Fare . . . 5G 49
Rye Dale. Asht . . . 2C 36
Rye Paddock La. Fawl . . . 1H 55
Rylandes Ct. Sotn . . . 6D 20

S

Saddlers Clo. Eastl . . . 1A 16
Sadlers La. Dib P . . . 5E 53
Saffron Ct. L Hth . . . 5C 48
Saffron Way. White . . . 5H 45
St Agathas Rd. Hamb . . . 3G 47

St Alban's Rd.
    Sotn 6D **30** (1G **5**)
St Andrews Bldgs.
    Hamb 5F **47**
St Andrews Clo.
    N Bad 2C **12**
St Andrew's Rd.
    Sotn 6C **30** (1E **5**)
St Anne's Gdns. Sotn 3G **41**
St Anne's Ho. Roms 6B **6**
St Annes M. Sotn 3C **30**
St Anne's Rd. Sotn 3G **41**
St Aubin's Av. Sotn 6A **32**
St Augustine Gdns.
    Sotn 2F **31**
St Austell Clo. Eastl 4E **17**
St Barbe Clo. Roms 6D **6**
St Bernard Ho. Sotn 5F **5**
St Blaize Rd. Roms 4E **7**
St Boniface Ct. N Bad 4E **13**
St Brelade Pl. Sotn 6B **20**
St Catherine's Rd.
    Eastl 2A **16**
St Catherine's Rd.
    Sotn 2F **31**
St Catherines Vw.
    H End 5G **33**
St Christophers Clo.
    N Bad 3D **12**
St Clements Clo. Roms 4B **6**
St Cuthbert's Clo.
    L Hth 3F **49**
St Cuthbert's La. L Hth . . .3F **49**
St Davids Clo. Cal 2C **26**
St David's Ct. N Bad 4E **13**
St Davids Rd. L Hth 4D **48**
St Denys Rd. Sotn 2D **30**
St Edmund Clo. Fare 6F **49**
St Edmunds Rd. Sotn 3F **29**
    (in two parts)
St Edwards Rd. Net A 6B **42**
St Elizabeths Av. Sotn 4B **32**
St Evox Clo. Rown 4D **20**
St Francis Av. Sotn 3B **32**
St Francis Clo. Black 6E **55**
St Francis Rd. Black 6E **55**
St Gabriel's Rd. Sotn 4B **32**
St George Clo. Burs 3F **43**
St George's Ct. N Bad 4E **13**
St Georges Rd. L Hth 4D **48**
St George's Ter.
    Sotn 1C **40** (4F **5**)
St Helena Gdns. Sotn 6H **23**
St Helens M. Eastl 2G **17**
    (off Stubbington Way)
St Helier Pl. Sotn 6C **20**
St James Ho.
    Sotn 2C **40** (5F **5**)
St James Pk. Cvn. Pk.
    Chan F 4C **8**
St James Rd. W End 2E **33**
St James's Clo. Sotn 2G **29**
St James's Pk. Rd.
    Sotn 1G **29**
St James's Rd. Sotn 2G **29**
St John's Cen. H End 5H **33**
St John's Cen. N Bad 2E **13**
St Johns Clo. Rown 2C **20**
St Johns Ct. March 4D **38**
St John's Ct. N Bad 4F **13**
St Johns Dri. March 4C **38**
St Johns Gdns. Roms 4C **6**
St John's Glebe. Rown 3C **20**
St Johns M. L Hth 4G **49**
St John's Rd. Eastl 3B **16**
St John's Rd. H End 1G **43**
St John's Rd. L Hth 5F **49**
St Johns St. Hythe 2E **53**

St Joseph Clo. L Hth 4F **49**
St Julien's Hospital Almshouses.
    Sotn 6E **5**
St Lawrence Clo.
    H End 1B **34**
St Lawrence Rd. Eastl 3A **16**
St Lawrence Rd.
    Sotn 2D **40** (6G **5**)
St Lukes Clo. H End 2A **34**
St Margarets Clo.
    Sotn 4B **32**
St Margarets Ho. Sotn 3B **30**
    (off Hulse Rd.)
St Margaret's Rd.
    Eastl 3C **16**
St Marks Clo. Chan F 4H **9**
St Martins Clo. Eastl 3D **16**
St Martins Clo. Sotn 6C **20**
St Mary's. Roms 6B **6**
    (off Banning St.)
St Mary's Chu. Clo.
    Sotn 5F **23**
St Mary's Pl.
    Sotn 1C **40** (4F **5**)
St Mary's Rd. Eastl 3D **16**
St Mary's Rd. Net A 1C **46**
St Mary's Rd.
    Sotn 5C **30** (1F **5**)
St Mary St.
    Sotn 6D **30** (2G **5**)
St Matthews Clo.
    Sotn 6D **30** (1F **5**)
St Michaels Clo. Black 4F **55**
St Michael's Rd. L Hth 5D **48**
St Michaels Rd. Tot 2F **27**
St Michael's Sq. Sotn 5D **4**
St Michael's St.
    Sotn 2B **40** (5D **4**)
St Monica Rd. Sotn 2A **42**
St Patrick's Ct. N Bad 4E **13**
St Pauls Rd. Sar G 1C **48**
St Peters Clo. Curd 3H **35**
St Phillip's Way. Sotn 4B **32**
St Simon Clo. L Hth 4F **49**
St Swithuns Clo. Cram 3G **7**
St Swithuns Ct. Sotn 5C **30**
    (off Cranbury Pl.)
St Thomas Ct. Eastl 2G **17**
St Tristan Clo. L Hth 5F **49**
St Vigor Way. Col C 4F **11**
St Winifred's Rd. Sotn 1G **29**
Salcombe Clo. Chan F 3D **14**
Salcombe Cres. Tot 5E **27**
Salcombe Rd. Sotn 4G **29**
Salcombe Rd. Tot 5E **27**
Salem St. Sotn 2G **29**
Salerno Ho. Roms 5E **7**
    (off Chambers Av.)
Salerno Rd. Sotn 5G **21**
Salisbury Clo. Eastl 3B **16**
Salisbury Ct. Eastl 3B **16**
Salisbury Rd. E Wel 6A **6**
Salisbury Rd. Sotn 6C **22**
Salisbury Rd. Arc. Tot 4F **27**
Salisbury St. Sotn 5B **30**
Salmon Dri. Eastl 5F **17**
Salona Clo. Chan F 6H **9**
Salterns La. Burs 1G **47**
Salterns La. Fawl 1H **55**
Saltmarsh Rd.
    Sotn 2D **40** (6H **5**)
Salt Mead. Sotn 1E **31**
Salwey Rd. Bot 6B **34**
Sampan Clo. Wars 6C **48**
Sandell Ct. Sotn 4D **22**
Sandhurst Rd. Sotn 5A **30**
Sandilands Way. Hythe 5E **53**
Sandlewood Clo. Cal 3C **26**

Sandown Rd. Sotn 2F **29**
Sandpiper Clo. March 4C **38**
Sandpiper Rd. Sotn 4E **21**
Sandringham Clo.
    Chan F 3B **14**
Sandringham Ct. Sotn 5E **29**
    (off Regents Pk. Rd.)
Sandringham Rd.
    Sotn 2G **31**
Sandycroft. Wars 6B **48**
Sandy La. F Oak 5H **17**
Sandy La. N Bad 2F **13**
Sandy La. Roms 1D **6**
Saracens Rd. Chan F 6H **9**
Sarisbury Ct. L Hth 3A **48**
Sarisbury Ga. Park G 2F **49**
Sarnia Ct. Sotn 5C **20**
Sarum Ho. Tot 2D **26**
Sarum Rd. Chan F 1G **15**
Satchell La. Hamb 1E **47**
Saturn Clo. Sotn 5C **20**
Savernake Clo. Roms 3E **7**
Saville Clo. Eastl 2D **16**
Saxholm Clo. Sotn 3B **22**
Saxholm Dale. Sotn 3B **22**
Saxholm Way. Sotn 3B **22**
Saxon Clo. Wars 6C **48**
Saxon Gdns. H End 6G **33**
Saxon Ho. Sotn 5E **31**
Saxon Rd. Black 4F **55**
Saxon Rd. Sotn 6H **29**
Saxon Wlk. Chan F 2G **15**
Saxon Way. Roms 5E **7**
Sayers Rd. Eastl 5D **16**
Scantabout Av. Chan F 6G **9**
School Clo. Chan F 3C **14**
School La. Chan F 3C **14**
School La. Hamb 6G **47**
School Pl. Sotn 1G **41**
School Rd. Burs 4G **43**
School Rd. Fawl 2G **55**
School Rd. Hythe 2E **53**
School Rd. Roms 3F **7**
School Rd. Tot 5G **27**
Schooner Way. Wars 6C **48**
Scotland Clo. F Oak 2H **17**
Scott Clo. Col C 5G **11**
Scotter Rd. Eastl 4D **16**
Scotter Sq. Eastl 4D **16**
Scott Rd. Eastl 5H **15**
Scott Rd. Sotn 4H **41**
Scullards La.
    Sotn 1B **40** (3D **4**)
Seacombe Grn. Sotn 2B **28**
Seafield Rd. Sotn 1B **28**
Seaford Clo. Burs 4F **43**
Seagarth Clo. Sotn 6H **21**
Seagarth La. Sotn 6H **21**
Sea Rd. Sotn 2F **41**
Seaton Clo. W End 2C **32**
Sea View Est. Net A 2B **46**
Seaward Gdns. Sotn 1G **41**
Seaward Rd. Sotn 1G **41**
Second Av. Sotn 3B **28**
Second St. Hythe 6H **53**
Sedbergh Ho. Sotn 2B **28**
Sedbergh Rd. Sotn 2B **28**
Sedgefield Clo. Tot 3C **26**
Sedge Mead. Net A 2B **46**
Sedgemead Ct. Net A 2B **46**
Sedgewick Ct. Eastl 4D **16**
Sedgewick Rd. Eastl 4D **16**
Sedgewick Rd. Sotn 6C **32**
Segensworth E. Ind. Est.
    Fare 2H **49**
    (in two parts)
Segensworth N. Ind. Est.
    Fare 2H **49**

Segensworth Rd. Fare 3H **49**
Segensworth W. Ind. Est.
    Seg W 2G **49**
Selborne Av. Sotn 3C **32**
Selborne Ct. Roms 3F **7**
Selborne Dri. Eastl 3A **16**
Selborne Rd. Tot 2D **26**
Selborne Wlk. Sotn 3C **32**
Selhurst Way. F Oak 3F **17**
Sellwood Rd. Net A 1C **46**
Selsdon Av. Roms 4E **7**
Selsey Clo. Sotn 6C **20**
Selwyn Gdns. Eastl 2A **16**
Sembal Ho. Sotn 5A **30**
    (off Handell Ter.)
Sengana Clo. Bot 5C **34**
Senlac Rd. Roms 5E **7**
September Clo.
    W End 2D **32**
Serle Clo. Tot 4B **26**
Serle Gdns. Tot 5D **26**
Setters Clo. Col C 5F **11**
Settle Clo. Sotn 3F **29**
Severn Rd. Sotn 3C **28**
Severn Way. W End 1D **32**
Seward Ri. Roms 4F **7**
Seward Rd. Hythe 3F **53**
Seymour Clo. Cal 2C **26**
Seymour Clo. Chan F 2G **15**
Seymour Clo. Sotn 6G **21**
Seymour Ho. Sotn 6H **21**
Seymour La. N Bad 3D **12**
Seymour Rd. Sotn 6G **21**
Shaftesbury Av.
    Chan F 3E **15**
Shaftesbury Av. Sotn 2D **30**
Shakespeare Av. Sotn 3D **30**
Shakespeare Bus. Cen.
    Eastl 3B **16**
Shakespeare Dri. Tot 1D **26**
Shakespeare Rd. Eastl 2H **15**
Shalcombe. Net A 6C **42**
Shalden Clo. Sotn 5G **21**
Shales Rd. Sotn 4B **32**
Shamblehurst La.
    H End 1A **34**
Shamblehurst La. N.
    H End 1B **34**
Shamblehurst La. S.
    H End 3A **34**
Shamrock Quay. Sotn 6F **31**
Shamrock Rd. Sotn 2F **41**
Shamrock Vs. Sotn 2E **31**
Shamrock Way. Hythe 1E **53**
Shanklin Cres. Sotn 2A **30**
Shanklin Rd. Sotn 1H **29**
Shannon Ho. Sotn 6E **31**
    (off Kent St.)
Shannon Way. Chan F 1C **14**
Shapton Clo. Holb 4B **54**
Sharon Rd. W End 1C **32**
    (in two parts)
Shaw Clo. Tot 4D **26**
Shaw Clo. W End 1A **32**
Shawford Clo. Sotn 5A **22**
Shawford Clo. Tot 4B **26**
Shayer Rd. Sotn 2G **29**
Shears Rd. Eastl 4E **17**
Sheffield Clo. Eastl 2D **16**
Sheldrake Gdns. Sotn 4F **21**
Shell Ct. March 3D **38**
Shellcroft. Wars 1B **50**
Shelley Ct.
    Sotn 6A **30** (1B **4**)
Shelley Rd. Eastl 6H **15**
Shelley Rd. Sotn 5D **32**
Shelley Rd. Tot 1D **26**
Shepherd Clo. Highc 4G **5**

Shepherdshey Rd. *Cal* 2B **26**
Shepherds Purse Clo.
   L Hth 5C **48**
Shepherds Way. *Nurs* . . .4A **20**
Sherborne Ct. *Eastl* 1H **15**
Sherborne Rd. *Sotn* 1D **30**
Sherborne Way. *H End* . . .5A **34**
Sherecroft Gdns. *Bot* 4F **35**
Sherfield Ho. *Sotn* 5A **30**
Sheridan Clo. *Sotn* 6D **32**
Sheridan Gdns. *Tot* 4D **26**
Sheridan Gdns. *White* 5G **45**
Sherley Grn. *Burs* 4G **43**
Sherringham Clo.
   Fawl 2H **55**
Sherwood Av. *H End* 1A **44**
Sherwood Clo. *Sotn* 6A **22**
Sherwood Gdns.
   Sar G 3C **48**
Sherwood Rd. *Chan F* 4G **9**
Sherwood Way. *Black* 6E **55**
Shetland Clo. *Tot* 3B **26**
Shetland Ri. *White* 6F **45**
Shinwell Ct. *Sotn* 2F **29**
Shipyard Est., The.
   Hythe 2F **53**
Shire Clo. *White* 6F **45**
Shires, The. *H End* 5G **33**
Shires Wlk. *Tot* 4B **26**
Shirley Av. *Sotn* 3G **29**
Shirley High St. *Sotn* 3F **29**
Shirley Pk. Rd. *Sotn* 3F **29**
Shirley Rd.
   Sotn 3G **29** (1A **4**)
Shirley Towers. *Sotn* 3G **29**
Shoblands Way. Hythe 5E **53**
   (off Sandilands Way)
Sholing Rd. *Sotn* 1G **41**
Shooters Hill Clo.
   Sotn 2B **42**
Shorefield Rd. *March* 3D **38**
Shore Rd. *Hythe* 2F **53**
Shore Rd. *Wars* 6H **47**
Shorewell. *Net A* 6C **42**
Shorewood Clo. *Wars* 6D **48**
Short Hill. *Roms* 2F **7**
Short's Rd. *F Oak* 5H **17**
Shotters Hill Clo.
   W End 2D **32**
Shraveshill Clo. *Tot* 2D **26**
Shrubland Clo. *Sotn* 3B **32**
Siddal Clo. *Sotn* 2C **42**
Sidings, The. *Net A* 2D **46**
Silkin Gdns. *Tot* 5D **26**
Silver Birch Clo. *Sotn* 1C **42**
Silver Birches. *Burs* 5F **43**
Silverdale Ct. *Sotn* 4A **30**
Silverdale Rd. *Sotn* 4A **30**
Silvers End. *Dib P* 5E **53**
Silvers Wood. *Cal* 2C **26**
Silverweed Clo. *Fare* 6B **8**
Silverweed Ct. *L Hth* 5C **48**
Simmons Clo. *H End* 3A **34**
Simnel St.
   Sotn 2B **40** (5D **4**)
Simon Way. *Sotn* 4E **33**
Sinclair Rd. *Sotn* 4E **21**
Singleton Way. *Tot* 3B **26**
Sir Christopher Clo.
   Hythe 2F **53**
Sirdar Rd. *Sotn* 6E **23**
Sir Galahad Rd.
   Chan F 4E **9**
Sir George's Rd. *Sotn* 5H **29**
Siskin Clo. *Sotn* 4E **21**
Sissinghurst Clo. *Sotn* . . .4A **42**
Six Dials. *Sotn* . . .6C **30** (2F **5**)

Six Oaks Rd. *N Bad* 3E **13**
Sixpenny Clo. *Fare* 6E **49**
Sizer Way. *Dib* 3A **52**
Skintle Grn. *Col C* 5F **11**
Skipper Clo. *March* 2E **39**
Skipton Rd. *Chan F* 3F **15**
Skys Wood Rd. *Chan F* . . .1B **14**
Slades Hill. *Black* 3F **55**
Slater Clo. *Tot* 3B **26**
Sloane Av. *Holb* 4D **54**
Sloane Ct. *Holb* 4D **54**
Sloe Tree Clo. *L Hth* 5G **49**
Slowhill Copse. *March* 2C **38**
Smith Clo. *Fawl* 3F **55**
Smithe Clo. *Eastl* 4A **16**
Smith Gro. *H End* 6A **34**
Smiths Fld. *Roms* 3D **6**
Smiths Quay. *Sotn* 1E **41**
Smythe Rd. *Sotn* 2D **42**
Snapdragon Clo.
   L Hth 5D **48**
Snellgrove Clo. *Cal* 1C **26**
Snellgrove Pl. *Cal* 1C **26**
Snowdrop Clo. *L Hth* 5D **48**
Solent Av. *Sotn* 5E **33**
Solent Breezes Cvn. Site.
   Wars 4C **50**
Solent Bus. Cen. *Sotn* 5F **29**
Solent Bus. Pk. *White* 6H **45**
Solent Clo. *Chan F* 1G **15**
Solent Dri. *Hythe* 2D **52**
Solent Dri. *Wars* 3B **50**
Solent Homes. *Sotn* 5E **33**
Solent Ind. Cen. *Sotn* 5G **29**
Solent Ind. Est. *H End* 2A **34**
Solent Meadows.
   Hamb 6G **47**
Solent Rd. *Dib P* 6C **52**
Solent Rd.
   W Dock 1A **40** (4A **4**)
Solway Ho. *Sotn* 5E **31**
   (off Kent St.)
Somborne Ho. *Sotn* 4H **41**
Somerford Clo. *Sotn* 5A **32**
Somerset Av. *Sotn* 4C **32**
Somerset Ct. *Sotn* 5G **29**
Somerset Cres. *Chan F* . . .4F **15**
Somerset Rd. *Sotn* 1E **31**
Somerset Ter. *Sotn* 5G **29**
Somerton Av. *Sotn* 4B **32**
Sommers Ct. *Sotn* 2F **41**
Sopwith Way. *Swanw* 5D **44**
Sorrel Dri. *White* 6H **45**
Sorrell Clo. *L Hth* 5D **48**
Sorrell Clo. *Roms* 3F **7**
Southampton (International)
   Airport. *Sotn* 2A **24**
Southampton Rd.
   Eastl 1A **24**
Southampton Rd.
   Hythe 2C **52**
Southampton Rd.
   Park G & Fare 2F **49**
   (in two parts)
Southampton Rd.
   Roms 5C **6**
Southampton St. *Sotn* 5B **30**
South Av. *Hythe* 2E **55**
Southbourne Av. *Holb* 4C **54**
Southbrook Rd.
   Sotn 6A **30** (2A **4**)
Southcliff Rd. *Sotn* 4C **30**
South Clo. *Roms* 3F **7**
South Ct. *Hamb* 5E **47**
South Ct. *Sotn* 3F **29**
Southdale Ct. *Chan F* 1E **15**
Southdene Rd. *Chan F* 2E **15**
S. East Cres. *Sotn* 1A **42**

S. East Rd. *Sotn* 1A **42**
Southern Gdns. *Tot* 4E **27**
Southern Rd.
   Sotn 1A **40** (3A **4**)
Southern Rd. *W End* 3D **32**
South Front. *Roms* 5C **6**
South Front.
   Sotn 1C **40** (3F **5**)
S. Hampshire Ind. Pk.
   Tot 1D **26**
S. Millers Dale. *Chan F* . . .6D **8**
S. Mill Rd. *Sotn* 4D **28**
South Pde. *Tot* 3F **27**
South Rd. *Sotn* 3E **31**
South St. *Eastl* 1A **24**
South St. *Hythe* 3E **53**
S. View Rd. *Sotn* 3H **29**
Southwood Gdns.
   L Hth 4D **48**
Sovereign Clo. *Tot* 3C **26**
Sovereign Cres. *Fare* 6E **49**
Sovereign Dri.
   H End & Bot 5B **34**
Sovereign Way. *Eastl* 1H **15**
Sowden Clo. *H End* 4H **33**
Spalding Rd. *Sotn* 6E **33**
Sparrowgrove. *Ott* 1C **10**
Sparrow Sq. *Eastl* 5F **15**
Sparsholt Rd. *Sotn* 5H **41**
Spear Rd. *Sotn* 3C **30**
Speedwell Clo. *Chan F* . . .2D **14**
Speedwell Clo. *L Hth* 5D **48**
Speggs Wlk. *H End* 5A **34**
Spencer Rd. *Eastl* 5G **15**
Spencer Rd. *Sotn* 5D **32**
Spenser Clo. *Wars* 1B **50**
Spicer's Hill. *Tot* 6E **27**
Spicer's Way. *Tot* 5E **27**
Spindlewood Clo.
   Sotn 3C **22**
Spindlewood Way.
   March 5D **38**
Spinney Dale. *Hythe* 4F **53**
Spinney Gdns. *Hythe* 4F **53**
Spinney, The. *Cal* 2C **26**
Spinney, The. *Eastl* 5G **17**
Spinney, The. *Sotn* 3B **22**
Spinney Wlk. *Sotn* 6H **23**
Spitfire Ct. *Sotn* 2E **41**
Spitfire Loop. *Sotn* 2H **23**
Spitfire Quay. *Sotn* 1E **41**
Spitfire Way. *Hamb* 5F **47**
Spring Clo. *F Oak* 2F **17**
Spring Clo. *Sotn* 1H **41**
Spring Ct. *Sotn* 6A **30** (1A **4**)
Spring Cres. *Sotn* 3D **30**
Springdale Ct. *Tot* 4F **27**
Springfield Av. *Holb* 4D **54**
Springfield Ct. *Sotn* 3H **41**
Springfield Dri. *Tot* 5E **27**
Springfield Gro. *Holb* 4D **54**
Springfields Clo. *Col C* 4F **11**
Spring Firs. *Sotn* 2H **41**
Springford Clo. *Sotn* 5F **21**
Springford Cres. *Sotn* 6F **21**
Springford Gdns. *Sotn* 5F **21**
Springford Rd. *Sotn* 6F **21**
Spring Gdns. *N Bad* 2D **12**
Spring Gro. *Burs* 4G **43**
Springhill Rd. *Chan F* 1E **15**
Spring Hills. *Sotn* 6C **32**
Spring Ho. Clo. *Col C* 4G **11**
Spring La. *Col C* 4F **11**
Spring La. *Eastl* 3D **16**
Spring Pl. *Roms* 5B **6**
Spring Rd. *Hythe* 2E **53**
Spring Rd. *Sar G* 1D **48**
Spring Rd. *Sotn* 5H **31**

Spruce Clo. *Wars* 1B **50**
Spruce Dri. *Sotn* 6E **33**
Spruce Dri. *Tot* 3B **26**
Square, The. *F Oak* 2F **17**
Square, The. *Fawl* 2H **55**
Square, The. *Hamb* 5G **47**
Squires Wlk. *Sotn* 4G **41**
Squirrel Clo. *Eastl* 5F **17**
Squirrel Dri. *Sotn* 2A **42**
Squirrels Wlk. *Dib P* 4D **53**
Stable Clo. *Fare* 5H **49**
Stables, The. *L Hth* 5E **49**
Stafford Rd. *Sotn* 4H **29**
Stagbrake Clo. *Holb* 5B **54**
Stag Clo. *Eastl* 5F **17**
Stag Gates. *Black* 4E **55**
Stainer Clo. *Sotn* 2D **42**
Staith Clo. *Sotn* 6C **32**
Stalybridge Clo.
   Park G 1E **49**
Stamford Way. *F Oak* 3F **17**
Stanbridge La. *Roms* 1A **6**
Standen Rd. *Sotn* 4A **20**
Standford St.
   Sotn 1D **40** (4H **5**)
Stanford Ct. *Sotn* 2D **42**
Stanier Way. *H End* 1A **34**
Stanley Rd. *Holb* 4D **54**
Stanley Rd. *Sotn* 2E **31**
Stanley Rd. *Tot* 2D **26**
Stannington Cres. *Tot* 3F **27**
Stannington Way. *Tot* 3F **27**
Stanstead Rd. *Eastl* 3H **15**
Stanton Rd. *Sotn* 4D **28**
Stanton Rd. Ind. Est.
   Sotn 4E **29**
Stapleford Clo. *Roms* 3E **7**
Staplehurst Clo. *Sotn* 4B **42**
Staplewood La. *March* 6H **37**
   (in two parts)
Starling Sq. *Eastl* 5F **15**
Station Hill. *Burs* 6H **43**
Station Hill. *Curd* 4G **35**
Station La. *Chan F* 1E **15**
Station M. *Roms* 4C **6**
Station Rd. *Burs* 5H **43**
Station Rd. *Net A* 2B **46**
Station Rd. *Nurs* 4G **19**
Station Rd. *Park G* 2E **49**
Station Rd. *Roms* 5B **6**
Station Rd. *Sotn* 3A **28**
   (SO15)
Station Rd. *Sotn* 2H **41**
   (SO19)
Station Rd. N. *Tot* 4H **27**
Station Rd. S. *Tot* 4H **27**
Steele Clo. *Chan F* 3F **15**
Steep Clo. *Sotn* 3C **32**
Steeple Way. *Fare* 4H **49**
Steinbeck Clo. *White* 5G **45**
Stenbury Way. *Net A* 6C **42**
Stephens Ct. Roms 6B **6**
   (off Middlebridge St.)
Stephenson Rd. *Tot* 6D **18**
Stephenson Way.
   H End 6H **33**
Steuart Rd. *Sotn* 4F **31**
Steventon Rd. *Sotn* 4C **32**
Stewart Ho. *Chan F* 4E **9**
Stinchar Dri. *Chan F* 2C **14**
Stirling Clo. *Tot* 3G **27**
Stirling Cres. *H End* 2A **34**
Stirling Cres. *Tot* 3G **27**
Stirling Wlk. *Roms* 5B **6**
Stockholm Dri. *H End* 6A **34**
Stocklands. *Tot* 1C **26**
Stockley Clo. *Holb* 5C **54**
Stockton Clo. *H End* 4B **34**

Stoddart Av. *Sotn* 5H **31**
Stoke Comn. Rd. *Eastl* . . .2E **17**
Stoke Heights. *F Oak* 4H **17**
Stoke Pk. Dri. *Eastl* 3D **16**
Stoke Pk. Rd. *Eastl* 3D **16**
Stoke Rd. *Sotn* 2E **29**
Stokesay Clo. *Hythe* 6E **53**
Stoke Wood Clo. *F Oak* . .5G **17**
Stonechat Dri. *Tot* 3B **26**
Stone Crop Clo. *L Hth* . . .5D **48**
Stoneham Cemetery Rd.
  Sotn 5H **23**
Stoneham Clo. *Sotn* 4F **23**
Stoneham Gdns. *Burs* . . .4F **43**
Stoneham La.
  Eastl & Sotn 6G **15**
Stoneham Way. *Sotn* 5F **23**
Stonymoor Clo. *Holb* 5C **54**
Stour Clo. *W End* 6B **24**
Stourvale Gdns.
  Chan F 2F **15**
Stowe Clo. *H End* 2B **34**
Stragwyne Clo. *N Bad* 2D **12**
Straight Mile, The.
  Roms 3G **7**
Strand. *Sotn* 1C **40** (4E **5**)
Strategic Pk. *H End* 4F **33**
Stratfield Dri. *Chan F* 4D **8**
Stratford Ct. *Sotn* 4C **22**
Stratford Pl. *Eastl* 3B **16**
Stratton Rd. *Sotn* 2G **29**
Strawberry Fields.
  H End 5G **33**
Strawberry Hill. *L Hth* 4D **48**
Strawberry Mead.
  F Oak 6H **17**
Streamleaze. *Fare* 5G **49**
Street End. *N Bad* 2F **13**
Strides Way. *Tot* 4B **26**
Strongs Clo. *Roms* 4E **7**
Stroudley Way. *H End* . . .1B **34**
Stuart Bridgewater Ho.
  Sotn 4A **32**
Stubbington Way.
  F Oak 2G **17**
Stubbs Drove. *H End* 4B **34**
Stubbs Rd. *Sotn* 3C **42**
Studland Clo. *Sotn* 2B **28**
Studland Rd. *Sotn* 3B **28**
Studley Av. *Holb* 4C **54**
Sturminster Ho. *Sotn* 2D **28**
Suffolk Av. *Sotn* 4H **29**
Suffolk Clo. *Chan F* 5E **15**
Suffolk Dri. *Chan F* 4E **15**
Suffolk Dri. *White* 6F **45**
Suffolk Grn. *Chan F* 5E **15**
Sullivan Rd. *Sotn* 1D **31**
Summerfield Gdns.
  Sotn 4F **23**
Summerfields. *L Hth* 6F **49**
Summerlands Rd.
  F Oak 2F **17**
Summers St. *Sotn* 5E **31**
Summit Way. *Sotn* 2H **31**
Sunningdale. *Hythe* 3D **52**
Sunningdale Clo. *Eastl* 5F **17**
Sunningdale Gdns.
  Sotn 4B **32**
Sunningdale Mobile Home Pk.
  Col C 4F **11**
Sunnyfield Ri. *Burs* 4G **43**
Sunny Way. *Tot* 4F **27**
Sunset Av. *Tot* 3E **27**
Sunset Rd. *Tot* 3E **27**
Sunvale Clo. *Sotn* 2B **42**
Surbiton Rd. *Eastl* 2B **16**
Surrey Clo. *Tot* 6D **26**
Surrey Ct. *Chan F* 4F **15**

Surrey Ct. *Sotn* 5G **29**
Surrey Rd. *Chan F* 4E **15**
Surrey Rd. *Sotn* 3F **41**
Surry Ho. *Chan F* 4F **15**
Sussex Rd. *Chan F* 4F **15**
Sussex Rd.
  Sotn 6C **30** (3E **5**)
Sutherland Clo. *Roms* 3E **7**
Sutherland Rd. *Sotn* 4D **20**
Sutherlands Ct.
  Chan F 1E **15**
Sutherlands Way.
  Chan F 6D **8**
Sutton Rd. *Tot* 2E **27**
Swale Dri. *Chan F* 6C **8**
Swallow Clo. *Tot* 5C **26**
Swallow Sq. *Eastl* 5F **15**
Swanage Clo. *Sotn* 1G **41**
Swan Cen., The. *Eastl* 5B **16**
Swan Clo. *Swanw* 6B **44**
Swan Ct. *Burs* 5A **44**
Swanley Clo. *Eastl* 2A **16**
Swanmore Av. *Sotn* 2B **42**
Swan Quay. *Sotn* 3F **31**
Swanton Gdns. *Chan F* . . .6D **8**
Swanwick Bus. Cen.
  Lwr S 6B **44**
Swanwick La. *Swanw* 5A **44**
Swanwick Shore Rd.
  Swanw 6B **44**
Swaythling Rd. *W End* . . .6B **24**
Sweethills Cres. *White* . . .5F **45**
Swift Clo. *Eastl* 5F **15**
Swift Gdns. *Sotn* 4F **41**
Swift Hollow. *Sotn* 4F **41**
Swift Rd. *Sotn* 4F **41**
Swincombe Ri. *W End* . . .2B **32**
Sycamore Av. *Chan F* 4E **9**
Sycamore Clo. *Burs* 5F **43**
Sycamore Clo. *Fare* 6G **49**
Sycamore Clo. *N Bad* 2D **12**
Sycamore Clo. *Roms* 6F **7**
Sycamore Dri. *Holb* 3B **54**
Sycamore Rd. *Hythe* 3D **52**
Sycamore Rd. *Sotn* 1E **29**
Sycamores, The.
  Hythe 2E **53**
Sycamore Wlk. *Bot* 4E **35**
Sydmanton Clo. *Roms* 6D **6**
Sydney Av. *Hamb* 4E **47**
Sydney Rd. *Eastl* 3D **16**
Sydney Rd. *Sotn* 2F **29**
Sylvan Av. *Sotn* 5C **32**
Sylvan Dri. *N Bad* 3D **12**
Sylvan La. *Hamb* 6G **47**
Sylvans, The. *Dib P* 3B **52**
Sylvia Cres. *Tot* 2E **27**
Symes Rd. *Roms* 5E **7**
Symonds Clo. *Chan F* 3F **15**

■ **T** ■

Tadburn Clo. *Chan F* 2F **15**
Tadburn Clo. *Roms* 5D **6**
Tadburn Grn. Roms 6B **6**
  (off Banning St.)
Tadburn Rd. *Roms* 5D **6**
Tadfield Cres. *Roms* 5D **6**
Tadfield Rd. *Roms* 5D **6**
Talbot Clo. *Sotn* . . .2C **40** (6E **5**)
  (SO14)
Talbot Clo. *Sotn* 5B **22**
  (SO16)
Talbot Rd. *Dib P* 5B **52**
Talisman Bus. Cen.
  Park G 2F **49**
Talland Rd. *Fare* 6F **49**
Tamar Gdns. *W End* 1B **32**

Tamar Gro. *Hythe* 3C **52**
Tamarisk Gdns. *Sotn* 3G **31**
Tamarisk Rd. *H End* 4H **33**
Tamella Rd. *Bot* 5C **34**
Tamorisk Dri. *Tot* 5C **26**
Tanglewood. *March* 4E **39**
Tangmere Dri. *Sotn* 5D **20**
Tanhouse Clo. *H End* 6B **34**
Tanhouse La. *Bot* 6B **34**
Tankerville Rd. *Sotn* 2F **41**
Tanner's Brook Way.
  Sotn 5D **28**
Tanners Rd. *N Bad* 4E **13**
Tanners, The. *Fare* 1G **51**
Tansy Mdw. *Chan F* 3B **14**
Tanyards, The. *Chan F* 4D **8**
Taplin Dri. *H End* 3A **34**
Taranto Rd. *Sotn* 5G **21**
Tasman Clo. *Ocn V* 3D **40**
Tasman Ct. *Sotn* 3D **40**
Tate Ct. *Sotn* 3A **28**
Tate M. *Sotn* 3A **28**
Tate Rd. *Sotn* 3A **28**
Tates Rd. *Hythe* 3F **53**
  (in two parts)
Tatwin Clo. *Sotn* 6D **32**
Tatwin Cres. *Sotn* 6D **32**
Taunton Dri. *Sotn* 4B **32**
Tavell's Clo. *March* 4C **38**
Tavell's La. March 4B **38**
Taverners Clo. *Sotn* 2D **42**
Tavistock Clo. *Roms* 3E **7**
Tavy Clo. *Chan F* 1D **14**
Taw Dri. *Chan F* 6D **8**
Taylor Clo. *Sotn* 4F **41**
Teachers Way. *Holb* 4B **54**
Teal Clo. *Tot* 4C **26**
Tebourba Way. *Curd* 4H **35**
Tebourba Way. *Sotn* 4C **28**
Tedder Rd. *Sotn* 3A **32**
Tedder Way. *Tot* 4D **26**
Tees Clo. *Chan F* 6C **8**
Tees Farm Rd. *Col C* 5F **11**
Tees Grn. *Col C* 5F **11**
Telegraph Rd. *W End* 3E **33**
Telford Gdns. *H End* 1B **34**
Telford Way. *Fare* 2G **49**
Teme Cres. *Sotn* 2C **28**
Teme Rd. *Sotn* 3C **28**
Templars Mede.
  Chan F 4D **14**
Templars Way. *Chan F* . . .3B **14**
Templecombe Rd.
  Eastl 6F **17**
Temple Gdns. *Sotn* 3H **41**
Temple Rd. *Sotn* 3H **41**
Tenby Clo. *Sotn* 3A **32**
Tenby Dri. *Chan F* 3C **14**
Tench Way. *Roms* 4C **6**
Tennyson Clo. *Holb* 3B **54**
Tennyson Rd. *Eastl* 6H **15**
Tennyson Rd. *Sotn* 3D **30**
Tennyson Rd. *Tot* 1D **26**
Tenterton Av. *Sotn* 4B **42**
Terminus Ter.
  Sotn 2D **40** (6F **5**)
Tern Clo. *Hythe* 4F **53**
Terrier Clo. *H End* 6H **25**
Terriote Clo. *Chan F* 6E **9**
Testbourne Av. *Tot* 4D **26**
Testbourne Clo. *Tot* 4D **26**
Testbourne Rd. *Tot* 4D **26**
Testlands Av. *Nurs* 3B **20**
Test La. *Sotn* 6H **19**
Test Mills. *Roms* 4A **6**
Test Rd. *E Dock* 4C **40**
Test Valley Bus. Pk.
  N Bad 1E **13**

Test Valley Small Bus. Cen.
  Sotn 1H **27**
Testwood Av. *Tot* 2E **27**
Testwood Cres. *Tot* 1D **26**
Testwood La. *Tot* 3F **27**
Testwood Pl. *Tot* 3G **27**
Testwood Rd. *Sotn* 5F **29**
Tetney Clo. *Sotn* 6C **20**
Teviot Ho. Sotn 5E **31**
  (off York Clo.)
Teviot Rd. *Chan F* 2C **14**
Thackeray Rd. *Sotn* 3D **30**
Thacking Grn. *Col C* 5F **11**
Thames Clo. *W End* 6B **24**
Thetford Gdns. *Chan F* . . .5C **8**
Thicket, The. *Roms* 6F **7**
Third Av. *Sotn* 4C **28**
Thirlmere. *Eastl* 5H **15**
Thirlmere Rd. *Sotn* 1C **28**
Thirlstane Firs. *Chan F* . . .3D **14**
Thistle Rd. *Chan F* 2B **14**
Thistle Rd. *H End* 5H **33**
Thomas Clo. *Tot* 5D **26**
Thomas Lewis Way.
  Sotn 3D **30**
  (SO14 & SO17)
Thomas Lewis Way.
  Sotn 2E **31**
  (SO17 & SO18)
Thomas Rd. *N Bad* 3E **13**
Thornbury Av. *Black* 5E **55**
Thornbury Av. *Sotn* 4A **30**
Thornbury Heights.
  Chan F 4H **9**
Thornbury Wood.
  Chan F 4H **9**
Thorn Clo. *Eastl* 2A **16**
Thorndike Clo. *Sotn* 1E **29**
Thorndike Rd. *Sotn* 1D **28**
Thorners Ct. *Sotn* 5B **30**
Thorner's Homes.
  Sotn 3F **29**
Thorness Clo. *Sotn* 2B **28**
Thornhill Av. *Sotn* 5D **32**
Thornhill Clo. *Fawl* 3F **55**
Thornhill Homes. Sotn . . .6D **32**
  (off Tatwin Clo.)
Thornhill Pk. Rd. *Sotn* 4D **32**
Thornhill Rd. *Fawl* 3F **55**
Thornhill Rd. *Sotn* 5H **21**
Thornleigh Rd. *Sotn* 3G **41**
Thornton Av. *Wars* 6A **48**
Thornycroft Av. *Sotn* 3F **41**
Thorold Rd. *Chan F* 4G **9**
Thorold Rd. *Sotn* 3G **31**
Threefield La.
  Sotn 2C **40** (5F **5**)
Three Oaks. *Sotn* 6E **33**
Thruxton Ct. *Sotn* 6G **31**
Thurmell Clo. *H End* 1A **44**
Thurmell Wlk. *H End* 1A **44**
Thurston Clo. *Chan F* 6F **9**
Thyme Av. *White* 5H **45**
Tichborne Rd. *Eastl* 1H **23**
Tichborne Rd. *Sotn* 3D **32**
Tickleford Dri. *Sotn* 4A **42**
Tickner Clo. *Bot* 6C **34**
Ticonderoga Gdns.
  Sotn 4G **41**
Tides Reach. *Sotn* 3F **31**
Tides Way. *March* 3D **38**
Tilbrook Rd. *Sotn* 3E **29**
Tillingbourn. *Fare* 4G **49**
Timberley Clo. *Holb* 4C **54**
Timor Clo. *White* 5F **45**
Timsbury Dri. *Sotn* 2D **28**
Timson Clo. *Tot* 5C **26**
Tindale Rd. *Sotn* 1C **28**

Tinker All. *Sotn* 2A **24**
Tintagel Clo. *Sotn* 3G **21**
Tintern Gro.
   Sotn 6A **30** (1A **4**)
Tiptree Clo. *Eastl* 2A **16**
Titchbourne Ho. *H End* 4A **34**
Titchfield Pk. Rd. *Fare* 4H **49**
Tithewood Clo. *Chan F* 3D **8**
Tivoli Clo. *Chan F* 6H **9**
Tolefrey Gdns. *Chan F* . . .1B **14**
Tollbar Way. *H End* 3G **33**
Tollgate. *Chan F* 5E **15**
Tollgate Rd. *Swanw* 5B **44**
Tomkyns Clo. *Chan F* 1B **14**
Toogoods Way. *Nurs* 4B **20**
Toomer Clo. *Fawl* 3F **55**
Toothill Rd. *Roms* 6A **12**
Topiary Gdns. *L Hth* 3F **49**
Torch Clo. *Eastl* 5H **17**
Torcross Clo. *Sotn* 3G **41**
Tormead. *Hythe* 3C **52**
Tornay Gro. *N Bad* 3D **12**
Torquay Av. *Sotn* 3H **29**
Torque Clo. *Sotn* 1E **43**
Torre Clo. *Eastl* 1A **16**
Torridge Gdns. *W End* 6B **24**
Torrington Clo. *Sotn* 1A **42**
Torwood Gdns. *Eastl* 5F **17**
Tosson Clo. *Sotn* 3C **28**
Totland Clo. *Sotn* 3C **28**
Totnes Clo. *Eastl* 2H **15**
Tottehale Clo. *N Bad* 4D **12**
Totton By-Pass. *Tot* 5F **27**
Totton Western By-Pass.
   Ower & Cal 4A **18**
Totton Western By-Pass.
   Tot 3A **26**
Tower Ct. *Wars* 6A **48**
Tower Gdns. *Sotn* 5B **22**
Tower Ho. *Sotn* 3G **41**
Tower Ind. Est., The.
   Eastl 6C **16**
Tower La. *Eastl* 5C **16**
Tower Pl. *W End* 2D **32**
Towers, The. *Net A* 2B **46**
Townhill District Cen.
   W End 1B **32**
Townhill Way. *W End* 1A **32**
Town Quay.
   Sotn 2B **40** (6D **4**)
Toynbee Clo. *Eastl* 4A **16**
Toynbee Rd. *Eastl* 4A **16**
Trafalgar Clo. *Chan F* 2D **14**
Trafalgar Ho. *Hythe* 3F **53**
Trafalgar Rd. *Sotn* 3C **40**
   (SO14)
Trafalgar Rd. *Sotn* 5G **29**
   (SO15)
Trafalgar Way. *Hythe* 5F **53**
Trafford Rd. *F Oak* 6H **17**
Tranby Rd. *Sotn* 1G **41**
Treagore Rd. *Cal* 2C **26**
Trearnan Clo. *Sotn* 3D **28**
Treeside Av. *Tot* 4G **27**
Treeside Rd. *Sotn* 3G **29**
Treloyhan Clo. *Chan F* 3F **15**
Tremona Ct. *Sotn* 1F **29**
Tremona Rd. *Sotn* 6F **21**
Trenley Clo. *Holb* 5C **54**
Trent Clo. *Sotn* 2H **31**
Trent Ho. *Sotn* 6E **31**
Trent Rd. *Sotn* 2H **31**
Trent Way. *W End* 1D **32**
Tresillian Gdns. *W End* 1B **32**
Trevone Clo. *Tot* 6E **27**
Trevose Clo. *Chan F* 3F **15**
Trevose Cres. *Chan F* 2F **15**
Trevose Way. *Fare* 6F **49**

Triangle Gdns. *Nurs* 6B **20**
Triangle La. *Fare* 5H **51**
Triangle, The. *Sotn* 2F **31**
Trimaran Rd. *Wars* 6C **48**
Trinity Ct. *Chan F* 1F **15**
Trinity Ct. *Col C* 5H **11**
Trinity Ct. *March* 3D **38**
Trinity Ct. *Sotn* 5G **29**
Trinity Ct. *Tot* 1E **27**
Trinity Ind. Est. *Sotn* 4D **28**
Trinity Rd. *Sotn* 6C **30** (1F **5**)
Tripps End Cvn. Site.
   H End 4B **34**
Tristram Clo. *Chan F* 3B **14**
Triton Cen., The.
   Roms 2B **12**
Trotts La. *March* 1A **38**
Trowbridge Clo. *Rown* 4C **20**
Truro Ri. *Eastl* 4E **17**
Tudor Clo. *Cal* 3C **26**
Tudor Gdns. *H End* 6G **33**
Tudor Wood Clo. *Sotn* 5B **22**
Tuffin Clo. *Nurs* 4A **20**
Tulip Gdns. *L Hth* 4D **48**
Tulip Rd. *Sotn* 5E **23**
Tumulus Clo. *Sotn* 1E **43**
Tunstall Rd. *Sotn* 1E **43**
Turners Oak Ct. *Sotn* 2G **29**
Turnpike Way. *H End* 3H **33**
Turnstone Gdns. *Sotn* 4F **21**
Tuscan Wlk. *Chan F* 1G **15**
Tussocks, The. *March* 3D **38**
Tutland Rd. *N Bad* 3D **12**
Tutor Clo. *Hamb* 4F **47**
Tweed Clo. *Chan F* 6C **8**
Twiggs End Clo. *L Hth* 3D **48**
Twiggs La. *March* 6C **38**
Twyford Av. *Sotn* 2G **29**
Twyford Rd. *Eastl* 4B **16**
Tyleshades, The. *Roms* 6D **6**
Tyne Clo. *Chan F* 2C **14**
Tyne Way. *W End* 1E **33**
Tyrrel Rd. *Chan F* 6E **9**
Tytherley Rd. *Sotn* 3C **32**

U

Ullswater. *Eastl* 6A **16**
Ullswater Av. *W End* 2B **32**
Ullswater Rd. *Sotn* 2C **28**
Undercliff Gdns. *Sotn* 5A **22**
Underwood Clo. *Sotn* 5A **22**
Underwood Rd. *Eastl* 3D **16**
Underwood Rd. *Sotn* 5A **22**
Union Rd. *Sotn* 5E **31**
Universal Marina.
   Sar G 1A **48**
University Cres. *Sotn* 6D **22**
University Parkway.
   Sotn 6G **13**
University Rd. *Sotn* 5D **22**
Unwin Clo. *Sotn* 4F **41**
Uplands Way. *Sotn* 1C **30**
Upmill Clo. *W End* 6B **24**
Up. Banister St. *Sotn* 5B **30**
Up. Barn Copse. *F Oak* 4H **17**
Up. Brook Dri. *L Hth* 5C **48**
   (in two parts)
Up. Brownhill Rd.
   Sotn 6D **20**
Up. Bugle St.
   Sotn 2B **40** (5D **4**)
Up. Crescent Rd.
   N Bad 2D **12**
Up. Deacon Rd. *Sotn* 5B **32**
Up. Mead Clo. *F Oak* 2G **17**
Up. Moors Rd. *Col C* 5F **11**
Up. Mullins La. *Hythe* 3C **52**

Up. New Rd. *W End* 2D **32**
Up. Northam Clo.
   H End 5G **33**
Up. Northam Dri.
   H End 5E **33**
Up. Northam Rd.
   H End 4G **33**
Up. St Helens Rd.
   H End 1H **43**
Up. Shaftesbury Av.
   Sotn 1D **30**
Up. Shirley Av. *Sotn* 2G **29**
Up. Spinney. *Wars* 1A **50**
Up. Toothill Rd. *Rown* 6C **12**
Up. Weston La. *Sotn* 3A **42**
Upton Cres. *Nurs* 2B **20**
Upton La. *Nurs* 4G **19**

V

Vale Dri. *Sotn* 2H **31**
Valentine Av. *Sotn* 2C **42**
Valentine Ct. *Sotn* 2C **42**
Valerian Rd. *H End* 5A **34**
Vale, The. *Hythe* 3D **52**
Vale, The. *L Hth* 5F **49**
Valley Clo. *Black* 4F **55**
Valley Clo. *Col C* 5F **11**
Valleydene. *Dib P* 4D **52**
Valley Ri. *Sar G* 3C **48**
Valley Rd. *Chan F* 6E **9**
Valley Rd. *Tot* 6F **27**
Vanburgh Ho. *H End* 3B **34**
Vanburgh Way. *Chan F* 4D **8**
Vanguard Rd. *Sotn* 3A **32**
Vardy Clo. *Sotn* 2D **42**
Varna Rd. *Sotn* 6G **29**
Vaudrey Clo. *Sotn* 2G **29**
Vaughan Clo. *Sotn* 6E **33**
Vaughan Rd. *Dib* 2A **52**
Veals La. *March* 6E **39**
Vear's La. *Col C* 5G **11**
Vectis Ct. *Sotn* 5B **22**
Vellan Ct. *Sotn* 2B **28**
Velmore Rd. *Chan F* 3D **14**
Velsheda Ct. *Hythe* 1E **53**
Ventnor Ct. *Sotn* 4E **23**
Venture Rd. *Chilw* 6H **13**
Verbena Way. *H End* 5B **34**
Verdon Av. *Hamb* 4E **47**
Verger Clo. *Fare* 4G **49**
Vermont Clo. *Sotn* 5B **22**
Vernon Wlk. *Sotn* 5B **30**
   (in two parts)
Verona Rd. *Chan F* 6G **9**
Verulam Rd. *Sotn* 4D **30**
Vespasian Rd. *Sotn* 4F **31**
Vespasian Way.
   Sotn 1G **15**
Vesta Way. *Chan F* 6G **9**
Vicarage Dri. *H End* 6H **33**
Vicarage La. *Curd* 4G **35**
Vicarage Rd. *March* 4D **38**
Viceroy Rd. *Sotn* 2A **42**
Victena Rd. *F Oak* 2F **17**
Victoria Clo. *L Hth* 6E **49**
Victoria Glade. *Net A* 2C **46**
Victoria M. *Net A* 2B **46**
Victoria Rd. *Eastl* 2B **16**
Victoria Rd. *Net A* 1A **46**
Victoria St. *Sotn* 6E **31**
Victoria Wlk. *W End* 1E **33**
Victor St. *Sotn* 2F **29**
Victory Clo. *Chan F* 2D **14**
Victory Cres. *Sotn* 4F **29**
Victory Rd. *Sotn* 5F **29**
Victory Sq. *Sotn* 4F **29**

Victory Way. *Rown* 2C **20**
Viking Clo. *Black* 5F **55**
Viking Clo. *Sotn* 4C **20**
Vikings, The. *Roms* 5F **7**
Villiers Rd. *Dib P* 6D **52**
Villiers Rd. *Sotn* 4G **29**
Vincent Av. *Sotn* 1E **29**
Vincent Rd. *Sotn* 3G **29**
Vincent's Gro. *Sotn* 3F **29**
Vincent St. *Sotn* 3G **29**
Vincent's Wlk.
   Sotn 1C **40** (4E **5**)
Vine Bank. *Sotn* 3B **32**
Vine Clo. *Sar G* 4B **48**
Vine Rd. *Sotn* 6E **21**
Vinery Gdns. *Sotn* 1G **29**
Vinery Rd. *Sotn* 1G **29**
Vineyard Clo. *Sotn* 2F **41**
Vineyards, The. *N Bad* 3E **13**
Viney Av. *Roms* 4E **7**
Violet Clo. *Chan F* 1C **14**
Violet Rd. *Sotn* 5C **22**
Vokes Clo. *Sotn* 6B **32**
Vulcan Clo. *Sotn* 4D **28**
Vulcan Rd. *Sotn* 4D **28**
Vyse La. *Sotn* 2B **40** (6D **4**)

W

Wade Hill Drove. *Cal* 5A **18**
Wadhurst Gdns. *Sotn* 5A **24**
Wadhurst Rd. *H End* 5A **34**
Wainwright Gdns.
   H End 6H **25**
Wakefield Ct. *Roms* 5C **6**
Wakefield Ct. *Sotn* 2A **32**
Wakefield Rd. *Sotn* 2A **32**
Wakeford Pl. *Wars* 6E **49**
Waldegrave Clo. *Sotn* 4F **41**
Waldon Gdns. *W End* 1B **32**
Walker Gdns. *H End* 2A **34**
Walkers Clo. *F Oak* 2G **17**
Walker's La. N. *Black* 4E **55**
Walker's La. S. *Black* 6F **55**
Wallace Rd. *Sotn* 4H **41**
Wallington Dri. *Chan F* 5D **8**
Walmer Clo. *Eastl* 6A **10**
Walnut Av. *Sotn* 4G **23**
Walnut Clo. *Chan F* 3E **9**
Walnut Clo. *Sotn* 2D **28**
Walnut Gro. *Sotn* 3D **28**
Walpole La. *Swanw* 5C **44**
Walsingham Gdns.
   Sotn 6H **23**
Waltham Cres. *Sotn* 5F **21**
Walton Rd. *Sotn* 1D **42**
Waltons Av. *Holb* 4C **54**
Wangfield La. *Curd* 2F **35**
Wansbeck Clo. *Chan F* 2D **14**
Warbler Clo. *Sotn* 3F **21**
Warblington Clo.
   Chan F 4C **14**
Warblington Clo. *Roms* 4E **7**
   (off Selsdon Av.)
Warburton Clo. *Sotn* 1E **43**
Warburton Rd. *Sotn* 6D **32**
Warden Clo. *W End* 2D **32**
Wardle Rd. *Highb* 6D **10**
Warlock Clo. *Sotn* 2D **42**
Warren Av. *Chan F* 2G **15**
Warren Av. *Sotn* 1E **29**
Warren Clo. *Chan F* 2G **15**
Warren Clo. *Sotn* 1E **29**
Warren Cres. *Sotn* 1E **29**
Warren Gdns. *Roms* 3E **7**
Warren Pl. *Cal* 1C **26**
Warren, The. *Holb* 3B **54**
Warrior Clo. *Chan F* 3D **14**

Warrior Pk. Ind. Est.
  Chan F 3D 14
Warrys Clo. Hythe 6E 53
Warsash Ct. Wars 6A 48
Warsash Rd.
  Wars & Fare 6B 48
Warwick Clo. Chan F 3C 14
Warwick Ho. Sotn 5E 31
  (off Princes Clo.)
Warwick Rd. Sotn 1H 29
Warwick Rd. Tot 3F 27
Waterbeech Dri. H End . .3A 34
Waterhouse La. Sotn 4F 29
Waterhouse Way.
  Sotn 4F 29
Water La. Dib P 4C 52
Water La. Sotn 6B 30 (1C 4)
Water La. Tot 3D 26
Waterloo Ind. Est.
  H End 2H 33
Waterloo Rd. Sotn 5G 29
Waterloo Ter. Sotn 5B 30
Watermans La. Dib P 5C 52
Waters Edge. H End 5H 33
Waterside. Hythe 1D 52
Waterside Rd. Roms 3D 6
Waterside Sq. Hythe 1D 52
Waterworks Rd. Ott 1C 10
Watkin Rd. H End 1B 34
Watley Clo. Nurs 4B 20
Watson Wlk. Tot 4C 26
Watton Rd. Holb 4C 54
Watts Clo. Sotn 1C 28
Watts Rd. H End 4A 34
Wavecrest Clo. March 2E 39
Wavell Rd. Sotn 4A 32
Waveney Grn. Sotn 2C 28
Waverley Av. Net A 2C 46
Waverley Clo. Roms 3E 7
Waverley Ct. Net A 2C 46
Waverley Rd. Sotn 6H 29
Wayfarer Clo. Wars 6D 48
Waylands Pl. H End 1H 43
Wayside. Lwr S 5B 44
Weald Clo. L Hth 3E 49
Weardale Rd. Chan F 3F 15
Weavers Pl. Chan F 4D 8
Weavills Rd. Eastl 5G 17
Webburn Gdns.
  W End 6A 24
Wedgewood Clo. Holb 4C 54
Welch Way. Rown 4D 20
Welland Gdns. W End 1B 32
Welland Grn. Sotn 3C 28
Wellbrooke Gdns.
  Chan F 6D 8
Wellers Clo. Tot 4B 26
Welles Rd. Chan F 1F 15
Wellington Av. Sotn 4B 32
Wellington Clo. Dib P 5B 52
Wellington Ct. Sotn 5H 29
Wellington Ct. W End 1C 32
Wellington Pk. H End 2G 33
Wellington Rd. Sotn 1F 31
Well La. Hamb 5G 47
Wellowbrook Clo.
  Chan F 1C 14
Wellow Clo. Sotn 4C 32
Wellow Gdns. Fare 5G 49
Wells Clo. White 5G 45
Wellsmoor. Fare 5G 49
Wells Pl. Eastl 5A 16
Wells Rd. Eastl 5B 16
Wembley Way. F Oak 3F 17
Wentworth Gdns.
  Holb 6D 54
Wentworth Gdns. Sotn . . .4B 42

Wentworth Gro. Holb 5D 54
Wesley Clo. Sotn 1D 42
Wessex Clo. Black 5F 55
Wessex Ct. Sotn 1A 42
Wessex Gdns. Roms 5E 7
Wessex La. Sotn 6F 23
Wessex Rd. W End 6B 24
Wessex Way. Col C 5G 11
W. Bargate.
  Sotn 1B 40 (4D 4)
W. Bay Rd. Sotn & W Dock
  . . . . .5E 29 (3A 4)
Westbourne Av. Holb 4C 54
Westbourne Cres.
  Sotn 2C 30
Westbourne Mans.
  Sotn 2C 30
Westbroke Gdns. Roms . . .3C 6
Westbrook Clo. Park G . . .1E 49
Westbrook Way. Sotn 5G 23
Westbury Ct. H End 6H 33
Westbury Rd. Sotn 4D 28
Westcliffe Wlk. Hythe 1D 52
  (off Waterside Sq.)
Westcliff M. Sotn 2F 41
Westcot Rd. Holb 5B 54
West Ct. Sotn 3F 29
West Dri. Eastl 3D 16
W. End Rd.
  Sotn & Burs 1F 43
W. End Rd.
  Sotn & W End 4A 32
Westering. Roms 3F 7
Westerley Clo. Wars 6C 48
Western Av. W Dock 6D 28
Western District Cut.
  Sotn 4H 29
Western Esplanade.
  Sotn 6A 30 (2B 4)
Western Rd. Chan F 4G 9
Western Rd. W End 2D 32
Westfield Clo. Hamb 5E 47
Westfield Comn.
  Hamb 5D 46
Westfield Corner. Sotn . . .4G 23
Westfield Cres. Chan F . . .3E 15
Westfield Rd. Chan F 4E 15
Westfield Rd. Sotn 4E 29
Westfield Rd. Tot 3F 27
Westgate M. W End 2E 33
Westgate St.
  Sotn 2B 40 (6D 4)
W. Hill Ct. Sotn 6A 30 (1B 4)
W. Hill Dri. Hythe 1D 52
W. Horton Clo. Eastl 5F 17
W. Horton La. Eastl 6F 17
West La. N Bad 2C 12
Westmarch Ct. Sotn 1E 31
W. Marlands Rd.
  Sotn 6B 30 (2D 4)
Westminster Gdns.
  Fare 4G 49
Westmorland Way.
  Chan F 2G 15
Weston Clo. Sotn 4H 41
Weston Cres. Sotn 4C 32
Weston Gro. Rd. Sotn 3F 41
Weston Homes. Sotn 5H 41
Weston La. Nurs 5G 19
Weston La. Sotn 5G 41
Weston Pde. Sotn 5G 41
Weston Rd. Eastl 4A 16
Westover Rd. Sotn 3A 28
W. Park Rd.
  Sotn 6B 30 (2C 4)
W. Quay Retail Pk.
  Sotn 1A 40 (3B 4)
W. Quay Rd. Sotn 1A 40

W. Quay Shop. Cen.
  Sotn 1B 40 (3D 4)
Westridge Ct. Sotn 2D 30
Westridge Rd. Sotn 2D 30
West Rd. Dib P 5H 53
  (East St.)
West Rd. Dib P 5B 52
  (Roman Rd.)
West Rd. H End 5F 33
West Rd. Sotn 3C 40 (SO14)
West Rd. Sotn 3G 41 (SO19)
Westrow Gdns. Sotn 4A 30
Westrow Rd. Sotn 4A 30
West St. Hythe 1D 52
West St. Sotn 2B 40 (5D 4)
Westward Rd. H End 3A 34
Westways Clo. Nurs 4B 20
West Wing. Net A 6A 42
Westwood Bus. Pk.
  Tot 6D 18
Westwood Ct. Sotn 3C 30
Westwood Ct. Tot 1E 27
Westwood Ct. W End 2D 32
Westwood Gdns. Chan F . .5G 9
Westwood Mans. Sotn 2C 30
Westwood Rd. Net A 6B 42
Westwood Rd. Sotn 3B 30
Wetherby Ct. Tot 3D 26
Wetherby Gdns. Tot 3C 26
Whalesmead Clo. Eastl . . .6F 17
Whalesmead Rd. Eastl 5F 17
Wharf Rd. Sotn 2F 41
Wharncliffe Ho. Sotn 2F 41
Wharncliffe Rd. Sotn 2F 41
Whartons Clo. Asht 2C 36
Whartons La. Asht 1C 36
Wheat Clo. Chan F 1B 14
Wheatcroft Dri. Sotn 2B 32
Wheatlands. Fare 3G 49
Wheatsheaf Ct. H End 5H 33
Wheelers Wlk. Black 5F 55
Wheelhouse Pk. Cvn. Pk.
  N Bad 4C 8
Whernside Clo. Sotn 3D 28
Whinchat Clo. Sotn 3F 21
Whinfield Rd. Dib P 5C 52
Whistler Clo. Sotn 2C 42
Whistler Rd. Sotn 2C 42
Whitcombe Clo. Tot 4E 27
Whitebeam Clo. Col C 5G 11
Whitebeam Rd. H End 5B 34
Whitebeam Way.
  N Bad 2E 13
Whitecroft. Hythe 4E 53
Whitefield Rd. Holb 5C 54
White Harmony Acres Ind. Est.
  W End 4E 25
White Hart Rd. F Oak 3F 17
Whitehaven Home Pk.
  Black 5E 55
White Heather Ct.
  Hythe 1E 53
Whitehill Clo. Sotn 3C 32
Whitehouse Gdns.
  Sotn 5E 29
Whitelaw Rd. Sotn 4F 29
Whiteley La. Bur 3F 45
Whiteley Way. White 1H 49
Whitenap Clo. Roms 6E 7
Whitenap La. Roms 6E 7
White Rd. Eastl 3D 16
Whites La. Fawl 2H 55
White's Rd. Sotn 6A 32
Whitestone Clo. Sotn 3D 28
Whitewater Ri. Dib P 4D 52
Whiteway M. Wars 6A 48
Whithedwood Av.
  Sotn 3H 29

Whithy Clo. Roms 4C 6
Whittington Clo.
  Hythe 4D 52
Whittle Av. Fare 2G 49
Whitwell. Net A 6C 42
Whitworth Ct. Sotn 3F 31
Whitworth Cres. Sotn 3F 31
Whitworth Rd. Sotn 3F 31
Whyte Clo. Holb 5B 54
Whyteways. Eastl 3A 16
Wicket, The. Hythe 4D 52
Wickham Ho. Sotn 2C 30
Wickham Rd. Curd 4G 35
Wicklow Dri. Chan F 2C 14
Widecombe Dri. Hythe . . .2C 52
Wide La.
  Sotn & Sotn I 4G 23
Widgeon Clo. Sotn 3F 21
Wild Arum Way.
  Chan F 2B 14
Wildburn Clo. Cal 1C 26
Wild Cherry Way.
  Chan F 1C 14
Wilde Clo. Tot 4D 26
Wildern Clo. L Hth 4D 48
Wilderness Heights.
  W End 2C 32
Wildern La. H End 3A 34
Wildground La. Hythe 5E 53
Wild Rose Cres. L Hth 5C 48
Wilks Clo. Nurs 4A 20
William Macleod Way.
  Sotn 2E 29
Williams Clo. Holb 5D 54
William St. Sotn 6E 31
Willis Av. N Bad 3F 13
Willis Rd. Sotn 4F 23
Willment Marine & Bus. Pk.
  Sotn 1F 41
Willments Ind. Est.
  Sotn 2E 41
Willow Clo. H End 5B 34
Willow Clo. W End 1E 33
Willow Ct. Sotn 6E 21
Willow Dri. March 5D 38
Willow Gdns. N Bad 2D 12
Willow Grn. Col C 5G 11
Willow Gro. F Oak 2G 17
Willow Herb Clo.
  L Hth 5C 48
Willows, The. Chan F 4E 15
Willows, The. W End 1E 33
Willow Tree Wlk. Sotn 2B 42
Wills Way. Roms 6D 6
Wilmer Rd. Eastl 5A 16
Wilmington Clo. Sotn 6H 23
Wilmot Clo. Eastl 2E 17
Wilson St. Sotn . . .6E 31 (1H 5)
Wilton Av. Sotn 5A 30
Wilton Ct. Sotn 3H 29
Wilton Cres. Sotn 2H 29
Wilton Gdns. Sotn 2H 29
Wilton Mnr. Sotn 5B 30
  (off Wilton Av.)
Wilton Rd. Sotn 1G 29
Wiltshire Rd. Chan F 4F 15
Wilverley Pl. Black 4E 55
Wimpson Gdns. Sotn 2D 28
Wimpson La. Sotn 3C 28
Winchester Clo. Net A 1B 46
Winchester Clo. Roms 3E 7
Winchester Hill. Roms 5D 6
Winchester Rd.
  Bish W & Wal C 1C 34
  Chan F 1E 15
Winchester Rd. Chilw 1C 22
Winchester Rd. Roms 5C 6

Winchester Rd. *Sotn* 2E **29**
Winchester St. *Bot* 3D **34**
Winchester St. *Sotn* 5B **30**
Winchester Way. *Tot* 4C **26**
Winchfield Clo. *Sotn* 4A **42**
Windbury Rd. *Sotn* 1C **28**
Windermere Av. *Sotn* 1B **28**
Windermere Gdns. *Tot* 3E **27**
Windermere Rd.
    W End 2B **32**
Windfield Dri. *Roms* 4E **7**
Windmill Ct. *Dib P* 5D **52**
Windmill La. *Burs* 3G **43**
Windover Clo. *Sotn* 5C **32**
Windrush Rd. *Sotn* 2C **28**
Windrush Way. *Hythe* 3E **53**
Windsor Ct. *Eastl* 3D **16**
Windsor Ct. *Sotn* 5E **29**
    (off Regents Pk. Rd., SO15)
Windsor Ct. *Sotn* 4G **31**
    (SO18)
Windsor Ga. *Eastl* 1A **16**
Windsor Rd. *Tot* 5G **27**
Windsor Ter. *Sotn* 2D **4**
Winfrid Ho. *Tot* 4D **26**
Winfrith Way. *Nurs* 4B **20**
Wingate Dri. *Sotn* 6B **32**
Wingate Rd. *Tot* 3D **26**
Wingrove Rd. *Asht* 2C **36**
Winifred Clo. *Eastl* 1F **17**
Winkle St. *Sotn* 3C **40**
Winnards Pk. *Sar G* 3B **48**
Winn Rd. *Sotn* 3B **30**
Winsford Av. *Eastl* 6G **17**
Winsford Clo. *Eastl* 6G **17**
Winsford Gdns. *Eastl* 6G **17**
Winstanley Rd. *Nurs* 4A **20**
Winston Clo. *Eastl* 3A **16**
Winston Clo. *Sotn* 1D **28**
Winstone Cres. *N Bad* 4E **13**
Winterbourne Rd.
    Roms 3E **7**
Winters Clo. *Holb* 5D **54**
Winton Ct. *W End* 2D **32**
Winton St. *Sotn* . . .6C **30** (2F **5**)
    (in two parts)
Witham Clo. *Chan F* 1C **14**
Witherbed La. *Fare* 3H **49**
    (in three parts)

Withewood Mans.
    Sotn 4G **29**
Wittering Rd. *Sotn* 4E **21**
Witt Rd. *F Oak* 2F **17**
Witts Hill. *Sotn* 2H **31**
Woburn Clo. *Eastl* 1A **16**
Woburn Rd. *Sotn* 4F **21**
Wodehouse Rd. *Sotn* 1G **41**
Wolseley Rd. *Sotn* 4G **29**
Wolverley Ct. *Sotn* 6H **21**
Wolverton Rd.
    Sotn 6D **30** (1G **5**)
Wolvesey Pl. *Chan F* 3C **14**
Wonston Rd. *Sotn* 5F **21**
Wood Clo. *Sotn* 2C **42**
Woodcote Rd. *Sotn* 6E **23**
Wood End Way. *Chan F* . . .1C **14**
Wooderson Clo. *F Oak* 4H **17**
Wood Glade Clo.
    March 4D **38**
Woodgreen Wlk. *Cal* 2B **26**
Woodhouse La. *Bot* 4B **34**
Woodland Clo. *Sotn* 4D **32**
Woodland Drove.
    Col C 2G **11**
Woodland M. *W End* 2D **32**
Woodland Pl. *Sotn* 4B **30**
Woodlands Clo. *Chan F* 3F **9**
Woodlands Clo. *Dib P* 5C **52**
Woodlands Clo. *Sar G* 1D **48**
Woodlands Ct. *Dib P* 5C **52**
Woodlands Dri. *Net A* 1D **46**
Woodlands Drove.
    Asht 2A **36**
Woodlands Gdns.
    Roms 3E **7**
Woodlands Rd. *Tot* 6A **26**
Woodlands Way. *Burs* 5F **43**
Woodlands Way.
    N Bad 3D **12**
Woodlands Way. *Sotn* 3B **30**
Woodland, The. *Chan F* . . .4C **8**
Woodland Va. *Sotn* 1B **42**
Woodland Vw. *Burs* 5F **43**
Woodlea Gdns. *W End* 2E **33**
Woodlea Way. *Amp* 3B **8**
Woodley Clo. *Roms* 2F **7**
Woodley Clo. Flats.
    Roms 2F **7**

Woodley Grange. *Roms* 3F **7**
Woodley La. *Roms* 4D **6**
Woodley Rd. *Sotn* 2F **41**
Woodley Way. *Roms* 2F **7**
Wood Lodge. *Cal* 2B **26**
Woodmill La. *Sotn* 6F **23**
Woodmoor Clo. *March* 4E **39**
Woodpecker Copse.
    L Hth 4F **49**
Woodpecker Dri.
    March 4C **38**
Woodpecker Way.
    Eastl 5F **15**
Wood Rd. *Asht* 3B **36**
Woodrush Cres. *L Hth* 5C **48**
Woodside. *Chilw* 5A **14**
Woodside Av. *Eastl* 4G **15**
Woodside Clo. *March* 4C **38**
Woodside Ct. *Sotn* 3D **30**
Woodside Cres. *Chilw* 5H **13**
Woodside Gdns. *Asht* 2C **36**
Woodside Rd. *Eastl* 3G **15**
Woodside Rd. *N Bad* 3D **12**
Woodside Rd. *Sotn* 3D **30**
Woodside Way. *H End* 6G **33**
Woodstock Clo. *H End* 6B **34**
Woodstock Dri. *Sotn* 2C **30**
Woodthorpe Gdns.
    Sar G 1D **48**
Woodview Clo. *Sotn* 3C **22**
Woodview Pk. Cvn. Pk.
    Curd 4G **35**
Woodville Rd. *Fawl* 2H **55**
Wooley Ho. *Sotn* 2F **5**
Woolston Rd. *Net A* 5B **42**
Woolwich Clo. *Burs* 4F **43**
Wootton. *Net A* 6C **42**
Worcester Pl. *Sotn* 3B **42**
Wordsworth Clo.
    White 4G **45**
Wordsworth Rd. *Sotn* 2G **29**
Workman's La. *Wars* 3C **50**
Wren Rd. *Eastl* 6G **15**
Wright's Hill. *Sotn* 3A **42**
Wrights Wlk. *Burs* 4F **43**
Wryneck Clo. *Sotn* 3E **21**
Wychwood Dri. *Black* 6E **55**
Wychwood Gro. *Chan F* . . .5G **9**
Wycliffe Rd. *Sotn* 2A **32**

Wykeham Clo. *Net A* 1B **46**
Wykeham Clo. *Sotn* 5A **22**
Wykeham Rd. *Net A* 1B **46**
Wylye Clo. *W End* 6B **24**
Wyndham Ct.
    Sotn 6A **30** (1B **4**)
Wyndham Pl.
    Sotn 6A **30** (1B **4**)
Wynter Rd. *Sotn* 3B **32**
Wynyards Gap. *N Bad* 3D **12**
Wyre Clo. *Chan F* 1D **14**
Wyvern Clo. *Chan F* 1F **15**

Y

Yardley Rd. *H End* 6H **33**
Yarmouth Gdns. *Sotn* . . .2F **29**
Yarrow Way. *L Hth* 5C **48**
Yaverland. *Net A* 1C **46**
Yelverton Av. *Hythe* 5E **53**
Yeoman Ind. Pk. *Sotn* . . .1H **27**
Yeoman Pk. *Sotn* 2A **28**
Yeomans Way. *Tot* 3F **27**
Yeovil Chase. *Sotn* 3B **32**
Yewberry Way. *Chan F* . . .1A **14**
Yew Rd. *Sotn* 3A **32**
Yew Tree Clo. *F Oak* 1F **17**
Yew Tree Clo. *H End* 5H **33**
Yewtree Clo. *Hythe* 6E **53**
Yew Tree Ct. *Swanw* 6F **45**
Yew Tree Ct. *W End* 2E **33**
Yew Tree Dri. *White* 6F **45**
Yewtree La. *Nurs* 6A **20**
Yonge Clo. *Eastl* 4B **16**
York Bldgs.
    Sotn 1C **40** (4E **5**)
    (in two parts)
York Clo. *Chan F* 3B **14**
York Clo. *Sotn* 5E **31**
York Clo. *Tot* 3G **27**
York Drove. *Sotn* 4B **32**
Yorke Way. *Hamb* 4E **47**
York Ga. *Sotn* 1C **40** (4E **5**)
York Ho. *Sotn* 5E **31**
York Rd. *Eastl* 1A **24**
York Rd. *Net A* 1A **46**
York Rd. *Sotn* 4G **29**
York Wlk. *Sotn* 1C **40** (4E **5**)

The representation on the maps of a road, track or footpath is no evidence of the existence of a right of way.

The Grid on this map is the National Grid taken from Ordnance Survey mapping with the permission of the Controller of Her Majesty's Stationery Office.